Coming Out of the Dark Into the Light

Coming Out of the Dark
Into the Light

An African American History of
Triune, Kirkland, and College Grove

Ovie Elaine Boleyjack Bell
and
Addie Marie Ridley Ogilvie
with
Rick Warwick
Williamson County Historian

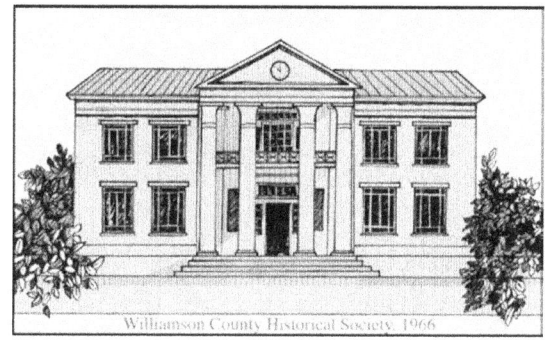

Williamson County Historical Society • Franklin, Tennessee
©2025

Coming Out of the Dark Into the Light
©2025, Williamson County Historical Society, All rights reserved.

ISBN: 979-8-9863055-3-0
Library of Congress Control Number: 2025916206

Marcia Fraser, editor, layout, and cover design

On the front cover:
Mrs. Nannie Lanier's Eighth Grade Class at Kirkland School
See page 128 for students' names.

Williamson County Historical Society
P.O. Box 71
Franklin, Tennessee 37065
www.williamsoncountyhistory.com

Contents

Introduction and Acknowledgements 1
Opening Thoughts
By Ovie Elaine Boleyjack Bell
3

iv

1. Picking Cotton 7
2. J.C. Patton, Jr. 11
3. Deception 15
4. Martha Ann House 17
5. Day in Court 20
6. Justice 23
7. Democracy 25
8. Coming Together 26
9. Kindness 28
10. My Recollections 29
11. Winner Take All 31
12. "Yes Sir, Mr. Tom" 33
13. Baseball 38
14. Arch Boleyjack 42
15. The Boleyjacks of Triune 45
16. The Hutton Vaughn Family 51
17. See Something, Do Something 53

18. Food for Thought 55

19. Minimum Wage 57

20. Robert Anderson Lee (1919-1951) 59

21. Bernita J. Hill 61

22. Embracing God's Assignment in Tennessee 63

23. Lawyer Peterson 66

24. What a Blessing! 68

25. Martha Louise Ridley Anderson 69

26. Addie Wilson Bostick 70

27. Mattie Lee Wilson Shaw 72

28. Mary Virginia Patton Williams 74

29. Ponell Cecil Williams 76

30. Charles Milton Glenn, Jr. 77

31. Henry Dozier 79

32. Strawberries 80

33. Juanita Ridley Jones Family 81

34. Frank James and Addie Marie Ridley Ogilvie 84

35. James and Araminta Shaw Ridley 86

36. Words Unspoken 90

37. Emmett and Ada Mae York Claybrooks 92

38. "Tunnie" 96

39. Margaret's Memories 98

40. Count It All Joy! 100

41. Memories of Green Grove School 101

Kirkland

42. Williamson County Public Schools 105

43. Schools in the Eastern Section of Williamson County 107
44. The Old Kirkland School 112
45. Kirkland Elementary School Memories 113
46. Kirkland Elementary School 115
47. Fond Memories 118
48. Kirkland Elementary Tigers 120
49. Kirkland School Students 137
50. The Majorettes 153
51. Gone Too Soon 155
52. New Beginnings 157
53. Looking Back at Kirkland School 160
54. John L. and Clatie Lytle Jordan 162
55. Those Were the Days 164
56. Aggie Jane Norris 166
57. Charles Lee and Nettie Mae Jones 167
58. Ella Virginia Anderson McClain 170
59. Margaret Jean McClain Coleman 171
60. Kirkland's Roadside Businesses 173
61. Kirkland Masonic Lodge 184
62. Familiar Faces Remembered 185

College Grove

63. The First 199
64. John and Pauline Rucker Cunningham 201
65. "Big Mama" 204
66. Maudell Parrish Dotson 206
67. Della Wilson Scales 207

68. The Sawyers, Howse, and Parrish Family 208
69. The Thompsons 212
70. Biracial Families in Southeastern Williamson County 215
71. Just the Two of Us 217
72. The Wilson Anderson Family 222
73. The John Frank Anderson Family 226
74. Lillian and Christine 230
75. The Wray Sisters 231
76. William B. Covington 233
77. Remembering William B. Covington 235
78. Let's Weigh In 237
79. Baxter Herbert Hardemon, Sr. 239
80. History of the Esmond Family 241
81. The Hatcher Family 243
82. Elder Jasper G. Hatcher 246
83. Rev. Judge Webb, Jr. 249
84. "Aunt Tish" 251
85. Life Goes On 252
86. My Thrill Upon the Hill 254
87. "They Called Me Mr. Carney" 256
88. Ebony and Ivory 258
89. Mammy and Pap 260
90. Astonished! 264
91. Planting a Seed 265
92. Imagine 266
93. Highlights and Challenges 268
94. Ministers and Evangelists 271

95. Green Grove Primitive Baptist Church   272

96. Shady Grove Primitive Baptist Church   276

97. Mount Pleasant Missionary Baptist Church   281

98. Locust Ridge Primitive Baptist Church   284

99. Our Service Men and Women   287

Acknowledgements   292

A Hopeful King
Ovie Elaine Boleyjack Bell
293

Take
Ovie Elaine Boleyjack Bell
294

Inaugural Address of President Barack Obama
January 20, 2009
296

Lift Every Voice and Sing
James Weldon Johnson
302

Into the Light   304

Index   305

In Gratitude

Rick Warwick, Williamson County Historian

We give special thanks to Mr. Rick Warwick. He was the wind beneath our wings throughout this endeavor. His guidance, wisdom, and patience carried us through the book's end. Sharing this with him has been a labor of love. We will never forget your kindness. God bless.

Introduction and Acknowledgements

As president of the Williamson County Historical Society and the County Historian, I am pleased to announce that another community history has been completed. I met with a group of Kirkland School alumni at the Green Grove Primitive Baptist Church in the fall of 2024 to discuss erecting a historical marker at the site of the Kirkland Elementary School on the Horton Highway. Sadly, the school no longer stands, but warm memories of the educational experiences still ring in their hearts. An agreement was reached with the understanding that the alumni would raise half of the $3,400 and the Historical Society would raise the rest. A committee was appointed to write the text, and the marker was ordered, soon to be erected.

Seeing the enthusiasm of the Kirkland alumni and the large collection of photos that was available from the first Kirkland School reunion in 2023, provided by Ovie Elaine Boleyjack Bell and Addie Marie Ridley Ogilvie, I suggested that we collaborate on producing a book about the history of the Black communities of Triune, Kirkland, and College Grove. Society members Ginger Shirling of Triune, Carolyn Smotherman of College Grove, Marcia Fraser of Franklin, and I would work with Ovie Elaine Bell and Marie Ogilvie, both of Triune, as a committee to collect histories of families and photos of former students of Kirkland. After weeks of collecting the necessary information and photos, we feel satisfied that we have done our best.

A genuine thank you goes to those who provided family photographs and histories of Black schools and churches in the area. A special thank you is due to Marcia Fraser for editing and designing the book. Carolyn Smotherman generously offered any material from her book on College Grove. Robbie D. Jones provided a preservation project entitled *Roadside Businesses of Kirkland, Tennessee*. Yet again, I am grateful to Thelma Battle for photographs and her willingness to help. Ovie Elaine Bell and Marie Ogilvie must be acknowledged for their work in canvassing the area for photos and material for this book. Ovie interviewed many of the people in the community and put their words to paper. A Biblical reference seems appropriate when referring to Ovie Elaine and Marie: "You shall know them by their works."

The personal stories dealing with the trauma of integration are an essential element of this book. I was surprised to hear of the mistreatment they experienced when entering College Grove High School in 1967. The general understanding at the time was that Black students were eager to enter a white school. Contrary to this thought, many expressed their love for Kirkland Elementary School, Natchez High School, and their respect for their Black teachers. Professor William B. Covington, principal of Kirkland School for decades, was admired for his ability as a teacher and kindness to his students. Mrs. Nannie Lanier, Mrs. Annie Patton, Mrs. Maudell Dotson, Mrs. Vella Moody, and Mr. Willie Wilson, Jr. are fondly remembered for their exceptional teaching abilities and encouragement, which inspired many students to follow in their footsteps.

I hope the readers of this book enjoy it as much as we have enjoyed putting it together.

Good Reading,

Rick Warwick

Opening Thoughts

By Ovie Elaine Boleyjack Bell

Ovie Elaine Boleyjack Bell

Many books have been written about the people of Williamson County. We hope that this one will open your mind to see life from a different perspective. Life is not always what you see, hear, or feel; it's simply life as it comes, one breath at a time.

That is how the people in this book had to survive the joy and pain of life after slavery. The Black families of Triune, Kirkland, and College Grove were hard-working and diligent people who envisioned a better future for their children, something they could not obtain due to all of the restrictions they endured along their journey.

As their offspring, we saw the path that our ancestors laid before us and went on to achieve great things in life. They taught us never to give up, even if the path is rocky and the mountain seems too high. We could always reach back and hear their voices telling us, "Just one more step, and we will reach our goal."

They had faith in us; we must pass that down to our children and grandchildren. Never let anyone tell your story because they may leave something out that the world may need to hear. So, now we pass the torch to you, our future generations. We know that you will build on the foundation that we have prepared for you and take it to greater heights because the blood still flows.

Triune

RELIGIOUS AND AGRICULTURAL COMMUNITY

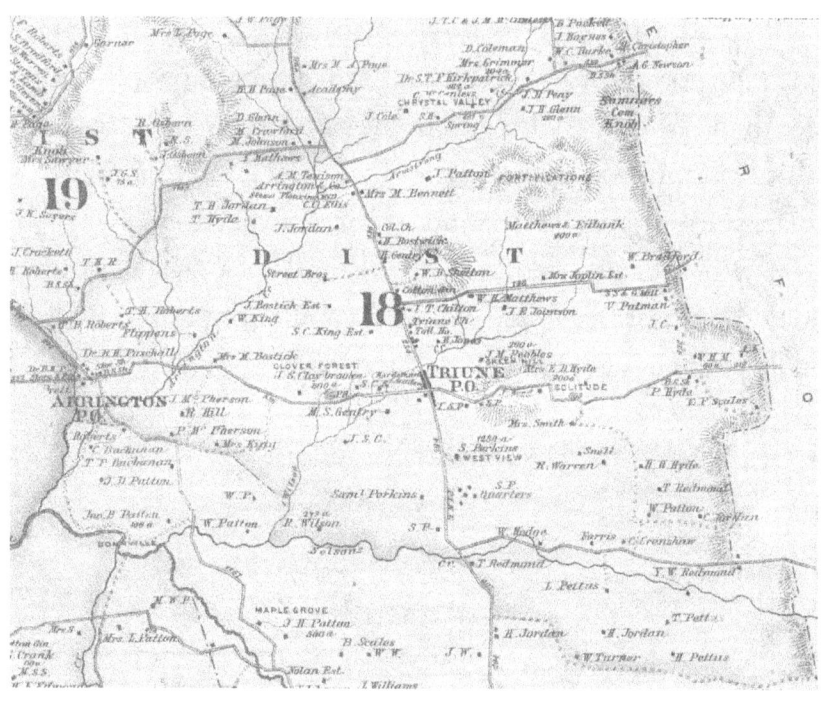

1878 Beers Map of Triune

Triune, Tennessee

According to records of the 1860s, Triune (18th Civil District) extended to the Harpeth River and included Petersburg (now Arrington) and Patterson (Possum Trot), both of which are now in Rutherford County. A 1935 newspaper article by John L. Jordan stated that Williamson County stood third in the state of Tennessee in taxable value in the 1860s and held more than twelve thousand slaves, as stated, "Of this number about twelve hundred slaves were held by residents in the 18th District, or Triune, or nearly one tenth of the entire number of slaves in the county."

By 1870, Triune had a population of one thousand and fifty-four people. Of the above number, four hundred and thirty-seven were White folk and six hundred and seventeen were Black and Mulatto folk. Of the six hundred and seventeen Black and Mulatto population, only two men (Peter Hyde and Brent Bostick) from that number held jobs other than farmers, cooks, and domestic servants. Both Hyde and Bostick were blacksmiths.

In 1889, Triune had a population of seven hundred and ninety-eight Black and Mulatto people. Of those, seven hundred and ninety-eight people, only nine of them held jobs other than farmers, cooks, and domestic servants. Those nine people were: Jack Carter, stone mason; Sam Fuller, school teacher; Archy German, woodchopper; Peter Hyde, blacksmith; Ephraim Yeargin, stone mason; Robert Parrish, shoemaker; Perkins, stoker; James Scales, works in mill; and Jack Shaw, stone mason. The statistics, among the eldest Black and Mulatto population, found Rachel Yeargin, age 85 in 1870, and Peter Hyde, age 97, in 1880.[1]

---

1. Battle, Thelma. *Triune, An African American Review: We've Come This Far By Faith*, 2003.

Picking Cotton

OVIE ELAINE BOLEYJACK BELL

Cotton pickers on T.B. Jones farm

There is a saying that black people use when asked, "How are you doing?" They respond by saying, "I'm still picking cotton." This means I am still working for the man, getting nowhere, losing hope, and getting frustrated.

In this country, after slavery, most black people felt that they were still picking cotton and not being paid for their labor. Most white people saw our freedom in a different light. They were without a field hand, cook, nanny, and housekeeper. Freedom to our people meant we could breathe, smile, and seek happiness.

As we look back at reality, freedom only existed in our minds. We never owned anything, just the clothing on our backs, because some of us didn't even have shoes on our feet.

We were placed back into that slave ship we arrived on without a thought for our well-being. You would probably say, "What ship are you talking about?" Our people were told they were free, yet there was no plan for us because no one ever thought this day would come. Our people had only traveled in the area of the Plantation. So, they were floating on the water, heading for an unknown destination.

The only alternative they had was to go back to the master and continue to pick cotton. Some looked for a different master due to the brutality they received or to get a new start in life. That didn't work for a large portion of the black population in Tennessee. They would leave and then come back to what was familiar because they had to stop going in circles.

Picking cotton at Duplex

Freedom will never come to fruition until you obtain power, and that will only come when you're in control of your life, realizing your potential and self-worth. Then, you will secure stability, the state of being stable. Our people, as a whole, to this day, have never been able to see this reality due to the fact that we own very little in this country, because of inequality.

When they would look for other opportunities in the north, blacks would have no other choice but to live in low-income housing in the ghetto, which placed them back into the slave ship, where they found no land in sight. What if we had been given what most white people have, a legacy that could be passed down from generation to generation? We worked the land and generated its worth; why shouldn't we share in the profits?

Most people in this country will never comprehend what we feel deep down inside.

We are told in the Declaration of Independence that all men are created equal and have rights, yet we have never been able to take advantage of this privilege. Why has it taken so long? I want you to understand that our people never want to take what you have; they only want the opportunity to have what you have. Our children have earned that right for all that we have gone through.

Imagine if we were willed property and money from our parents and grandparents. We would be prospering as you are, and we would be on a level playing field. Our future would look quite different, wouldn't you say? In this year of our Lord 2025, we're still pursuing that elusive dream of equality. O' say, can you see America!

Cotton pickers on the T.B. Jones farm

Share-Croppers

Just a herd of Negroes
Driven to the field,
Plowing, planting, hoeing,
To make the cotton yield.

When the cotton's picked
And the work is done
Boss man takes the money
And we get none,

Leaves us hungry, ragged
As we were before.
Year by year goes by
And we are nothing more

Than a herd of Negroes
Driven to the field –
Plowing life away
To make the cotton yield.[1]

– *Langston Hughes*

---

1. Hughes, Langston (1902 – 1967), Shakespeare in Harlem [poetry], Alfred A. Knopf, 1942.

J.C. Patton, Jr.

OVIE ELAINE BOLEYJACK BELL

Back: Mary Patton Williams, J.C. Patton, Sr., and Mamie F. Patton Polk; Front: Annie Margaret Vaughn and J.C. Patton, Jr.

J.C. Patton Jr. is the son of J.C. Patton Sr. and Henry Ester Jordan and the grandson of George and Martha Ann Patton of Triune. The Patton family worked as sharecroppers on Lee Caldwell's and Mr. Williams' farms. They worked in the tobacco and hay fields and shared in the crops after they were harvested, as many black families did in this part of the country.

J.C. went to Green Grove School until the 4th grade and revealed his and his friend's exploits during those years. One day, they had to gather wood for the heater to warm the school. Something that took place almost every day in the winter. They would pick up sticks from around the area and place them under the building where they were stored. They thought they would have a little fun playing in the woods on this particular day and lost track of time. When the teacher called for them to come in, they knew they were in trouble, so they took wood from beneath the school and made her think they had gathered it. "None the Wiser."

After the fourth grade, J.C. attended Kirkland Elementary School in Kirkland, Tennessee. New schools, new rules, and teachers, like Mr. W. B. Covington, Mrs. Maudell Dotson, Mrs. Reams, and Mrs. Lanier. He said he missed his old school, but this was a better facility with restrooms and a heating unit. J.C. had great memories of how much fun he had playing baseball on the hill; it was a part of the playground, but separate for playing ball. When he was in the eighth grade, the boys tried to convince Professor Covington, their teacher, to allow them to play ball in the middle of the day. He would give in on occasions because he loved the game as much as they did, and they played until it was time to go home.

After J.C. advanced from the eighth grade, he went to Franklin Training School, which was renamed Natchez High School. He played on the football team with Jimmy Anderson, Julius Cisner, and William James Jones, friends from Kirkland. He said they were given used football uniforms and equipment from the white school in Franklin that was torn and broken, which made it difficult to wear. Surprisingly, they received new uniforms and all the equipment they needed in their senior year. They were so proud of how they looked and felt, he said I think it made us play a little harder. It must have worked because they became the 1962 champions in the Shrine Bowl, which was played at Tennessee A&I College in Nashville (now TSU). Jimmy Anderson received a full scholarship in football to play at the same college where his dream began. This was an exciting time in their young lives.

Natchez High School 1962 Champions. 1st row: Charles Fitzgerald, Harold Moore, Leon Hodge, Zack Hodge, William Dalton, Charles Hardeman, Edward Fleming, William Burns, Walter Selmer, William Pope, and Jimmy Anderson; 2nd row: Douglas Lane, Claude Perkins, John Woods, William Brooks, Richard Southall, Julius Cisner, David Grimes, Vel Lucas, Ellis Lockridge, Coach Hayes, Head Coach Bill Reynolds, and Principal C.B. Spencer; 3rd row: George Esmon, Edward Robinson, J.C. Patton, William Scruggs, Ike Norris, John Murdic, and Billy Murdic.[1]

Following J.C.'s graduation from high school, he went to work for a cement company with his friends Bud Glenn and J.W. Boyd for a year. Later, he obtained employment with the Rudy Farms Corporation. During his employment there, he started a softball team with the men he grew up with in Nolensville, Tennessee. They were called the Outlaws. They were having great success but needed a sponsor to help with finances. He asked the manager at Rudy Farms if he would be interested in helping them, and

---

1. Natchez High School Yearbook. Franklin, Tennessee. 1963.

he agreed to be their sponsor. They paid for the uniforms and all the equipment, even the balls. J.C. said they played at Sunset Park and Sulphur Dell Park in Nashville. J.C. was the coach, and James K. Perkins was the team's assistant coach. They won many games and trophies during the time they played together. The memories of those years will be forever in their hearts and minds.

The Rudy Farm Softball Team

Deception

George Boleyjack's Car Repair

OVIE ELAINE BOLEYJACK BELL

Will "Babe" Ridley

James Johnson's service station in Triune, Tennessee, was a hangout for many black and white young men. They would drink beer and have a good time. Mr. Johnson also hired blacks to pump gas and clean the cars' windshields. Will "Babe" Ridley worked there for several years. Many people brought their cars to be worked on at his station. My oldest brother, George Boleyjack Jr., was told that Mr. Johnson was a great mechanic, so when he was having trouble with his car, he took it to him to check it out. He looked the car over and told George what parts he would need to fix it. He also said he would need to order the parts and how much they would cost.

George permitted him to do what was necessary and left the car with him. When he returned to pick up his car, he paid him what he was told and drove off. A few days later, when he came to fill his car with gas, one of the white guys told him that Mr. Johnson had put used parts in his car and said, "Please don't tell him it was me."

My brother confronted him and said, "You need to show me where you put the new parts in my car." He confessed that he had put used parts in the car and said they worked fine. George said, "You need to give me my money back." After he received his money, he told him, "You will never get my business again because I can't trust you." We were never to question a white man, even if he was wrong. However, my brother was honest, and he expected Mr. Johnson to have integrity, of which he had none. Some of those same interactions continue to this day in one form or another.

"These were things that black people had to go through quite often in the South."

– Elaine Bell

Martha Ann House

ANN BETTS

"Is that you, sugar? I can't see on cloudy days."

The speaker is small, spry, and alert. She stands in the doorway of her cottage overlooking Henry Horton Highway, on a farm where she has spent the better part of her life. The speaker is Martha Ann House, and she is 97 years old. Born in a house on Spanntown Road in Triune, Mrs. House cannot remember a time when she was not working. "My mother had me driving the turkeys to roost when I was just a little girl," she recalls. "We took in washing, and I had to wash men's socks in a cedar tub."

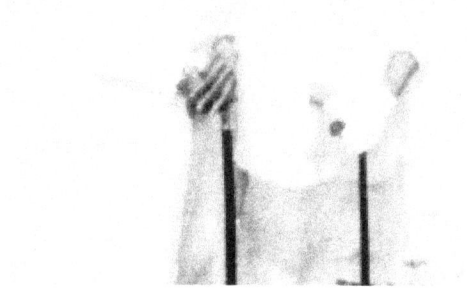

Martha Ann Bostic House, on left, with Lucy Johnson McClaren

Memories of her mother include a story about the Civil War. "Mama told me she saw Yankee soldiers coming ... coming up the hill. She ran away from them. The only place she could find to hide was behind a tree that had a cord of firewood stacked beside it. She hid behind that firewood from the Yankees."

High on the hill above Martha Ann's cottage looms the stately Page home, the former residence of the late Mr. and Mrs. Millard (Cora Page) Hopkins.

"I did everything in that house," says Martha Ann. "Miss Cora promised me a home on this place for as long as I lived. Miss Cora and I got along just fine. If she sassed me, I never sassed her back. I'd just look up, and she'd say, "What are you looking at?" I'd say, I'm just looking to the Lord!" The Lord is Martha Ann's strong shield and staff.

The home of Mrs. Cora Page Hopkins

"I go through this house singing praises," she smiles. "Once late in the night, I dreamed I was talking to the Lord," I said, "Lord, I can't read, and I can't write. What can I do? A voice came back to me and said, 'Look in the Gospel of John. In the beginning was the Word, and the Word was with God.' That came to me in my sleep."

Martha Ann is the oldest living member of the Green Grove Baptist Church. A plaque attesting to her more than 50 years of service is proudly displayed on the bedroom wall.

"I was baptized in Wilson Creek," she says. "I had been baptized a Methodist first, but the feeling came over me that I had to be a Baptist. That was a long time ago."

Well-known in the area for her culinary skills, Martha Ann recalls picnics and dinners she catered at the Page-Hopkins place.

"Miss Cora used to give those big parties, and everybody would come. Mr. and Mrs. Leslie Osburn, Miss Sue, and Mr. Claude Moss. Now, there was a mighty nice man,"

When asked about her preferences in food, Martha Ann quickly replies, "I eat everything but chitterlings. I used to fry a lot of chitterlings for Miss Cora, but I don't like to eat them."

She was eager to talk about her family. "I had two children," she says, "and 54 grandchildren, step-grandchildren, and great-grandchildren."

They all visit frequently, and one granddaughter is a special help to Martha Ann. "Mary Davis, my granddaughter in Nolensville, does all my paperwork for me – insurance and the like."

Martha Ann does all her own housework and cooks for herself and her grandson, Babe Ridley. "I've had him all his life," she says proudly. Ridley, an employee of the Nolensville Utility District, shares the little house with his grandmother.

Mrs. House says, "I never miss a meal. I eat a big meal at noon, and just some grits or oatmeal at night."

What was the worst time in her life? "There never was a worst time; I loved it all."

Her secret for longevity is simple. "I've walked with the Lord," she says, "and tried not to do wrong. Nobody has ever heard me say a smutty word."

Firmly, she delivers a piece of advice for those who wish to match her life span. "Live a Christian life. Keep your foot in the middle of the road, and don't step out of either side."

Martha Ann House is a small woman, but her spirit is ten feet tall.[1]

"Wisdom is passed down from generation to generation through the ones that came before us. Mrs. Martha Ann House told her family, and anyone else who would listen, how to live a godly life. Her giving spirit filled a room with joy. She left so many memories for her children, grandchildren, and friends."

– Addie Marie Ridley Ogilvie, granddaughter of Mrs. Martha Ann House.

---

1. Betts, Ann. "The Lord Praised for 97 Years of Living," October 5, 1982 (page 41 of 50). *The Tennessean* (1972-) Retrieved from https://www.proquest.com/historical-newspapers/october-5-1982-page-41-50/docview/1908449433/se-2

Day in Court

The Life of Thomas Jefferson Wilson

OVIE ELAINE BOLEYJACK BELL

Thomas Jefferson Wilson

Thomas Jefferson Wilson was born in 1864, just before slavery ended. He married Sallie Ezell, and to their union, four daughters and a son were born: Ovie Jane Wilson Thompson, Mattie Lee Wilson Shaw, Addie Wilson Bostick, Della Wilson Scales, and William McKinley (Buddy) Wilson.

During Thomas's latter years, he worked on many farms throughout the area, where he lived in Williamson County. He would raise tobacco crops in Triune for many years while sharecropping on the Atha Thomas farm.

In 1936, his life ended in a tragic accident on Nolensville Road, close to where I live today. It was a cold night in December. As he often did, he was walking home because he didn't own a car. While on his journey, a man driving a Chevrolet hit him from behind and dragged him 15 feet down the road. Injuring him severely, he received a gash in the back of his head, a broken arm, and a deep wound to his back. R.G. Smith, a local mail carrier of College Grove, was the man who hit him. He got out of his car and saw what he had done. Then, he placed Thomas in his car and took him all the way to Nashville. I can imagine the pain that he was feeling riding to Hubbard Hospital, located at Meharry Medical College, the only hospital that black people could go to in the 1930s. He stayed in the hospital for a few days, where he suffered and died.

Sallie Ezell Wilson   Ovie Jane Wilson Thompson   Royden G. Smith, Sr.

His family was devastated by their loss. They knew they had to do something, but in the 1930s, black people had very few options. It was almost impossible to take a white man to court and have him acknowledge his part in his death, but that is what my grandmother and her family did. They wanted justice for their father, even though they worried about the consequences, because of so many hate crimes during the 1930s. I was so proud of them for not giving up before they had their day in court. They had an all-white jury that delivered the verdict, " Guilty." They received very little of what they requested, but it was never about the money. It was about making him accountable for their father's death.

This is the article I found in the newspaper. It took three days to find it in the archives. When I gazed upon the words, "NEGRO IS HURT ON HIGHWAY," I had to take a deep breath and then look for his name.

A few weeks ago, I found a picture of R. G. Smith with the help of a friend. He was the mail carrier who brought my great-grandfather's mail each week. The family had to see him each and every day during this time. I knew that my grandmother came from a praying family, and oh, how they needed the Lord to pull them through. Many people thought the Wilson family was passive and accepting of what was being done to them. That was far from the truth because they showed courage under pressure.

I'm named after my grandmother, and I hope that I am making her proud. I am telling her story because I'm so proud of her for fighting for what was right. It may have been an accident that took place that night, but in the light of day, there was an empty place at the table.

Charles Darwin once said, "The species that survive aren't the strongest nor the most intelligent, but rather the ones who best adapt to change." I am so glad my family was brave enough to reshape the life they envisioned for the next generation. Now, let us shine a light on the truth as we move forward, filled with pride because of the blood that runs through our veins.

I would like to tell everyone who is reading this story to always listen to your parents and grandparents when they tell stories about their past, and maybe you will find the truth in black and white.

– Ovie Bell

Justice

OVIE ELAINE BOLEYJACK BELL AND BETTY BOLEYJACK MURRAY

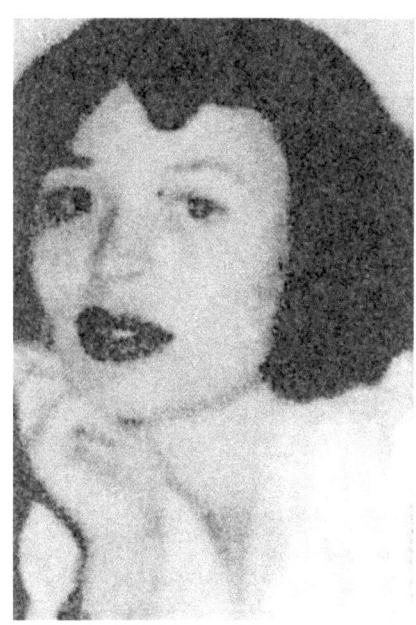

Betty Boleyjack Murray

There was a time when black people couldn't try on clothing in a department store. I had a difficult time understanding this fully until I read a story that explained it to me. The people who owned the store felt that if a black person tried it on, no white person would want to purchase the item. But, in some stores, they would allow the black clientele to put the item over the clothing they were wearing so that It wouldn't touch their skin.

In the "Jim Crow" South, this form of racism was tolerated in many different ways, even in the 1970s. Black people had to wait until the white people were waited on. I know that this is true because it happened to me, Ovie, and my sister, Betty.

In 1972, I went to a store called "Three Sisters." I picked out four outfits and went to pay for the items. I was third in line, but the sales lady asked a white woman to come before me each time it was my turn to check out. After they had been waited on, she motioned for me to come. I put all the items on the counter and said, "You can put them back." I walked out of that store and never went back.

My sister Betty had a different experience. She was shopping in Nashville at Cain Sloan Department Store during the Christmas holiday season. A white man walked into the store and wanted to buy a gift for his wife. As the salesperson was helping him, he turned to Betty and said, "You're the same size as my wife. Would you try these dresses on for me." Betty said, "Of course, I will." The sales lady looked shocked but didn't say a word. Betty entered the dressing room, where she was never allowed to go. She came back out and modeled each one of the dresses for the man. He took all three and left the store. Betty smiled at the sales lady and purchased one of the same dresses for herself.

The man never knew she was black because of her fair skin color.

As the saying goes, "Never judge a book by its cover," or should I say skin color. No harm was done, so it was "none the worse for wear."

Democracy

LANGSTON HUGHES

Democracy will not come
Today, this year
     Nor ever
Through compromise and fear.

I have as much right
As the other fellow has
     To stand
On my two feet
And own the land
I tire so of hearing people say,
Let things take their course.
Tomorrow is another day.
I do not need my freedom when I'm dead.
I cannot live on tomorrow's bread.

>*Freedom*
>
>*Is a strong seed*
>
>*Planted*
>
>*In a great need.*
>
>*I live here, too.*
>
>*I want freedom*
>
>*Just as you.*

Coming Together

JOHN H. BOLEYJACK

In the rural area of Triune, Tennessee, the young men in the community during the 1950s and 1960s had to look for jobs near home. Black and white guys worked together in the fields, cutting tobacco, gathering corn, and cutting hay. There was no segregation when it came to hard work. We drank from the same water cooler and went to the same toilet with the half-moon on the door. When it was time for lunch, we found a cool spot under a tree where we ate and complained about the day's activity.

The only problem the black guys had was receiving the same salary as the whites. We couldn't get angry because we were initially told how much money we would be given. Yet, the wheels in my mind were turning. The next time they called for me to work, I would say no if I didn't get equal pay. The following day, I decided to test my theory, which worked as I had hoped. From then on, we were given the same pay as the white guys.

At the end of each day, we were all very tired and wanted to go home, but when someone mentioned, let's play one game of baseball, we were no longer tired. Our family was living on the Horace Windrow property, and we had a large field in the backyard where we were staying. We didn't put together a black versus white team. We chose who was best for our team.

We had so much fun playing the game that we loved. Some of the players on the team included Bill and Tom Ewing, Charles and Oneal Vaughn, Albert, James, and George Boleyjack, Larry and Charlie Brown, Dan Pierce, and George Jones. Even though my brother Joe and I were young, they would allow us to play from time to time. I often wonder why the world wasn't always like this.

Triune

Because you see no color when you're laughing, talking, and having a good time, we all think about those days we spent together.
Or has the world changed so much that we would like to bury the past and the joy?

Kindness

The Ferguson Family

JOHN H. BOLEYJACK

John and Martha Ferguson

There is a family that I will never forget, and that is the Ferguson family. Especially Mr. John Ferguson. He lived on Old Murfreesboro Road, not far from where we lived. I recall one afternoon, my brothers Joe, Howard, and I were getting ready to go to a football game at Natchez High School in Franklin. Mr. Ferguson was at our home talking with our dad, and we interrupted their conversation to ask for two dollars to get into the game. Dad said you don't need to go to that game because he didn't want to give us the money. Mr. Ferguson said, "Give them the money, Scoonie." Dad did.

Then Mr. Ferguson took some money from his pocket and gave us three dollars. He said you may want to buy your girlfriend something at the game. You can come to the farm tomorrow and do some work to earn extra money. I will never forget his kind gesture. We worked for him quite often during high school. He is no longer with us, but his memory lives on. His daughter, Ann Ferguson Frank, still lives on the Ferguson farm, and she is just as kind as her father.

My Recollections

LT. COL. JOHN L. JORDAN

Lt. Col. John L. Jordan

There is no more enjoyable sport than opossum and raccoon hunting at night in the fall of the year. I enjoyed this perhaps above all others when the coon dog would tree a coon and necessitate the climbing of the tree by one of the of the party. I have climbed some of the highest trees in the forest at night after a coon. Opossums, in general, climb a small tree or hide in the hollow of a tree. They are not often difficult to reach, although it is sometimes necessary to smoke them out. Old negroes I went with could always tell whether a dog would chase a rabbit, and this earned him a good whipping as quickly as he returned. I have caught fine opossums in the woods in the daytime. I regard them as good food when barbecued and baked with sweet potatoes, but in recent years, I have never found one cooked so that I cared for it.

The 18th Civil District in which Triune was situated contained over 1,200 people in the 1870s and 80s about half of them were negroes. The Negroes voted freely with the aid of some white man who selected his ticket. There was always a spirited contest for constables and justices of the peace. The best element, composed of the leading citizens of the old families, had to combat with a component composed of what could be described as poor whites. Some of them were of unsavory reputation, combined with a majority of the negroes. Many old ex-slaves stood loyally by their old families and voted with them in local elections.

Old Uncle Edward Jamison who lived on Uncle John Jordan's place on Arrington Creek, adjoining ours, made the startling prediction in 1878 that within five years, a Negro be as a great a curiosity in Williamson County, Tennessee, as an elephant because many were then emigrating to Kansas. Old Uncle Edward went with his family but there were and still are perhaps a hundred Negroes in the Triune community. Saloons existed in several places in the district then, but early in the eighties, they were legislated out by the famous "Four Mile Law".

In those days, there was more litigation due perhaps to the saloons, more disorder than now, but the moral tone of the community was high. My father, who was a justice of the peace in the county and a member of the county court for many years, perhaps thirty in all, told me that in the first term beginning in 1876, he had many times as many cases on his docket as in the nineties. There were no white Republicans in the district until about 1880, when Hiram Hooper came and built a home and livery stable at the corner of Spanntown Road. To this day, there is only one white Republican in the community.[1]

---

1. Warwick, Rick. *Triune: Two Centuries at the Crossroads*, excerpts by Lt. Col. John L. Jordan, Williamson County Historical Society, 2004.

Winner Take All

The Raccoon Hunters

JOHN H. BOLEYJACK

George "Scoonie" Boyleyjack with his grandsons, Keith and Marcus Murray, and coon dogs.

There were many coon (raccoon) hunters in the rural area of Williamson County, and my father George "Scoonie" Boleyjack was an avid hunter. He would stay up all night in the woods just to hear the sound of his dog tree a coon. He had many black and white friends who would go on that journey with him. On one particular night in the fall of the year, 12 hunters and 22 dogs sat out to find a coon. They decided to make the hunt a contest. Each group put money into a hat and the first group that found a coon would be the winner. Many sounds were coming from the dogs in the woods. George and his partner Dave Rutledge felt good about their chances of finding the coon first. George's dog Jim was on the trail of something near the tree, and he started to howl and dig around the root. George felt that the coon was in the hole, so he cut the root, and Jim pulled the coon out.

George and Dave shouted, "We've got him." All the other Hunters came running, and their worst nightmare came true. George and Dave would brag about this forever. Alton Ferguson had to see where he found the coon. They showed him the hole where the coon went in.

Alton said, "You helped your dog by cutting the root off the tree. You cheated."

George said, "Who is holding the coon, me or you?"

Everyone started to laugh. Alton said, "I knew you would find a way to win."

Dad would tell that story repeatedly through the years and laugh until he cried. He had the best memories of his life with the guys he hunted with. I would like to name a few of them: Alton Ferguson, Walter Beasley, Dave Rutledge, Bubba Gentry, Doris Hardeman, Mr. Derryberry, Hamp Thomas, and Dan Fuller. Dad hunted from Mississippi to Indiana and loved every minute of it, including the friends he met along the way.

Triune Coonhunters: Alton Ferguson, John Ferguson, unknown, and George Boleyjack

"Yes Sir, Mr. Tom"

Jim Crow Etiquette

OVIE ELAINE BOLEYJACK BELL

Dan Fuller

When I had the opportunity to talk with Mr. Dan Fuller, my father's hunting buddy, he expressed to me that he didn't understand why my father called him Mr. Dan and said "Yes, Sir" to him. Dan was a young man at that time, and my father was much older than he was.

I was quite baffled by his statement, and it took me a little while to form the words in my mind to respond to his question. As I started to explain from my perspective, I thought, how did he not see what was going on in our country and community? I pushed that aside and said Dad was born in 1908 and grew up under the Jim Crow laws.

Dad was always in survival mode, and this was ingrained into him as a child due to a racially oppressive society, where white people held the power. He felt pressured to conform to what he knew was wrong and humiliating. I want everyone to know it didn't take anything away from my father's character or his dignity. What he showed on the outside was not what he felt on the inside. He was a proud man who was never broken because he had real power. He could play the game and come out on the other side and live a happy life for 97 years.

I discern that Mr. Fuller wanted to give my father the respect he felt he deserved, being an older man. The times would not allow my father to let down his guard, because it could have brought about conflict. As the saying goes, he "went along to get along."

There is another expression that says, "Time heals all wounds." Time doesn't heal all wounds. Time only breaks it down into fragments as they drift around, causing the wound to be irritated and bringing about more pain.

As you read the following article, you will better understand why Black people formed this habit, simply for survival. If someone had authority over your life, what would you do?

JIM CROW ETIQUETTE

Most southern white Americans who grew up prior to 1954 expected black Americans to conduct themselves according to well-understood rituals of behavior. This racial etiquette governed the actions, manners, attitudes, and words of all black people when in the presence of whites. To violate this racial etiquette placed one's very life, and the lives of one's family, at risk.

Blacks were expected to refer to white males in positions of authority as "Boss" or "Cap'n" — a title of respect that replaced "Master" or "Marster" used in slave times. Sometimes, the white children of one's white employer or a prominent white person might be called "Massa," to show special respect. If a white person was well known, a black servant or hired hand or tenant might speak in somewhat intimate terms, addressing the white person as "Mr. John" or "Miss Mary."

All black men, on the other hand, were called by their first names or were referred to as "Boy," "Uncle," and "Old Man" — regardless of their age. If the white person did not personally know a black person, the term "nigger" or "nigger-fellow," might be used. In legal cases and the press, blacks were often referred to by the word "Negro" with a first name attached, such as "Negro Sam." At other times, the term "Jack," or some common name, was universally used in addressing black men not known to the white speaker. On the Pullman Sleeping cars on trains, for example, all the black porters answered to the name of "boy" or simply "George" (after the first name of George Pullman, who owned and built the Pullman Sleeping Cars).

Whites much preferred to give blacks honorary titles, such as Doctor, or Professor, or Reverend, in order to avoid calling them Mister. While the term "nigger" was universally used, some whites were uncomfortable with it because they knew it was offensive to most blacks. As a substitute, the word "niggra" often appeared in polite society.

Black women were addressed as "Auntie" or "girl." Under no circumstances would the title "Miss" or "Mrs." be applied. A holdover from slavery days was the term "Wench," a term that showed up in legal writings and depositions in the Jim Crow era. Some educated whites referred to black women by the words "colored ladies." Sometimes, just the word "lady" was used. White women allowed black servants and acquaintances to call them by their first names but with the word "Miss" attached as a modifier: "Miss Ann," "Miss Julie," or "Miss Scarlett," for example.

This practice of addressing blacks by words that denoted disrespect or inferiority reduced the black person to a non-person, especially in newspaper accounts. In reporting incidents involving blacks, the press usually adopted the gender-neutral term "Negro," thus designating blacks as lifeless and unknown persons. For example, an accident report might read like this: "Rescuers discovered that two women, three men, four children, and five Negroes were killed by the explosion."

In general, blacks and whites could meet and talk on the street. Almost always, however, the rules of racial etiquette required blacks to be agreeable and non-challenging, even when the white person was mistaken about something. Usually, it was expected that blacks would step off the sidewalk when meeting whites or else walk on the outer street side of the walk, thereby "giving whites the wall." Under no circumstances could a black person assume an air of equality with whites. Black men were expected to remove their caps and hats when talking with a white person. Those whites, moreover, who associated with blacks in a too friendly or casual manner ran the risk of being called a "nigger lover."

Blacks and whites were not expected to eat together in public. It was okay for blacks to enter a restaurant to buy food to take out or to stand at the end of a lunch counter until their order was taken. Usually, they would then leave and wait outside for their food to be brought to them. Some places allowed blacks to eat in the kitchen. Nor were black customers always allowed to use store implements such as plates or dishes or even boxes. Black customers commonly brought their own tin pails and buckets to be filled.

The white owners of clothing stores did not allow blacks to try on clothing as a general rule, fearing that white customers would not buy clothes worn by African Americans. Some stores did allow blacks to put on clothing over their own clothes or to try on hats over a cloth scarf on their heads. Shoes were never tried on as a general rule, but most white clerks did allow exact measurements to be made. In most towns, black customers knew which stores could be expected to treat them with respect while not breaking the rules of racial etiquette.

Many public places, parks, and entertainment centers excluded blacks altogether after 1890, frequently by law if not by custom. Signs were often posted equating blacks with animals: "Negroes and dogs not allowed." In some communities, blacks could attend public performances but only by using separate entrances in the back or via an alley. In public halls, theaters, and movie houses, they always sat upstairs in the so-called "nigger heaven" or "buzzard roost." Even the annual state fairs would have a "colored day", allowing the black population to attend only on that specific day.

Law rather than custom separated the races in public transportation, but local habits of racial etiquette usually determined how the statutes were implemented. Some towns and municipalities put blacks in the rear of the streetcars while others required them up front where they could be watched by the car's operator. Custom did not allow motormen or conductors to assist black women with bags or parcels. Some municipal codes required blacks to be seated from the front to the rear, while others allowed blacks to sit anywhere they wanted in the black section. In general, it was expected that blacks would give up their seats to white passengers during peak or crowded times.

Some towns required separate entrances to public buildings, with blacks using one entry and whites another. In most cases, white clerks in stores and ticket stands always served white customers first, although no state or municipal law required this practice. Signs in the black section of waiting rooms at train stations, for example, customarily warned against loafing, spitting, and unacceptable behavior. No such signs were usually displayed in the white sections. Nor did blacks generally eat in the dining cars on trains, and, if they were allowed to eat there, a drawn curtain separated the one or two "colored tables" from the rest of the car. These rules did make exceptions, however, for black nurses and nannies who accompanied white children or elderly white people on trains and streetcars.

The color line and the codes of racial etiquette were also strictly observed in public hospitals, with separate wards for whites and blacks. Black nurses were allowed to minister to whites but not the other way round. If a black person needed an ambulance, for example, a private, black-owned-and-operated wagon or auto would have to be obtained. No exceptions were allowed, no matter the extent of the injury or emergency. A similar Jim Crow code of conduct applied even in the U.S. Army. It was not until Eleanor Roosevelt intervened in WWII that black nurses were allowed to care for white soldiers, even though a serious shortage of nurses existed. The black nurses were used prior to Roosevelt's intervention to attend to German prisoners of war rather than U.S. soldiers.

The whole intent of Jim Crow etiquette boiled down to one simple rule: blacks must demonstrate their inferiority to whites by actions, words, and manners. Laws supported this racist code of behavior whenever racial customs started to weaken or break down in practice — as they did during the Reconstruction era. When the laws were weakly or slowly applied, whites resorted to violence against blacks to reinforce the customs and standards of behavior. Indeed, whites commonly justified lynchings and the horrible murders of blacks during the Jim Crow era as defensive actions taken in response to black violations of the color line and rules of racial etiquette.[1]

Ronald L.F. Davis, Ph. D.
California State University, Northridge
September 2006

---

1. Davis, Ronald L. F., Ph.D., *Jim Crow Etiquette*, September 2006. Accessed online at Jim Crow Museum, Grand Rapids, MI: https://jimcrowmuseum.ferris.edu/question/2006/september.htm, on June 23, 2025.

Baseball

OVIE ELAINE BOLEYJACK BELL; DELORES VAUGHN MATTHEWS; AND JOHN H. BOLEYJACK

The Kirkland Baseball Team

The love of baseball transcended color and race; it was the nation's favorite pastime, at least in the area of Triune, Kirkland, and College Grove, Tennessee.

Delores Vaughn told me a story about her when she was a little girl. Her mother had dressed her for church in a pretty little dress and her Sunday shoes, and she was waiting for someone to pick her up to take her to church, but no one came. Her grandfather was getting dressed to go to the Sulphur Dell ballpark in Nashville. He told her I guess you're going with us to the game. He stopped, picked up his friend, Mr. George Boleyjack (Scoonie), and headed to the game. My grandfather would never let anything stand in his way regarding baseball. The New York Yankees played ball that day, and I felt special being with my grandfather.

Delores Vaughn Matthews, Hutton Vaughn, and Mary Ann Floyd Claybrooks

Before 1947, baseball was segregated, we had the white and Negro leagues around the country. The young men and boys in Williamson County found this an enjoyable experience. Some dreamt of becoming a professional baseball player. For the black youth in this area, it was thought to be a pipe dream, but it didn't stop them. They would practice as if it were valid. Several baseball teams sprouted up in the surrounding communities.

John Leslie Vaughn was a pitcher on a baseball team in the Possum Trot area in the late 1940s and 1950s. I don't know the team's name, but the initials were B.G. His daughter (Delores) gave me this picture of the team. That day was very special for John; he pitched a no-hitter, and his teammates put him on their shoulders and carried him off the field. Many more teams followed in their footsteps.

After Jackie Robinson broke the color barrier, every black male child wanted to emulate his style and presence. The Brooklyn Dodgers were the talk of every household. George Boleyjack Sr. and Walter Sawyers created a team in Triune, Tennessee, that brought together many students who went to Kirkland Elementary School. Joe and Jimmy Anderson, Wesley Anderson, Joe and

John Boleyjack, William James Jones, Taylor Grant Ewing, Sam Williams, James Floyd, James Shaw, George Ogilvie, John Willie Bostick, Jerome Covington, Jessie Anderson, and Thomas Williams. They played baseball on Sunday afternoon on a field in Triune, which the white players were no longer using, and they allowed us to play there for free. It's the area where they still have horse shows to this day.

After church, we would all gather together, enjoy each other's company, and cheer for our favorite team. We would also capture the wonderful smells in the air of food being prepared by Annie Boleyjack, Lelia May Odom, and Ella Rucker. Ella would be frying fish while Annie and Lelia May scooped ice cream and fixed hot dogs and hamburgers, and we can't forget the fried peach pies. Those were the good old days.

Annie Boleyjack

Ella Rucker

I want to acknowledge a few more young black men who played during this time and were good at their game. John and Henry Perkins, James K. Perkins, William Hubert Thompson, and James Cunningham. J. C. Patton of Triune was also a coach for the teams called the Outlaws and Rudy Farms, and they won quite a few trophies.

I also want to thank all of the parents and teachers who encouraged the young men and gave their support, enabling them to become the self-sufficient men they are today. Special thanks go out to Professor William B. Covington. He saw their abilities and drive at an early age. Because he was the principal at Kirkland Elementary School and because he had a love for baseball, he would bring a television to school when it was time for the World Series. He would then allow the young men in the 7th and 8th grades to watch the games with him as long as they had completed their classroom assignments.

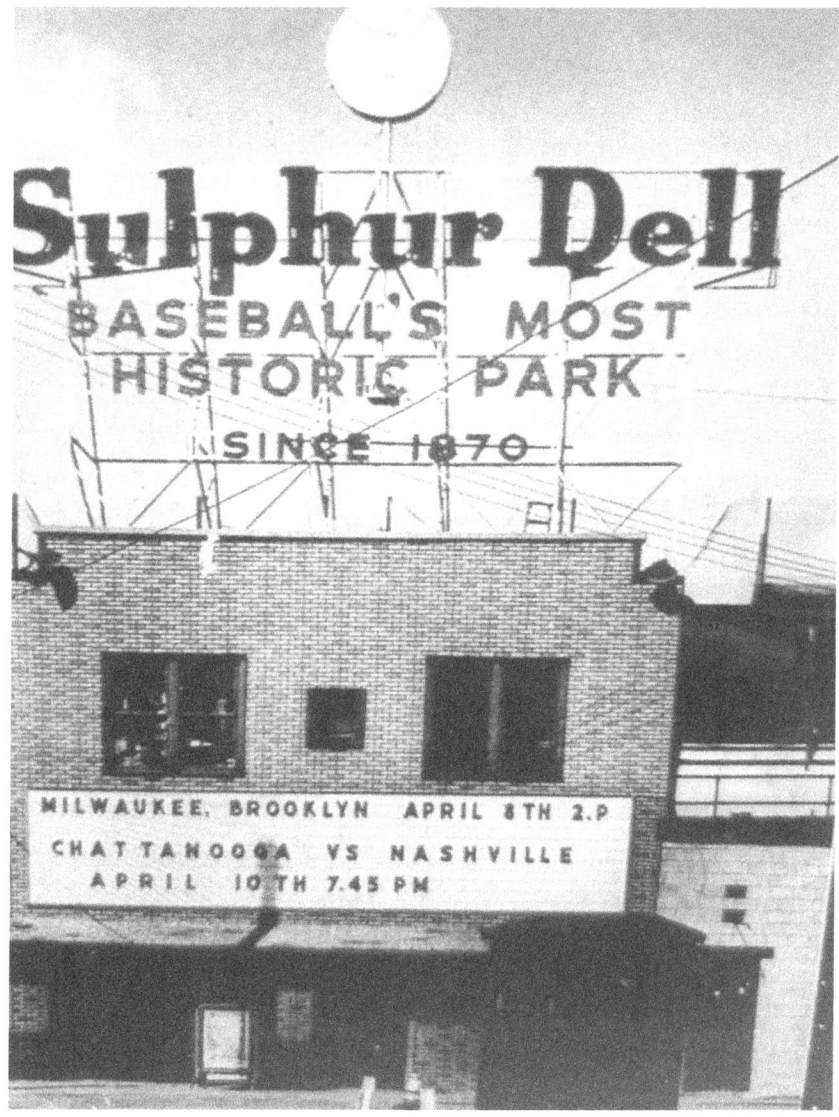

Sulphur Dell

Arch Boleyjack

OVIE ELAINE BOLEYJACK BELL

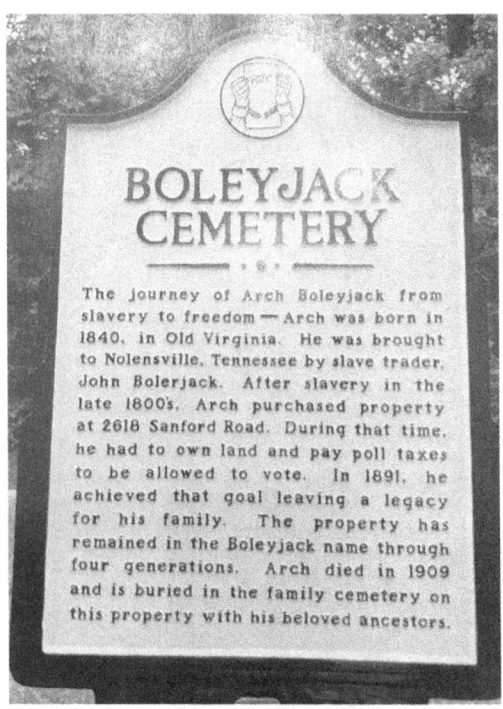

Arch Boleyjack Historic Marker

I have a tough time putting myself into my ancestors' shoes. It is hard for me to imagine getting beaten with a whip and being made to work from sunup to sundown. This is hard to comprehend.

I want to tell you about one such man, Arch Boleyjack, my great-grandfather. He was born in Virginia in 1840. As a young man, he was bought and paid for by a slave trader named John Bolerjack. His brothers were also taken simultaneously and brought to Nolensville, Tennessee. Arch told his family about that day. He said his mother was crying and wringing her hands, as her children were being taken away from her forever.

I know nothing about his life as a slave; I can only imagine what he may have gone through. I know that he was married at the end of slavery in 1865 and had one son. He later married my great-grandmother, Sally, and had five children. One of the children was named Margaret, and she was my grandmother, and her oldest son was my father, George Boleyjack Sr. My father would often tell us stories about Arch. He said he was a hard worker and purchased property on Sanford Road in Nolensville, Tennessee, in the late 1800s.

It gives me so much joy walking on the land where my ancestors walked. My great-grandfather and many of my ancestors are buried in the cemetery on the property. I wish there were a way for him to see me now. I hope he would be proud of me, because I'm so proud of him, for one special reason. He was a voter! The reason I know this is because he faithfully paid his poll taxes. He paid $2 in the 1880s so that no one could take away his chance to vote. When I think about him, I try hard to fight for what is right because his blood runs through my veins.

THIS IS WHY I VOTE!

THIS IS WHY MY GREAT-GRANDFATHER PAID TO VOTE!

THIS IS WHY WE MUST NEVER PASS UP THE CHANCE TO VOTE!

"Liberty, freedom, and democracy are very fuzzy words, but human rights is very specific."

— Joichi Ito

Never say, "I don't have time to vote." Our ancestors died for this right.

Do not dishonor their memory in that way.

— Ovie Bell

Descendants of Arch Boleyjack

Dr. William and Elaine Boleyjack Bell

I want to thank my great-grandfather for living and for enduring all the pain, so that I can live the life that I'm living today. I will never forget that from which I came.

The Boleyjacks of Triune

OVIE ELAINE BOLEYJACK BELL

George "Scoonie" Boleyjack and Annie L. Thompson Boleyjack

George "Scoonie" and Annie L. Thompson Boleyjack planted firm roots in Williamson County for most of their lives. It all started with George's grandfather, Arch Boleyjack. He was brought to Nolensville during slavery from Virginia. He and his family remained in the same area after slavery was over. Arch purchased land and established a lasting foundation for his family to build on. Life was not always easy, but they persevered with God's help. George was brought up in Nolensville, and Annie was born in Triune.

They got married at an early age, just teenagers. They started their family in 1930, during a difficult time for African Americans. There weren't many quality jobs for people of color. George didn't have many skills, being so young, yet he was very industrious. He had learned how to be self-sufficient as a young boy. At age ten, he started a business, cutting wood and placing it on a wagon he made, pulled by a goat. He sold the wood to neighbors in the area, and his family taught him how to work the land.

Now that he had taken on the responsibility of husband and father, he needed to work with urgency because the children were coming back to back. They were now living in the home where his grandfather, Arch, lived. They had only six acres of land, which wasn't enough to produce what was needed to provide for his family.

John W. Little

It became necessary to seek other opportunities. They later moved to Louis Williams' farm on York Road in Nolensville. This was the first time he worked as a sharecropper. They stayed there for a few years, then relocated to the Herschel Adams farm in Arrington, Tennessee. George continued to work as a sharecropper, learning many skills along the way.

Next, the Boleyjack family moved to the John Little Farm in Kirkland. On this farm, he would sharecrop, train, and groom horses. They would stay there for many years as their family grew. This was one of the places where George could expand his wings, grow different crops, and earn more money for the family.

George was always seeking other endeavors to better himself, which brought him the old Joe Covington farm in Triune, now owned by Horace Windrow and Fannie Covington Windrow. He was the principal of East High School in Nashville, Tennessee, and his wife taught school in College Grove, Tennessee.

In the mid-40s, times were changing, and sharecropping was transformed into something other than a step up from slavery. It was time to negotiate the terms and rules of staying on someone else's property. The Boleyjack family would share equally in all aspects of the farm work. They would provide the labor for rent and then share the cost of what was being planted. Everything would be split down the middle, and both parties would keep records. In doing this, George could put money away for the future. The last five children were born during this time, bringing the total to fifteen. Annie had her hands full raising her family.

Horace Windrow

Fannie Lou Covington Windrow

There was no television to entertain us; we listened to the radio for a few years. Annie would tell stories and act out the parts. We would sit on the porch at night, sing songs, and watch the fireflies dance throughout the yard. She was a loving, caring mother who showed us by example how important it is to serve the Lord. She would often read to us from the Bible during our childhood. George would give his wife a break on Sunday afternoons in the summer, take us to the backyard, and assemble a baseball team. He was always the umpire so that he could help the younger kids in the family. We had so much fun; we were never lonely because there was always someone to talk to and play with. That is the blessing of having a large family.

There were many black families like ours throughout Williamson County. We worked harder than we should have, trying to get ahead and doing jobs we would never allow our children to do. Life was not easy; we were called names and treated with disrespect just because of the color of our skin, yet that didn't stop us. In 1963, Dave and Mary Scales McMurray's farm was put up for sale on Old Murfreesboro Road, and my father and mother would purchase that 50-acre farm and have something we could call our own.

We could not receive our 40 acres and a mule after slavery, but we did work hard to acquire our 50 acres and a tractor. We had land where we could put down roots and decide what to plant and what cattle to buy. Racism would rear its ugly head occasionally because we were prospering and moving forward. George dealt with it and always made us feel safe. He had many black and white friends to whom he would give support in their time of need, and they would return the favor. Our parents taught us always to judge people by their character because they felt there was good in everyone if you look for it.

Two of George and Annie's sons, John and Larry, still live on some of the property today. We will always be thankful for our home, filled with beautiful memories that will last a lifetime, and for the love of God that brought us through it all.

George "Scoonie" Boleyjack

Triune

George William Boleyjack, Jr.

Betty Jane Murray (Raymond)

Margaret Ann Randolph (James)

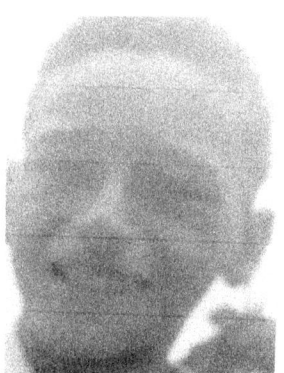

Albert Lee Boleyjack

Ellowese Sowell (William)

James Andrew Boleyjack (Alma)

Hattie Ruth Lane (Cornell)

Howard Landis Boleyjack

Joe Clifton Boleyjack (Carla)

COMING OUT OF THE DARK INTO THE LIGHT

John Haley Boleyjack (Lena)

Alma Muse Scales (Eugene)

Linda Darnell Williams (Steve)

Thomas Jefferson Boleyjack (Shelia)

Ovie Elaine Bell (William)

Larry Neal Boleyjack (Shirley)

The Hutton Vaughn Family

DELORES VAUGHN MATTHEWS

Dolores Vaughn Matthews

Hutton Vaughn and his wife, Mary Frances, were the head of our family. We call them Papa Hutton and Mama Frances. We would always take their advice because we respected their judgment. They had seven children: John Leslie, Richard, Thomas "Jack," Virgil O'Neal, Ada Mae, Lillian, and Robert "Monk."

My father was John Leslie Vaughn, and my mother was Winnie Vaughn. They had four children: Geraldine, Delores, Wesley, and Gloria. My father, John, drove a milk truck and would drive from home to home, collecting milk from the farmers in the area. My sister Geraldine and I would occasionally ride with him, and some of the farm people would give us candy and cookies. We had so much fun! We lived on Mr. Willie Pate's property because my father was also a sharecropper.

Mr. and Mrs. Pate were nice to my sister and me. Mrs. Georgia would take us into her home when we were outside playing, when it was cold, to keep us warm, and she would make small biscuits for us to eat. They tasted so good. She would also give us gifts. Once she went on vacation to Washington, D.C., and when going through Virginia, she picked up pens for my sister and me. It was filled with lead. I was in the second or third grade, and I still have the pen. I will never forget her kindness.

We lived in Triune, Kirkland, and Nashville. My mother was the first cook at the new Kirkland Elementary School. She had to take a course at Tennessee A&I College in the 1950s to learn how to cook nutritious and well-balanced meals for the students. This was a requirement of Williamson County Schools.

The Hutton Vaughn family

John, Robert, Jack, and Richard Vaughn

Delores Matthews, Ada Mae Floyd, Erskine Vaughn, Geraldine Fletcher, Charles Vaughn, Mary Ann Claybrooks

Winnie holding Delores and John Leslie holding Geraldine Vaughn

See Something, Do Something

What Mary Elizabeth Scales McMurray Did!

JOHN H. BOLEYJACK

As told by George Boleyjack, Sr., father of John Boleyjack

W.P. Scales

George "Scoonie" Boleyjack

Epp Starnes, bus driver

Mrs. Mary Scales McMurray (1888-1962) lived with her husband on Old Murfreesboro Road in Triune, Tennessee. She was a neighbor of the Boleyjack family. During that time, she often saw the children walk for miles in the rain and cold weather to get to school. There were no school buses allocated in Williamson County for black students. There were days her husband, Dave, would take them in his horse and buggy.

She took it into her own hands and called her brother, Mr. W.P. Scales, the Superintendent of Schools in Williamson County. She told her brother that it was wrong for the colored children not to have a bus like the whites. Mr. Scales talked with Mr. Boleyjack about the situation and devised a plan. He said he could get a bus but needed a bus driver. He asked Mr. Boleyjack, if he knew of anyone, and he replied I think I can get Mr. Epp Starnes to drive. The problem was solved because Mrs. Mary Scales McMurray wouldn't take no for an answer.

She was a small woman with a big voice that changed many lives in the area of Triune, Arrington, and College Grove.

"Action is the foundational key to all success."

– Pablo Picasso

Food for Thought

Memories of the Ed Brown Family

OVIE ELAINE BOLEYJACK BELL AND THE BOLEYJACK FAMILY

DURING OUR JOURNEY OF SEGREGATION, MANY PEOPLE CAME INTO OUR LIVES AND LEFT A LASTING IMPRESSION IN UNEXPECTED WAYS ...

There was a small store at the end of Old Murfreesboro Road and Nolensville Road in Triune, Tennessee. The owner of that establishment was Mr. And Mrs. Ed. Brown. They had six children: Mary, Katie, Linda, Shirley, Charley, and Larry. It's no accident that I remember their names because we played together, Black and White. While our parents were shopping in the Brown's grocery store. One of our favorite games was hide and seek.

The Ed Brown Family

The Ed Brown Store in Triune

The mothers would purchase the food, and fathers would gather around the potbelly heater and talk about hunting coons and rabbits, and sometimes they would play cards. So, we had time to have a little fun just being kids.

The store was only a few miles from where we lived, and we would walk there at least twice a week to buy snacks and pick up groceries for our mother. She would tell us to tell Mr. Brown to put it on Dad's tab. He would pay for it at the end of the week or month. This is the way things were done in our area from the 1940s to the 1970s. Our neighbors looked out for each other, and we had an unspoken trust. If we needed one another, all we had to do was ask.

I will always have fond memories of Mr. Brown and his family. I still see Shirley, on occasion, and we give each other warm hugs as we talk about our families, and days gone by.

There was one other notable business near the same area on Nolensville Road – the Puckett Brothers grocery store – owned by James and Milton Puckett. They would serve the community in the same manner as the Brown family did. Their location would become a gathering place on Saturday afternoon and early Sunday morning. Many of the Black men sit on the porch and had a conversation about what was going on in their lives while their wives were doing the grocery shopping. Here are a few names you may recognize: Mr. Brown Lee, Mr. J.C. Patton Sr., Mr. Fred Johnson, Mr. Tom Perkins, Wash Perkins, and Mr. Frank Ogilvie Sr. They would laugh and talk for hours. Some of the White men would join in, and it would last throughout the day.

Puckett Brothers Store in Triune

Puckett's Store with James Puckett in Triune

Minimum Wage

Doing Chores at the Hopkins Home

ADDIE MARIE RIDLEY OGILVIE

Marie Ridley Ogilvie

When I was young, I often visited my great-grandmother Martha House, with my sisters and brother, Annie Mary, Martha, and James. She lived on Mr. and Mrs. Hopkins's property in Triune. In the late 1950s and early 1960s, we spent time at her home with our cousins.

When we were there in the summer months, Mrs. Cora Hopkins would step outside her door, which wasn't far away. She repeatedly called our great-grandmother's name, "Martha Ann, Martha Ann!" until she responded.

Mrs. Hopkins would tell her to send the children to her home because she had chores for them to do. She would always ask us to help with things like getting her mail. She wanted us to pull the weeds from her flower garden that day. We ran to her as fast as our legs could carry us.

When we arrived, she instructed us to pull the weeds. She said, "Don't pull up my flowers, just the weeds, but it was hard to tell one from the other. She stayed outside to watch us for a while. As we started to pull, she shouted, "Don't pull up the flowers!" We finally recognized the weeds from the flowers and went to work.

She told us before she went back into the house, "You're going to be paid, so do a good job." We started to work fast because the sun was beaming down, and we were starting to sweat. We worked for at least two hours, and when the job was completed, she came out to pay us. She gave each of us ten cents. We would look at each other with shock on our faces, but when Mr. Millard Hopkins said he would take us to Puckett's store, we were all in. We all bought different kinds of candy so that we could share them with each other. It was hard work, but we loved spending time together and making memories that would last forever.

Robert Anderson Lee (1919-1951)

Robert Anderson Lee

Robert Anderson Lee, a heavyweight boxer in the military during World War II, has a connection to Williamson County. He was a family member of Brown Lee and Lena Hardison Boleyjack of Triune, a little-known fact that has brought pride to the Lee family.

Corporal Lee's obituary appeared in *The Tennessean* on April 8, 1951. It reads as follows:

"Funeral services for Cpl. Robert Anderson Lee, believed to be the first Korean War fatality, returned to this area, were held in Williamson County Friday.

"Military services for the Negro soldier, an army heavyweight champion boxer, were held at the First Baptist Church in Franklin. Burial was in a family cemetery near Duplex, Tenn. [Spratt Cemetery]

"Corporal Lee died in an army hospital in Japan on Feb. 28, about six hours after he had been wounded by shrapnel in Korea. He was flown to Japan after being hit.

"He had been in the army for eight years. He served at Pearl Harbor during World War II and was in the 25th Infantry Division in Korea.

"He is survived by his widow, Mrs. Hettie Fudge Lee; two sons: Robert Howard Lee and James Alexander Lee; his mother, Mrs. Frances Lee Baugh; eight sisters: Mrs. Elizabeth Bonner, Mrs. Sarah Owen, Mrs. Henrietta Cheairs, Mrs. Emma Dudley, Mrs. Florence McLemore, Mrs. Janie Overton, Mrs. Mary Lee Wilson, and Dinah Lee; and three brothers: Monroe Lee, Will Lee, and Joseph Lee.

"The Nashville Officers' Reserve Corps furnished an honor guard and a firing party, on hand from Fort Campbell."[1]

Rites Conducted For Cpl. R. A. Lee

Funeral services for Cpl. Robert Anderson Lee, believed to be the first Korean war fatality returned to this area, were held in Williamson county Friday.

Military services for the Negro soldier, an army heavyweight champion boxer, were held at the First Baptist church in Franklin. Burial was in a family cemetery near Duplex, Tenn.

Corporal Lee died in an army hospital in Japan Feb. 28 about six hours after he had been wounded by shrapnel in Korea. He was flown to Japan after being hit.

He had been in the army eight years. He served at Pearl Harbor during World War II. In Korea he was in the 25th infantry division.

He is survived by his widow, Mrs. Hettie Fudge Lee; two sons, Robert Howard Lee and James Alexander Lee; his mother, Mrs. Frances Lee Baugh; eight sisters, Mrs. Elizabeth Bonner, Mrs. Sarah Owen, Mrs. Henrietta Cheairs, Mrs. Emma Dudley, Mrs. Florence McLemore, Mrs. Janie Overton, Mrs. Mary Lee Wilson, and Dinah Lee; and three brothers, Monroe Lee, Will Lee, and Joseph Lee.

The Nashville officers' reserve corps furnished an honor guard and a firing squad was on hand from Fort Campbell.

Tennessean, April 8, 1951

---

1. Robert Anderson Lee Obituary. April 8, 1951 (page 58 of 114). (1951, Apr 08). Nashville Tennessean (1923-1972) Retrieved from https://www.proquest.com/historical-newspapers/april-8-1951-page-58-114/docview/1905546957/se-2

Bernita J. Hill

Bernita J. Hill

Evangelist Bernita J. Hill is a native Nashvillian, the third of five children born on May 31st, 1958, to the late Deacon Eddie L. Hill and Zula M. Garnett Hill. She is a proud graduate of Hillsboro High School in Nashville, Tennessee. She attended the University of Memphis for two years and Nashville Tech, where she received several certificates. On October 5, 2016, she received her Associate Degree in Theology from Life Christian University, graduating Magna Cum Laude.

Evangelist Hill accepted Christ at age nine under Pastor Charles Hogue and was baptized at Mt. Calvary Missionary Baptist Church on Herman Street in Nashville, Tennessee. In 1974, Evangelist Hill and her entire family united with the Shiloh Missionary Baptist Church family under the Pastorate of Elder James Mitchell until he resigned, and Pastor Elton Lee Waller was installed. She was a faithful member for 33 years.

On her road to evangelism, she has been a Sunday school teacher, interim superintendent of the Sunday School, singer in the choir, and Vacation Bible School teacher for over 40 years.

Her first unofficial sermon was at Green Grove on April 8, 2006, when she spoke on one of the Fruits of the Spirit – JOY – requested by First Lady Bertha Lloyd. This day would change her life and cause her to accept God's call to preach his word.

On February 25, 2007, the Holy Spirit led her to join the Green Grove Church family under the covering of Elder Richard Lloyd. She preached her first public sermon on November 25, 2007, at Green Grove titled, *Keep On Walking and Don't Look Back*, taken from Philippians 3:13-14. Evangelist Hill is living proof that your past can't hold you back if God has a calling on your life. To this day, she is still walking.

She currently serves in several ministries, but her most passionate responsibilities are as the director of evangelism and outreach and Bible study teacher. She considers herself a street preacher, as her pulpit is wherever the Lord sends her. She believes in the great commission given in Matthew 28:16-20 that instructs us to GO. Her passion for and teaching God's word to God's people in a plain and practical way led her to the Nashville Rescue Mission, where she preached God's word on the first Saturday night of every month for over 10 years. She also led the outreach team that fed at the Women's Mission, had worship services at the Tennessee Prison for Women, and spearheaded the food and Turkey drives for the Rescue Mission's Thanksgiving meal.

Her heart desires to be a servant and for all mankind to be saved and come to know the Love of Jesus Christ. She continues to serve at Green Grove under the recently installed Pastor, Elder Charles Claybrooks.

Embracing God's Assignment in Tennessee

PAMELA COTTON

Minister Pamela Cotton

Minister Pamela Cotton relocated from Milwaukee, Wisconsin, to Murfreesboro, Tennessee, in 2012, where she found her spiritual home at Green Grove Primitive Baptist Church. Under the leadership of *The General* himself, Pastor Elder Richard A. Lloyd, and First Lady Bertha Lloyd, Minister Cotton began walking steadfastly in the divine assignment placed on her life.

At Green Grove PBC, she humbly serves as the Minister of Music, utilizing her gift of playing the piano to minister through music and uplift the congregation, thereby honoring God. Her commitment extends beyond the pulpit as she continues to spread the gospel, show love to all, and work diligently to reach lost souls.

Minister Cotton is also the founder and organizer of Global Walk in Forgiveness, Inc., an organization dedicated to helping individuals and groups understand the dynamics of forgiveness. The organization provides conferences and specialized services for church organizations, married couples, individuals, and corporate groups, fostering healing and reconciliation.

Additionally, Minister Cotton offers music therapy at local mental health facilities, youth and alcohol rehabilitation centers, and homeless shelters. Her work brings comfort, healing, and encouragement to those in need, demonstrating her unwavering passion for service and ministry.

Reflecting on her journey, Minister Cotton shares, "I've discovered that southern hospitality is real." Her dedication to her calling and community continues to be a testament to her faith and a blessing to all those she serves.

It's been a wonderful journey and below you will find a few of the names of people who had a great impact on my life since I relocated to Tennessee: Pastor Elder Richard A. Lloyd, First Lady, Bertha Lloyd, Elders Shaun and Annette Gaffney of Disciples for Christ, Deacon Herald Span, Sandy Thomas Alsup, Cheryl Womack, Minister Angeline Burns; Pastor Terry and Sirvela Terry of Clarksville, Pastor Gerald Oglesby, Treva Gordon, Melbra Simmons, Martitia Woullard, Curry and Gail Peacock, Dr. Lee of Lloyd C. Elam Mental Health Clinic, Dr. Novella Williams, Dr. Stephanie Nipper, Lady Corder, Sandra Waterway, Charleen Cobbs, Dr. Cornelius Hill, Quintin Coleman, Pastor James McCaroll of First Baptist Church, Murfreesboro, and William Richardson.

Ladies of the Green Grove Primitive Baptist Church

Green Grove Ladies

Ameerah Cotton, daughter of Rev. Cotton

Ladies of Green Grove with Rev. Pamela Cotton

Lawyer Peterson

OVIE ELAINE BOLEYJACK BELL

John Boleyjack, Ann Peterson, Ovie Elaine Boleyjack Bell, and Judge Jim Peterson

We would always hear this name when my father, George Boleyjack, had a legal question or a problem that needed to be solved in the courts. He always knew that Lawyer Peterson would guide him in the right direction and trusted his judgment.

My brother John and I were asked to tell our story for the monthly *Porch Talk* hosted by the African American Heritage Society of Williamson County. The talk was generally held at the McLemore House in Franklin, but that afternoon, it was held at the Williamson County Public Library. Alma McLemore was in charge of the program.

I was surprised when a gentleman and his wife approached me and said, "I'm Mr. Peterson, your father's lawyer." It brought such joy to my heart. He said he saw the article in the paper and had to be here. We discussed his memories of my father and looked at our family's pictures. It was a blessing to have him with us and to share this moment.

As I learned later, my family was not the only Black family with fond memories of Mr. Peterson. The Emmett Claybrooks family told me how he helped their family and did the legal work for Green Grove Church. Good works will always be remembered.

What a Blessing!

Mildred Johnson

Mrs. Mildred Johnson, at 103 years, is still counting! She is the mother of Mary Ruth, William B., and Deborah Johnson. She lived in the Triune community for many years. She is a member of Green Grove Church and served on the Mother Board. A very quiet lady, she never missed a chance to shake hands with all of her church members on Sunday. It is a blessing to still have her with us, celebrating life.

Martha Louise Ridley Anderson

Martha Ridley Anderson

I was born on January 5, 1950, to James and Araminta Ridley, the third of nine children. I attended Kirkland Elementary School from grades 1 to 8, then Natchez High School from grades 9 to 10, and completed my education at College Grove from grades 11 to 12.

I married Powell E. Anderson, Jr., in August 1970, and we have two children, Jeffrey and Shawn. I am also a grandmother of three grandchildren: Carlos, Ashley, and Gabrielle. I worked for the state at Clover Bottom Developmental Center for 32 years.

I have been a member of Green Grove Primitive Baptist Church for over fifty-seven years and have served on the Usher Board. I have lived in Smyrna, Tennessee, for the past fifteen years.

Addie Wilson Bostick

OVIE ELAINE BOLEYJACK BELL

Addie Wilson Bostick

As told by Addie Bostick Hardin and John H. Boleyjack.

Addie Wilson was born in Marshall County, Tennessee, in 1894. She was the third child of Thomas and Sallie Wilson. She was educated in Williamson County. She married Edward Bostick in 1912, and two sons were born from their union: James Robert (Guy) and Edgar Benson Bostick. She was a member of Mt. Pleasant Missionary Baptist Church in Kirkland, Tennessee.

Her granddaughter, Addie (Edgar's daughter), told me a story about Addie Bostick. She told me her grandmother was an easy-going, quiet spirit. In the summer, she would spend two to three weeks with her grandmother. She would go with her to the Homecoming Celebration at Mt. Pleasant Church, where they had a good time with their family.

Her grandmother would also make outfits for her and her two sisters. They enjoyed having skirts and tops just alike, made by their grandmother's hands. She often watched her pumping on that old sewing machine. When Addie married, her grandmother would come to have Thanksgiving dinner and help her prepare the turnip greens. She was a great cook. She was loved by her sons, twelve grandchildren, and many great-grandchildren.

Later, she moved to Nashville to live with her son, E. B., and his wife, Mattie. She left her beloved family in 1977 and is buried in Greenwood Cemetery in Nashville.

John Boleyjack told us a story about Aunt Addie's lemonade. The family was having a reunion sometime during the 1960s. Aunt Addie was to bring the lemonade, and she would always put more than enough lemons to make it taste great, but she would never put enough sugar, and her niece, Annie, knew that. So, she told our dad to go to the store to get more sugar. Without Aunt Addie knowing it, she added the sugar. Everyone was telling Aunt Addie how good the lemonade tasted, and she was so happy. She watched as my brothers and friends drank dipper after dipper of her lemonade. No one ever told her why they loved it so much. They just told her it was the best she had ever made.

Mattie Lee Wilson Shaw

ROSIE DAVIS CARNEY

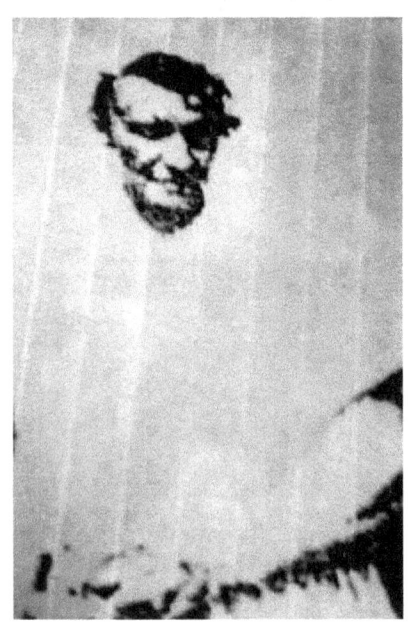

Mattie Wilson Shaw

Mattie Lee Wilson Shaw was born on December 24, 1891, in Williamson County, Tennessee. The second child of Thomas Jefferson Wilson and Sallie Ezell Wilson.

In the 1910 census, she was 18 years old, and her occupation was a cook for a private family. She had a third-grade education, and she could read and write. Mattie married Willie Dee Shaw on Sept. 3, 1911, in Williamson County, to this union they had twelve children, Jennie Mae, Woodrow, George, Sallie, Louise, Ovaline, Walter, Mack, Araminta, Martha, Robert and Thomas.

Mattie died in 1954. She was affectionately known by her family as "Big Mama." Here are a few stories they told about her:

Big Mama would always tell us to clean the house. Martha and I would never listen to her, and we would keep on talking and playing. She would tell us, "You don't want me to come in there." That is probably why we use that phrase today when talking to our children.

One day, when it snowed outside. Big Mama went to work, and May Lizzie, and I made some ice cream. We didn't clean up after ourselves, and when she came through the door, she started hitting us with a dishcloth and pulling our ears. She may have been hard on us, but after our mother Jennie Mae passed away, we stayed with our grandmother for a while, and we had many good times together.

Mattie was a beautiful lady, who made clothes without a pattern to go by. She would get the material from a flour sack.

She also loved planting flowers and cooking for her family.

George Shaw and Thomas Shaw

Ovaline Shaw Johnson and Araminta Shaw Ridley

Rosie Marie Davis Carney

Martha Shaw Morton

Robert Shaw and Louise Shaw Fitzgerald

Mary Virginia Patton Williams

Mary Virginia Patton Williams, photo courtesy of Thelma Battle.

Mary Virginia Patton Williams was born on September 19, 1935, in Triune, Tennessee, to the late Henrie Ester and J.C. Patton, Sr. She peacefully closed her eyes on December 1, 2006, at Centennial Medical Center and entered into eternal rest. In addition to her parents, Mary was preceded in death by her husband, Ponell Cecil Williams; daughter, Beverly Ann Pope; son, Kenneth Eugene Williams; and grandson, Joshua Matthew Morton. Mary was educated in the Williamson County School System. She accepted Christ in 1972 under the leadership of Elder Henry Dozier at Green Grove Primitive Baptist Church, where she remained a dedicated member until her health began to fail.

She was united in holy matrimony to the late Ponell Williams on March 29, 1958; seven children were born to this union. She was employed at Genesco as a seamstress for 28 years and retired in January 1998. Mary was a very devoted wife and mother, a loving grandmother and great-grandmother, a caring sister and aunt, and a dear friend. She enjoyed sewing, cooking, watching television, and was always ready to go at a moment's notice. She had a warm, compassionate heart of gold that was so overwhelming. She was one of the nicest people you would ever want to come in contact with. She was always willing to help or do whatever she could for anyone. Her loving smile, heart, and kindness will be missed by all her family, friends, and church family.

Mary V. Williams

Mary leaves to cherish her memories: four sons, Larry Williams and Alexander Perkins, of Nashville, Tennessee, Carl and Charles Williams, of Nolensville, Tennessee; two daughters: Jacqueline (Elder Mack) Morton of Franklin, Tennessee, and Hattie (Lemon) Shaw of Nolensville, Tennessee; ten grandchildren: Zoelithia (Jerry) Martin, Lemon Shaw II, Anthony Williams, Deonna Harlan, Martez Williams, Shatonya Williams, Brianna Oglesby, Ke'aria Perkins, JarKaveus Morton, and Carlton Williams, Jr.; one great grandchild, Naveysha Williams; three sisters: Mamie (Frank) Polk, Sr., Annie Vaughn, and Vivian (George) Moreland; one brother, J. C. (Carrie) Patton, Jr.; one aunt, Elizabeth Patton; one sister-in-law, Sophia Boykin; four brothers-in-law: LeRoy (Cheryl) Williams, Brady Williams, Leslie Carraway, and Essex (Shirley) Williams; God-mother, Lorenzia Credle; four play-sisters: Mary Elizabeth Anderson, Ella Mae Patton, Marie Ogilvie and Mary Britton; two devoted cousins: Evelyn Hogans and William J. Washington; a host of nieces, nephews, cousins and friends.[1]

REMEMBER ME

To the living, I am gone. To the sorrowful, I will never return. To the angry, I was cheated. But to the happy, I am at peace. And to the faithful, I have never left.

I cannot be seen, but I can be heard. So, as you stand upon a shore gazing at the sea, remember me. Remember me as you look in awe at a mighty forest and its grand majesty. As you admire the beauty of flowers, remember me.

Always keep me in your thoughts and your heart. Remember the good and the bad times we shared, the laughter and the tears, and the special moments we spent together. And remember, if you always think of me, I will never truly be gone. – Margaret Mead

---

1. Mary Virginia Patton Williams Obituary, *The Thelma Battle Funeral Program Collection*, Williamson County Public Library. Accessed online at wcpltn.org on May 24, 2025.

COMING OUT OF THE DARK INTO THE LIGHT

Ponell Cecil Williams

Ponell Cecil Williams (1934-2006) married Mary Virginia Patton Williams (1935-2006) in 1958. He was a devoted member of the Green Grove P.B. Church. They were survived by children: Larry Williams, Alexander Perkins, Carl Williams, Charles Williams, Jacqueline Morton, and Hattie Shaw. Two of their children preceded them in death: Beverly Ann Pope and Kenneth Eugene Williams.

His funeral program and obituary are available in the Special Collections Department at Williamson County Public Library.

GOD CARES WHEN WE LOSE SOMEONE SO SPECIAL

We may never understand why someone caring, kind, and good
would have to leave us long before we ever thought they would.
Yet comfort comes from knowing God is with us every day
and grieves with us when one so full of goodness slips away.
And so, we trust His steadfast love through sorrow, pain, and fear
as he holds us gently in his arms and wipes away our tears.
— Sadly missed by your children

Charles Milton Glenn, Jr.

Charles Milton Glenn, Jr.

Charles Milton Glenn, Jr. was born March 9, 1945, and died November 16, 2023. He is the child of the late Charles M (Bud) Glenn Sr, Louise Batey Muhanda, and Savannah Floyd. In December 1965, Charles was united in matrimony with Willie Mae Scruggs. To this union, they were blessed with five children: Charles Milton III, Antoine Decarlo, Andreaco Ramaun, Steffon Milano, and Nikitra Shantel Glenn. In later years, he married Carleesa Marshall, and to this union, Charles was blessed with a stepson, Kenneth Jackson, and a son, Dasmine. Charles M. Glenn resided in Triune, TN. Charles attended and was educated in the Williamson County school system – Green Grove School and Kirkland School. He worked for Gates Tire Company, Kroger (as a driver), and in the construction business, first with his father and then with his brother James Batey, Sr. In his free time, he enjoyed working on cars and trucks. Charles loved spending time with and talking to his grandchildren, and watching Matt Dillon and Western movies.

GLENN, Carleesa Marshall—Age 39. Departed on December 17, 2004, at Southern Hills Hospital after a brief illness. Born December 4, 1967. She leaves behind a very loving and devoted husband, Charles Milton Glenn, Jr.; two loving children, Kenneth

Jackson and Dasmine Glenn; devoted stepchildren, Charles M. Glenn III, Antoine (Brandy) Glenn, Andreaco, Steffon, and Nikitra Glenn; ten grandchildren; devoted sister, Mary Campbell-Webb; siblings, Patricia Campbell, Ann Mercer III, Norma Taylor, Fulton Campbell, George, Jason, and William Turner; grandparents, William and Ruthie Turner, brothers-in-law, James Batey, Kent Phillips; sisters-inlaw, Anastasia Batey, Ann Morris, and Judith Phillips; devoted uncle and aunt, James and Linda Glenn; devoted family members, Joerina and Farolyn Hawkins, very devoted friends, Rev. Frank and Marie Olgivie and Family, Staff at Southern Hills Hospital CCU and Nurse Charmine, and Love United Church. Visitation Today, noon til 7 p.m., at Terrell Broady Funeral Home. Visitation with Family Tuesday, December 21, 2004, from 6-7 p.m., funeral to follow at Love United Missionary Baptist Church, 427 Humphreys St., Nashville, TN 37203. Officiated/Eulogy: Elder Alvin White. Services entrusted to TERRELL BROADY FUNERAL HOME, 3855 Clarksville Pike, Nashville, TN 37218, Tennessean, December 20, 2004.[1]

---

1. Carleesa Marshall Glenn Obituary, December 20, 2004 (page 15). The Tennessean, Retrieved from https://www.proquest.com/historical-newspapers/december-20-2004-page-15/docview/2733175758/se-2

Henry Dozier

Elder Henry and Mary Dozier's family, pictured left to right. Front Row: Patricia Dennis, Mother Mary Dozier, Dorothy Lockridge, and Annette Powell. Second Row: Samuel Dozier, Elder Henry Dozier, and James Dozier. Elder Henry Dozier pastored Green Grove Primitive Baptist Church from 1967 to 1972.

Strawberries

JOHN H. BOLEYJACK

John Weakley Covington

When the Boleyjack family lived on the Horace Windrow and Fannie Covington Windrow property, the boys would occasionally work for Mr. John Weakley Covington, the brother of Fannie Windrow.

John told a story of picking strawberries for Mr. Covington. Many young men worked for Mr. Covington gathering his crop of berries. I remember the Goins brothers; on this particular day, Wayne and I picked the strawberries and ate them simultaneously. They were so sweet and juicy, we couldn't resist.

Mr. Covington was watching and came over to inform us that we would be paid for what we picked. No more berries were going into my mouth, so I started to pick faster and faster, putting them into the crate.

Mrs. Covington called us for lunch, and they had a table under a tree. We all ate together, black and white. We talked as we ate, but we must have stayed too long at the table because Mr. Covington told us it was time to go back to work. I didn't mind because I was thinking about the money.

We had three days to complete the job. When we finished, I had the most berries, but Mr. Covington questioned the amount I had picked because I had more than anyone else. I said, "You told me to work, and I did, and I need my money.' He frowned and gave me the money I earned.

Juanita Ridley Jones Family

From left: Leo Lamont Jones, Trina Jones (1974-1921), Shanna Michelle Anderson, Katherine Chera Jones, and Thomas Edward Jones, Jr.

Juanita Ridley Jones attended Kirkland School, College Grove School, and Riverdale High School in Murfreesboro. She enjoys cooking and baking, spending time with her grandchildren, and teaching them how to cook and bake her famous yellow cake and caramel icing.

Anthony Jones, son of Thomas Jones, Jr.

Michael Jones, son of Thomas Jones, Jr.

Jalen Jones, son of Lamont Jones

Chance Jones, daughter of Lamont Jones

Emoni and Emaji Rawls, daughters of Chera Jones

Cohen Jones, son of Anthony Jones

Ezekiel Key, son of Chera Jones

Serenity Anderson, daughter of Shanna Anderson

Corbin Jones, son of Anthony Jones

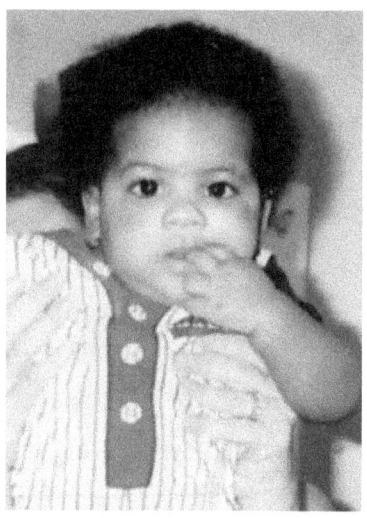

Keland Jones, son of Thomas Jones, Jr.

Tanaa Jones, daughter of Thomas Jones, Jr.

Frank James and Addie Marie Ridley Ogilvie

ADDIE MARIE RIDLEY OGILVIE

Frank James Ogilvie, Jr. and Addie Marie Ridley Ogilvie

Parents: Minnie Anderson and Frank Ogilvie, Sr.

Elder Frank J. and Addie Marie Ridley Ogilvie were married for 42 years. From this union, three children were born: two daughters and a son: Evangelist Valerie Ogilvie, Minister Frank Ogilvie (wife, Sara), and Dr. Candace Ogilvie; four grandchildren: Libbie, Addie, Kennedie, and Frankie Ogilvie.

Valerie R. Ogilvie

Frank and Sara Ogilvie, III

Candace Ogilvie

Libbie, Addie, Kennedie, and Frankie Ogilvie, children of Sara and Frank Ogilvie III

James and Araminta Shaw Ridley

ADDIE MARIE RIDLEY OGILVIE

Elder James Ridley, Jr., Father of Addie Marie Ridley Ogilvie

Araminta Shaw Ridley and James Ridley, Jr., parents of Marie Ogilvie

Marie's Family Notes

My siblings and I all attended Kirkland School. Annie, Martha, and I would go to school early to help peel the potatoes for lunch. This is how we could pay for our family to eat. I'm so thankful for the memories. And to my nieces and nephews, what a blessing to have you in my life!

Annie Mary Ridley

The oldest. She enjoys keeping a clean house. Growing up, she would throw you out of the house if you messed it up.

Martha L. Anderson

She was born after me. I remember one time when we were in the car (nine of us), and she did not want anyone to touch her.

James W. Ridley

He had a kind heart and enjoyed laughing.

Juanita Ridley

Enjoys cooking and baking.

William Ridley

Also known as "Tater." He enjoyed spending time training horses and being outside.

Dorothy J. Ridley

She was always into something. She enjoyed working with her hands. Fixing things and growing flowers.

Frank J. Ridley

He enjoyed life. He passed away when He was five.

George E. Ridley

He reminds us always to look our best. He has his own Florist shop – Creations by G. Ridley.

"I attended Kirkland School. My favorite teacher was Mrs. Annie Patton. She would wear cat-eyed glasses. To my parents, grandparents, and great-grandparents, thank you for your love and support and for teaching me about the goodness of God. At age 25, I became a business owner – A Village of Flowers and now Creations by G. Ridley. I have one daughter, Shawna Lee Ridley, and three grandsons: Torey Wayne Wilkerson Jr, Mon'Torre Dewane Wilkerson, and Mackenzie Dai'Shawn Price. I have one God-Grandson, Tevin Woods, two great granddaughters – Gianna Reign Wilkerson and Sisoukrath Xander Price. I am Thankful to God for them all." – George Ridley

FLOWERS and George Edward Ridley

George Ridley and Natalie Cole

When George told you about his life, he left out what an accomplished florist he is. He was an apprentice for a while, then ventured out independently, attending school to become a florist and starting a business solo. He has met many people along his journey. He did the floral arrangements for Natalie Cole's wedding, and they became very close friends. She would invite him and bring him to many award shows, like the Stellar Gospel Music Awards.

He has worked with many country, gospel, and R&B singers, including Pattie LaBelle, Whitney Houston, Reba McEntire, Garth Brooks, and Dolly Parton. He also decorated many homes, churches, and businesses during Christmas. The newspaper has written articles about his business.

One would never have imagined that a quiet-spoken Kirkland Elementary school kid from Triune, Tennessee, could take his dreams to such heights, but George Ridley did just that.

James W. Ridley, Juanita Jones, Martha Anderson, George Ridley, Araminta Shaw Ridley, Annie Mary Ridley, William Ridley, and Marie Ridley Ogilvie

Frank J. Ridley

George E. Ridley and his daughter, Shawna Ridley

Annie Mary Ridley

Words Unspoken

OVIE ELAINE BOLEYJACK BELL

Reading the newspaper was a ritual for most families in small towns and communities, during the early 1900's. This is how we got our news, which kept us informed about what was going on in our neck of the woods as the saying goes.

We learned about the crops, schools, state fairs, recipes, and what was on sale in the grocery stores. And we can't forget reading "Dear Abby." It was like a soap opera. There was one section that no one could pass up: the *Obituaries* section. In the rural area, it was called *Death Notices*. Ours was put in a special area, labeled *Colored Death Notices* and printed separately, coming after the White obituaries. It felt like coming in the back door. It wasn't until 1909 that we as Black people could legally receive a death certificate. It was also difficult to purchase a headstone for our loved ones, even if we had the money to pay for it. Let us not forget the cemetery, I guess that was separate but equal also.

I knew that our people were considered second-class citizens, but why must we always be labeled and sit apart from other ethnic groups? When we paid our taxes, we were separated in the ledger, but I'm sure when the money was counted, it was all put together because it had the same value.

I only wish that was the way of the world. When we have a conversation with White people, they always point out the person's color when they're Black. You would very seldom hear a Black person talk about a person's color unless you ask them to identify the person.

I know this is the way that we have been brought up in this country, but it's time for a change. We are all just human beings trying to make it through this complicated life. We cooked your food, but couldn't sit down to enjoy the meal with you. That is why we needed people like Dr. Martin Luther King, Jr., and John Lewis to fight for the rights that are vanishing before our very eyes today. We're supposed to live in a free society, yet we still have a long way to go, due to our selective memory. If we could only see things as they are, and not travel back into the past, wishing for a bygone era that will never come again.

It's unrealistic to think that one can move forward while looking backward to what has been, instead of embracing what is and praising what we have accomplished as a nation. This is how we grow, with an open dialogue from all Americans. So many people have been afraid to have a conversation about race and culture because they don't know where to start. Tell your story and be unapologetic about how the history books have unfolded, knowing that so much has been excluded. Now is the time to get it right. We lived it, and we should be able to tell it in our own words.

The world is evolving into something unrecognizable, books are being banned, and free speech is on the chopping block. There is no better time to speak the truth and stand for honesty. Living in a global society, where everything is spoken freely, right or wrong, every day, we have nothing to hide. Reach out to your neighbor, and maybe you can find common ground, if you're open and ready to have a meaningful experience on race relations in the good old U.S.A. I think you will be the better for it, and you may find you have more in common than you think. If not, I hope you can learn to see another's journey through their eyes and give homage.

Death Notices

Triune, Tenn.

CLAIBORNE, Charlie F.—Age 75, Thursday morning, December 11, 1975 at Williamson County Hospital. He is survived by a brother, A.L. Claiborne, of Arvin, Calif.; several nieces and nephews. Remains are at the Waller Chapel in Nolensville where funeral services will be held Saturday morning at 10:30am with The Rev. Chris Wilson officiating. Friends and neighbors will please serve as honorary pallbearers. Active: Julius Porter, Horace Windrow, Tom B. Toomes, Leon Sherrod, Gordon Lamb, J.D. Maupin, John Kruzan, Herman Skelley. Interment Triune Cemetery. WALLER & CO., 776-

Colored Death Notices

BOSTICK—Friday morning, April 8, 1949 at the residence of her daughter, Mrs. Viola McKinnon, 1035 Second ave., S. Mrs. Nancy Bostick. Survived by husband, Mr. Frank Bostick; son, Rev. Robert L. Bostick; two daughters, Mrs. Blanche Ferguson and Mrs. Viola McKinnon; sister, Mrs. Lennes Williams of Chicago, Ill.; granddaughter, Mrs. Mary E. Jones; two great-grandchildren; two nieces; two nephews; two sons-in-laws, Will Ferguson and Archie McKinnon of Indianapolis, Ind.; daughter-in-law, Mrs. Rosie B. Bostick; one grandson-in-law; other relatives and friends. Remains will be at the above address Sunday morning. Services Monday evening at 2 o'clock from the Tabernacle Baptist church, conducted by her pastor, Rev. Evans. Remarks by Rev. L. E. Parks and Rev. Wright. Interment at Greenwood cemetery. Johnson and Brown, 90 Lafayette st. Phone 6-3271. Walter

Emmett and Ada Mae York Claybrooks

Emmett Claybrooks, holding Charles Claybrooks, and Ada Mae York Claybrooks

When Emmett Charles Claybrooks was born on May 1, 1922, in Tennessee, his father, James, was 39, and his mother, Sophia, was 34. He married Ada Mae York on October 17, 1948, in Giles County, Tennessee. He retired after working for more than 40 years with the L & N Railroad, and Ada was a homemaker. They had four children. He died on October 12, 1991, at the age of 69, and was buried in College Grove, Tennessee.

Emmett Charles Claybrooks Jr. was born on December 1, 1949, in Franklin, Tennessee. His father, Emmett Sr., was 27, and his mother, Ada, was 21. He married Malinda Gwen Jackson, and they had one daughter together. He also had three sons from another relationship. He died as a young father on March 6, 1979, in Nashville, Tennessee, at the age of 29, and was buried in College Grove, Tennessee.

Delores Claybrooks was born on October 18, 1951. Her father, Emmett, Sr., was 29, and her mother, Ada, was 23. She had two brothers and one sister.

Deborah Claybrooks was born in Franklin, Tennessee, on September 14, 1953. She had two brothers and one sister.

Kenneth Wayne Claybrooks was born in Franklin, Tennessee, on August 7, 1962. His father, Emmett, Sr., was 40, and his mother, Ada, was 34. He married Wanda Lane Ellis on December 31, 1999, and Linda Faye Baugh on February 10, 2006. He died on December 19, 2019, and was buried in College Grove. He had two sisters and one brother.[1]

CLAYBROOKS, Emmett Charles—Departed this life Tuesday, March 6, 1979 at a local infirmary at age 29. He is survived by wife, Mrs. Gwendolyn Claybrooks; one daughter, Miss Delicia Lashann Claybrooks; three sons, Masters Derrell, Kevin and Terrence Claybrooks, all of Franklin, Tenn.; parents, Mr. and Mrs. Emmett Charles Claybrooks, Sr.; two sisters, Misses Delores and Deborah Claybrooks; one brother, Mr. Kenneth Wayne Claybrooks, all of College Grove, Tenn.; mother and father-in-law, Mr. and Mrs. Dudley Jackson; two sisters-in-law, three brothers-in-law, and a host of aunts, uncles, cousins, other relatives and friends. The family will receive friends this Thursday, March 8, from 7 to 9 p.m. at Green Grove P.B. Church, Triune, Tenn. Funeral services Friday morning at 11 a.m. from the above church, conducted by Elder J.E. Taylor. Pallbearers and Flowerladies selected from friends. Interment Locust Ridge Cemetery College Grove, Tenn. WRIGHT'S FUNERAL HOME, in Charge, 255-8735

College Grove, Tennessee
CLAYBROOKS, Deacon Emmett Charles, Sr.— Entered into eternal rest on Saturday, October 12, 1991. Survived by devoted wife, Ada Mai Claybrooks; daughters, Delores and Deborah; son, Wayne; sister, Louise Spann of Murfreesboro, TN.; brother, Rev. Fred W. Claybrooks of Chicago, ILL.; four grandchildren; a host of nieces and nephews; other relatives and friends. The body will lie in state at Cumberland Association Tabernacle, 232 Whitsett Road, Nashville on Wednesday, October 16, 1991 from 9-10 a.m. Visitation from 10-11 a.m. Funeral following at 11 a.m. Services conducted by his Pastor, Elder Richard Lloyd. Interment Locust Ridge Cemetery, College Grove, TN. LEWIS AND WRIGHT FUNERAL DIRECTORS, 2500 Clarksville Hwy., 255-2371. Richard A. Lewis and William H. Wright, Directors[2]

---

1. Emmett Charles Claybrooks, Jr. Obituary. March 8, 1979 (page 102 of 120). (1979, Mar 08). The Tennessean (1972-) Retrieved from https://www.proquest.com/ historical-newspapers/march-8-1979-page-102-120/docview/1908238876/se-2.
2. Emmett Charles Claybrooks, Sr. Obituary. October 16, 1991 (page 19 of 85). (1991, Oct 16). The Tennessean (1972-) Retrieved from https://www.proquest.com/historical-newspapers/october-16-1991-page-19-85/docview/1909498577/se-2

Vivian with baby, Joyce and Donald Claybrooks

Kenneth Wayne and Faye Claybrooks

Susie Bell, James Arthur, and Annie Louise Claybrooks

Wayne Claybrooks

Elder Charles Claybrooks

Delores Claybrooks

Irene Claybrooks

"Tunnie"

My Granny, Annie Margaret Patton Vaughn

NICHOLAS AUSTIN THOMPSON

Nicholas Thompson and Granny Tunnie Vaughn

Granny Tunnie and Nicholas Thompson

Annie Margaret Patton Vaughn was born on October 27, 1940, to J. C. Patton Sr. and Henrie Ester in Triune, Tennessee. She died on April 13, 2023, and is buried in Green Grove Cemetery. I am her grandson, Nicholas Austin Thompson.

My granny was so special to me. Everyone called her "Tunnie." I once asked her, "Where did you get that name?" She said, "My mother called me Tunnie, but my father called me Margaret."

I have so much gratitude in my heart for what she taught me about faith in God and people. She was a true example of faith in action. Every person she met along her journey was showered with kindness that they will never forget. Her love filled our home and touched everyone who came in contact with her. Granny always went out of her way to show me that I was valued and my life had meaning. There wasn't a week that went by that I didn't see Granny, and she would show up with a $20 bill! That simple act helped carry me through high school. I want to thank Granny for loving me, and I will never forget her.

Annie Margaret Vaughn, also known as G Money and Tunnie. Granny has truly left a legacy for me and Mom. Even now, we look at each other and say, "It's going to be all right." I think back to how Granny would say those exact words to us, and I don't think she ever realized the lasting gift she was leaving us. Those words still bring us comfort and strength, and will live in our hearts forever.

Margaret's Memories

MARGARET BOLEYJACK RANDOLPH

Margaret Boleyjack Randolph

I was born in Nolensville, Tennessee, in 1935. We lived on the property once owned by Dad's grandfather, whose name was Arch Boleyjack. I lived there with my mom, Annie, my dad, George, my brother George Jr., and my sister Betty. I was told that while mom was carrying me, she took care of a cousin named Ira Morton who had tuberculosis. Dad built a one-room house for him there on the property.

We later moved to York Road on the property of Louie Williams. Dad sharecropped with him and also helped raise a prize-winning dairy herd of cattle called Jerseys. They would take their best-looking one to show in the Tennessee State Fair. I was told that George had fun playing with Louie's daughter, Betty Lou. While living there, Albert, Ella, and James were born.

After a few years, we moved to the Adams farm in Triune on Highway 96. It's hard for me to remember, but I was told that George, Betty, and I attended the Black school, located on the property of Green Grove Church in Triune.

Many years later, we lived on the John Little farm on Horton Highway and Patterson Road. Dad raised crops and worked with walking horses. While living there, I went to Nashville to live with my grandmother Margaret [Boleyjack], whom I was named after. I attended the J. C. Napier school from the first to the seventh grade. I would come home in the summer, work on the farm, and learned to cook. Dad made me a stool so that I could reach the top of the stove.

There was no electricity in the house. We used kerosene for the lamp light, and had a battery-operated radio. Mama was very good at making things work. When the battery would get low, she would heat it up in the oven for awhile, so that it would give more listening hours, and it worked. That woman was a genius! In the summer, Dad would plant a big garden, and the kids would chop the weeds out to help everything grow. We would gather the vegetables so Mama could cook some and can the rest.

In the winter, we had vegetables, and Dad would kill hogs, rabbits, and goats, and Mama would kill chickens so that we could have meat to eat with our meals.

Mama taught me to cook at the age of nine, the same age her mother taught her. Having a large family, she always instructed me to cook more than was needed just in case someone came for a visit. Those may have been hard times for us, but we were taught how to work and take care of the ones we loved.

When I was 12 years old, I stopped staying in Nashville and attended school in Kirkland. Our school was on the property of Mt. Pleasant Baptist Church. It was a two-room school heated with a potbellied heater. We had to carry our lunch, sometimes our grandmother Ovie would bring us lunch.

After the eighth grade, my sister and I were ready for high school. There was only one school bus for us, and it had to cover the whole eastern part of Williamson County. It was driven by Mr. Epp Starnes. The bus didn't come by where we lived, so my sister Betty and I stayed with our grandparents, Clarence and Ovie Thompson, whose home was on the bus route.

It took two years before the bus picked us up at our home. We enjoyed living with Mammy and Pap, as we called them. Pap enjoyed helping us with our math, and he was very good at it. Mammy was a great cook, and she and my mother taught me everything I know about preparing meals, but it is still hard to duplicate the good taste that they put into the food. I guess it was seasoned with so much love.

My sister and I went to Franklin Training School, later known as Natchez High School. We had many beautiful memories and lots of friends that we will never forget. Sometimes it's good to travel back in time to appreciate what the Lord has given us.

Count It All Joy!

DR. CANDACE OGILVIE

What joy a child has knowing that he could teach his mother something that she doesn't know how to do. That is what Frank J. Ogilvie Jr. was feeling when he was showing his mother, Minnie, how to ride his bike for the first time.

Minnie Mary Anderson Ogilvie and Frank J. Ogilvie Jr.

Frank J. Ogilvie Sr. and Minnie Mary Anderson Ogilvie

Memories of Green Grove School

Green Grove students with Mrs. Pattie Davis Taylor. Kneeling, unknown, 2nd Row: unknown, Robbie Morton Nevils, Labora "Rick" Lee, unknown, 3rd Row: unknown, Fannie Bell Lee Patton, Mrs. Taylor, unknown.

Memories by J.W. Boyd

The school was a small one-room white building set on the hill near the church, overlooking Horton Highway. Among the schoolteachers at Green Grove School were Mamie Bostick Starnes, Miss Cotton, Mrs. Shelton, and Mrs. Pattie Davis Taylor.

During winter, the school was heated by a big, tall Warm Morning™ heater. It was located in the center of the room. A flue was built above the ceiling, and a stove pipe connected the stove to the flue. The county would bring the coal to heat the school and the boys would gather the kindling to start the fires. The first of the older children to arrive at school were the ones who made the fires in the mornings.

In the early 1940s, the small grades were separated from the higher grades. The smaller grades were taught in Green Grove Church. Mrs. Videll of Nashville was the first teacher to teach the separate class assigned to the church. Mrs. Pattie Davis Taylor continued to teach the higher grades in the one-room school.

Memories by Mary Boyd Vaughn

They toted the drinking water from Mr. Epp Starnes' house most of the time. After they brought the water into the school, they would sit the buckets down on one long bench. Each student brought their own drinking glass, which was turned upside down on a newspaper. The students' initials were written in fingernail polish outside of their own glasses. They used a dipper to dip the water into each glass. The dipper was white with a long red handle.[1]

Memories by Thomas Shaw

The boys would go down to Zephiniah and Short Bostick's farm and get students milk for school. One of the Bostick men would milk the cows in the mornings and keep it cool until the boys came before lunch to pick up the milk and carry it to school. The milk was kept in two tin buckets with tops. The teacher would send two boys at a time to get the milk. Some of the boys who took turns carrying the milk were Ed McClain, William Boyd, Will Ridley, and Ed Bostick.

Finally, a little kitchen was built onto the side of the one-room schoolhouse. The county furnished the food, and the big girls did the cooking. But before they added that little kitchen, everybody brought their own food. The students' lunches would be wrapped in newspaper or wax paper. There was a shelf in the school where everybody

---

1. Battle, Thelma. *Triune: An African American Review, We've Come This Far By Faith:* "Recollections of Former Students," 2003.

put their lunches. The students would write their names on their lunches. The bread that was used for their sandwiches were mostly biscuits.[2]

RECOLLECTIONS BY THOMAS SHAW

Green Grove School Boys: Edward McClain, Woody Lee, William Boyd, Jr., Will H. "Babe' Ridley, unknown, and unknown

I was the son of Will D. and Sallie Wilson Shaw and attended Green Grove School for about five or six years. I am now 74 years old.

My first-grade teacher was Elizabeth Green. My second-grade teacher was Mattie B. Bates. My fourth-grade teacher was Lillian Redmond. My fifth-grade teacher was Pattie Davis. I reckon Miss Pattie Davis taught up at Green Grove longer than any other teachers.

Most teachers stayed at the preacher's home during the week. But some of the teachers had someone to pick them up from school every day. The preacher during that time was Elder Robert Bostick. He lived down the little lane behind the church.

One exception to where the teachers boarded was Miss Louise Beal, later Mrs. Thomas Patton. She recollects that she boarded with Epp Starnes, a widower, and his cousin, Mamie Turpin.

---

2. Battle, Thelma. *Triune: An African American Review, We've Come This Far By Faith:* "Recollections of Former Students," 2003.

COMING OUT OF THE DARK INTO THE LIGHT

Kirkland

Center of the Black Community

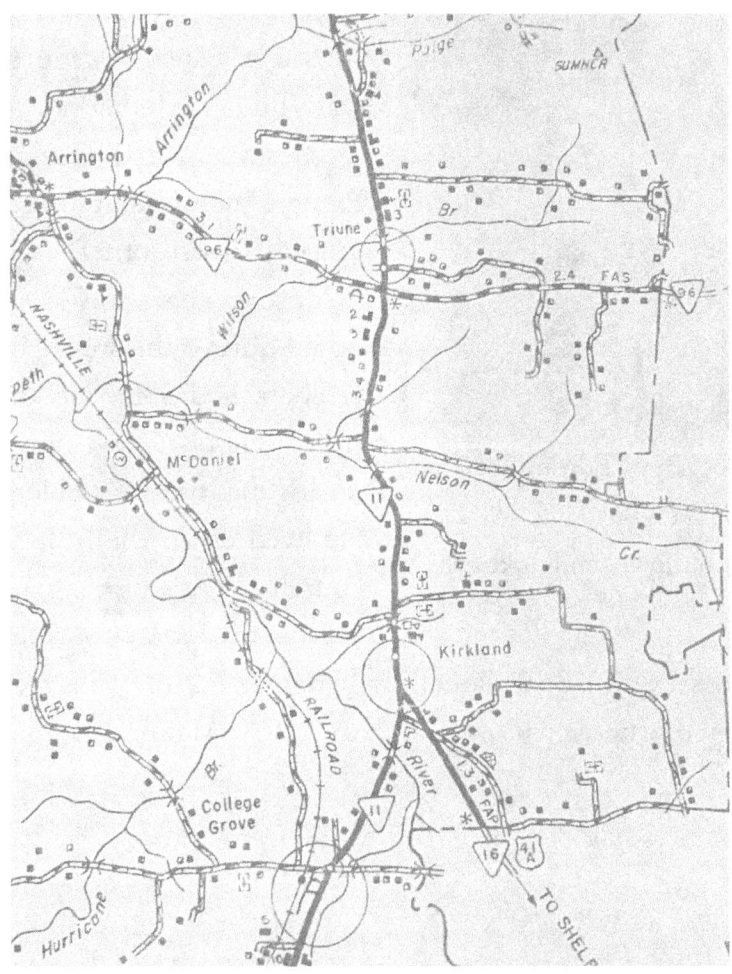

1951 Map of Kirkland

Williamson County Public Schools

At the request of the Williamson County Board of Education, the Survey of the Public Schools of Williamson County, Tennessee was undertaken by the Division for Teachers at Field Services, George Peabody College for Teachers. Nine specialists carried out the fieldwork and prepared the report from August 15, 1950, to March 15, 1951. The survey is comprehensive in scope, including a study of community, resources, organization, and administration, school personnel, curriculum, instruction in elementary schools and high schools, physical facilities, transportation, finance, and business management.

Elementary Schools for Negro Children

Williamson County has twenty-two elementary school centers for Negro children. One of these is operated in Brentwood, Davidson County, but only Williamson County pupils are reported to be enrolled. All of these schools are too small to provide an adequate program of education, and by the very nature of their size and inadequacy, the Board of Education spends more per pupil and gets less in return for its school dollars than on any other expenditures it makes. Only five of the schools have two teachers each. All of the others are one-teacher schools.

The appraisal of adequacy, as shown in Table 12, presents a disturbing picture. No county-owned elementary school facilities for Negro children are better than "poor," as represented by the highest rating of 47 given to Thompson Station and Westwood Schools. Scores of 41 were assigned to Lee-Buckner and Nolensville Schools. All other centers are evaluated as being unsatisfactory. Among the poorest are Fitzgerald, Hillsboro, Mt. Lavergne, Pearly Hill, Cedar Hill, Green Grove, and Kirkland. The Hillsboro Center probably should not be appraised as a school since it ostensibly is a church building.

The following, Table 12, illustrates the poor conditions of white and black schools throughout Williamson County.

Name of School	No. of Teachers	Total Score	1	2	3	4	5	6	7	8	9	10	11	12	13	14	15	16	17	18	19	20
New Hope	3	54	4	3	3	3	2	1	4	3	2	2	3	4	2	1	1	3	3	3	3	4
Nolensville	4	59	3	3	4	3	4	3	2	3	3	3	3	2	3	2	3	3	3	3	3	3
Peytonsville	3	77	4	2	4	5	4	4	5	4	4	4	4	4	3	4	3	3	4	3	4	4
Post Oak	1	39	3	2	3	3	2	1	0	2	2	2	1	1	1	1	0	3	3	3	3	3
Rudderville	1	38	3	3	2	2	1	2	1	2	2	2	1	1	1	1	2	3	3	3	2	1
Shoals Branch	1	56	3	3	4	4	2	1	2	3	4	3	3	3	3	1	0	3	3	3	4	4
Southall	1	38	2	1	2	2	2	1	1	2	2	2	1	2	2	1	1	3	3	3	3	2
Starkey	1	32	4	1	1	1	1	1	0	0	2	1	1	2	1	1	0	3	3	3	3	3
Thompson Sta.	5	39	4	2	2	2	1	1	1	2	2	1	2	2	1	1	2	3	3	3	3	1
Triangle	3	37	4	3	3	1	1	1	1	2	2	0	2	1	1	1	2	3	3	3	2	1
Trinity	5	79	3	2	5	4	5	4	5	5	4	4	5	4	5	2	4	3	4	3	4	4
Franklin High		58	4	3	4	3	3	3	3	3	2	3	3	2	2	3	2	3	3	3	4	3
Schools for Negroes																						
Allison Chapel	1	38	3	1	2	3	2	3	1	0	2	2	2	1	1	1	0	3	3	3	3	2
Beechville	1	33	3	1	2	2	1	2	0	0	2	2	1	1	1	1	0	3	3	3	3	2
Brentwood†	2	48	3	2	3	3	2	2	3	2	2	2	4	2	3	1	0	3	3	3	3	2
Cedar Hill	1	26	3	1	1	1	2	1	0	0	1	1	1	1	0	0	0	3	3	3	3	1
Fitzgerald	1	24	1	0	1	1	1	1	0	0	2	1	1	1	0	0	0	3	3	3	4	1
Florenceville	1	31	2	1	2	2	1	1	0	0	2	3	1	1	1	0	0	3	3	3	3	2
Goose Creek	1	31	3	1	1	1	1	2	0	0	2	3	1	1	1	1	0	3	3	3	3	1
Green Grove	2	27	1	1	1	1	1	2	0	0	2	2	1	1	1	0	0	3	3	3	3	1
Hillsboro	1	24	2	1	1	1	1	1	0	0	2	1	1	0	0	0	0	3	3	3	3	1
Hills Valley	1	33	3	1	2	2	2	1	0	0	1	2	1	1	1	2	0	3	3	3	3	2
Holts	1	33	2	1	2	2	2	2	0	0	2	3	2	1	1	1	0	3	3	3	3	1
Huntsville	1	35	2	1	1	2	1	2	1	0	2	3	1	2	2	0	0	3	3	3	4	2
Kirkland	2	27	2	1	1	1	1	2	0	0	2	1	1	1	1	0	0	3	3	3	3	1
Lee-Buckner	2	41	3	1	3	2	2	2	1	2	2	2	3	1	1	1	1	3	3	3	3	2
Locust Ridge	1	37	2	1	2	3	1	2	0	0	2	3	2	2	1	0	2	3	3	3	3	2
Mt. Lavergne	1	24	2	1	1	1	1	1	0	0	1	1	1	1	1	0	0	3	3	3	3	1
Nolensville	2	41	4	3	4	1	1	1	1	1	2	3	3	1	1	0	1	3	3	3	3	2
Pattons Chapel	1	31	4	2	1	1	1	2	0	2	1	2	1	1	0	0	0	3	3	3	3	1
Pearly Hill	1	26	2	1	1	1	1	1	0	0	2	1	1	1	1	0	0	3	3	3	3	1
Perkins	1	36	2	1	2	2	1	1	2	0	2	3	1	2	1	1	0	3	3	3	3	3
Thompson Sta.	2	47	4	3	3	2	1	2	1	2	2	3	2	2	2	2	2	3	3	3	3	2
Westwood	1	47	3	1	3	3	2	2	1	2	2	3	2	2	1	2	2	3	3	3	4	3
Franklin Trg.		72	3	2	5	5	4	4	5	4	3	5	4	3	3	3	4	2	5	2	2	4

*Appraised as one 12-grade school.
†In Davidson County.

Though Williamson County has always been one of the richest counties in Tennessee, it has ranked below average in funding for public schools. Local elected county officials prided themselves on keeping the school budget on a starvation level. In 1899, Superintendent Fred J. Page reported that there were 135 schools in the county, many one-room structures, and an average pay of thirty dollars a month for the teachers. In 1950, Williamson County ranked 13th in wealth per capita and 49th in expenditure for public education. Williamson County elementary teacher's average annual pay was $1,726, and $2,527 for high school teachers. In the 1955-56 school year, there were 19 schools for White children and 11 schools for Black. Of the 125 teachers, only 45% of them held a college degree.[1]

---

1. *Public Schools of Williamson County, Tennessee.* Division of Surveys and Field Services, George Peabody College for Teachers. Nashville, Tennessee, 1951.

Schools in the Eastern Section of Williamson County

In the Fall of 1954, the new Kirkland School opened, with Allison's Chapel, Huntsville, Locust Ridge, Green Grove, and Patton's Chapel Elementary Schools being sent to the new school. Nolensville Elementary School, which had been for Black students, was integrated into Nolensville School for White children in 1967. The following photographs reveal the poor conditions these schools were in.

Allison Chapel School was located on Owen Hill Road on the Homer Demonbreun farm. This is the first school and an A.M.E. Church building.

Allison School. Longtime teacher, Maudell Dotson, is shown with her female students in front of the new schoolhouse. The students were mostly from the Demonbreun and Hatcher families.

Locust Ridge School, located on Arno-College Road, in 1948.

Mamie Bostick King Starnes, beloved teacher at Green Grove. Photo courtesy of Thelma Battle.

Green Grove School, 1948

Patton's Chapel School

1st Row: R.L. Jordan, Robert Easley, Mackene Tucker, Anna Margaret Patton, Mamie Patton, Sallie Ann Tucker, Billy Tucker, Sam Hartan, and Baby Dalton; 2nd Row: Mary E. McClain, Olvie Tucker, Louis Tucker, Willie Starnes, Mal Starnes, Jr., and John Willie Jordan; 3rd Row: Walter Dalton, Jimmie Patton, Mary Patton, Mrs. Bybee House, and Etter Dalton.

Patton's Chapel School was on Cox Road, one-half mile from Murfreesboro Road. The building offered poor lighting, a coal-burning stove, and drinking water from Searcy Covington's well next door.

Huntsville School

Huntsville School was located on Trinity Road between Murfreesboro Road and Wilson Pike. Two windows provided daylight, a coal-burning stove provided heat, and drinking water had to be carried from a neighbor's well.

The Old Kirkland School

MARY L. JONES OGILVIE

Mary L. Jones Ogilvie

I attended the old Kirkland School.

My father was Lolie Jones, and he and his brother, Colie Jones, were identical twins, both of whom are now deceased. My mother was Frances Biggers Jones, and she was the only girl in her family of seven children.

When I was very young, I walked to school with my cousins and friends. It wasn't easy, but we made it fun.

Sometimes, we would walk through the woods behind the schoolhouse. For lunch, I would bring a big sack of food and share it with my play sisters and others who didn't have anything to eat.

Our family moved to Nashville, but I would catch a ride with Miss Moody and a teacher at Green Grove School. Some of my teachers taught me how to crochet and knit.

These were some of the best years. I made friends that have lasted a lifetime. I wouldn't change a thing.

Kirkland Elementary School Memories

MARY ELIZABETH CUNNINGHAM ANDERSON

Mary Elizabeth Cunningham Anderson

In 1951, George Peabody College for Teachers in Nashville prepared a report on the status of schools in Williamson County, Tennessee, and made recommendations for the future. A plan of reorganization was put forth for Negro elementary schools, closing smaller schools and combining their students in five centers with a minimum of 150 students at each school. The paper concludes with this statement:

The program will require transportation for Negro elementary school pupils, a responsibility which the county has not faced in the operation of its deplorable and even disgraceful existing school centers.

I started Kirkland School in the third grade, about 1950. We lived in College Grove and walked about four miles to Kirkland. College Grove had a stoker-warmed building as the school for the white children. Kirkland was a two-room school where heat was provided by a stove, and the students gathered kindling to start the fire.

Soon after that, Green Grove in Triune and Patton Chapel School in Arrington were closed, and the students were sent to Kirkland, but no extra rooms were provided.

In about 1952, Kirkland School burned down. We attended school in the Mt. Pleasant Church and an old house. Circumstances were even worse there concerning heat and the lack of a suitable playground. We had very good teachers – Mrs. Lucinda Rucker and Professor William B. Covington. Still, with four grades in each room, it was almost impossible for them to provide all the students with a good education. There were no desks; students held their books and tablets in their laps while sitting on church pews.

There were no school lunches in those days; students brought what they brought from home. Sometimes, Mrs. Covington, the principal's wife, would bring soup or some other hot food and serve us. Sometimes, a truck from the county would bring us orange juice and prunes.

In 1954, a new Kirkland Elementary School was built, costing $71,000. Other Black schools in the county received repairs and additions in an effort to bolster the claim that separate but equal facilities were provided.

In 1955, desegregation appeared in the school board minutes for the first time.

On August 16, 1962, *The Review-Appeal* listed the facilities for Black students. Those listed for Kirkland were Professor William B. Covington, principal, Maudell Dotson, Vella Moody, Nannie Lee Lanier, Pattie Taylor, Annie Elizabeth Patton, and Hattie Louise Reams.

In addition to the brick building and increased faculty, a custodian named Judge Webb, Jr. was employed, bus transportation was provided, and a kitchen and cooks prepared hot meals daily. Some of the cooks at that time were Annie Well Scales, Winnie Vaughn, Eula Jones Johnson, and Tish Webb. Willie B. Thompson and Pauline Cunningham filled in when substitutes were needed. Bus drivers included Preston Scales, Ross Norris, Jimmy Thompson, Albert Jordan, and Edd Scales.

Kirkland Elementary School

A History

JOSIE ANN SCALES

The Formulation of Kirkland Elementary School

Following the Civil War, the Freedmen's Bureau established schools in Williamson County, Tennessee, to educate newly freed slaves. In 1873, the county established public schools, and children attended segregated schools, often in one-room buildings. Kirkland Elementary School resided in Kirkland, Tennessee, and was established to provide education to African American children during the era of segregation. Like much of the South, Williamson County enforced segregationist policies, requiring separate educational facilities for Black and White students. Many Negro schools in Williamson County were established in churches within predominantly Black communities.

In the mid-1870s, Kirkland Elementary School began its early years on several sites on the Scales Family Farm. On April 4, 1887, Absalum and Eliza D. Scales donated land for a public school for colored children in the Kirkland community. Later, the school moved to another location on Horton Highway, to a church then called Scales Chapel, later renamed Mount Pleasant Missionary Baptist Church. In the early 1950s, when the church burned down, Kirkland Elementary School relocated to the Mr. Hetley Scales Home. Mr. Scales, an African American businessman who owned a grocery store, theater, and club in Kirkland, offered his home for the school.

COMING OUT OF THE DARK INTO THE LIGHT

The New Kirkland Elementary School

In the mid-1950s, Williamson County Board of Education Officials decided to build a new school for colored children. The county acquired 4.8 acres of land from Abb Scales to construct the new Kirkland School. Abb Scales was an African American farmer and a successful businessman who owned several hundred acres of farmland in Kirkland, Tennessee. He was a strong advocate for education. This new school became a cornerstone of the African American community in Kirkland, symbolizing the transformative power of education. Abb Scales' vision and generosity ensured that countless Negro children received the education they deserved, enabling them to pursue better opportunities and contribute positively to society.

Josie Scales, Professor, Tennessee State University

He attended public school in a one-room schoolhouse on the Absalum and Eliza D. Scales Farm and emphasized the essential role that education plays in empowering people in the community. There was an agreement between Abb Scales and the Williamson County Board of Education Officials that the school would always remain, or the building and acreage would serve the school and community at large. Peabody College for Teachers in Nashville, Tennessee, conducted a study recommending the reorganization of schools in the surrounding communities to be included in the new Kirkland Elementary School. These schools included Allison's Chapel Elementary, Huntsville Elementary, Kirkland Elementary, Locust Ridge Elementary, Green Grove Elementary, and Patton Chapel Elementary.

The new Kirkland School opened in 1954 on 4.8 acres and consisted of a building with six classrooms, a kitchen, a cafeteria that also served as an auditorium, and a playground. The faculty included Principal Professor W.B. Covington and six teachers: Vella Moody, Pattie Taylor, Hattie Louise Reams, Maudell Dotson, Nannie Lanier, and Annie [Elizabeth] Patton. Teacher's aides included Earline Lanier, Sue Sawyers, and Jessie Covington, who also served as the school's secretary. Kitchen staff members initially, Sadie B. Demonbreun, and Lucille Wray, later Winnie Vaughn, and succeeded by Annie Well Scales, and Tish Webb, substitutes were Willie B Thompson and Pauline Cunningham. Judge Webb served as the custodian for many years, later succeeded by Preston Scales, Jr. Transportation was provided and several bus drivers were hired to transport the students to Kirkland School, including Preston Scales, Jr., Ross Norris, Jimmy Thompson, Marshall Rogers (transported students from Kirkland School to Natchez High School in Franklin), John L. Jordan served as a substitute, and Epp Starnes, provided transportation to Franklin Training High School located in Franklin.

Integration and Closure of Kirkland Elementary School

In 1968, Williamson County Schools were fully integrated. Before full integration, Negro students who chose to attend White schools were permitted to do so. With full integration, grades one through four were housed in the Kirkland School building, while grades five through eight and high school students attended College Grove High School. In 1975, with the opening of Page High School, all elementary students were sent to College Grove, leading to the closure of Kirkland Elementary School. The Williamson County Board of Education Officials closed and sold the school and acre in an auction on December 11, 1976, breaking the hearts of the members of the Kirkland and surrounding communities that had long cherished the school because it was a center for cultural and social activities, fostering a sense of community.

Fond Memories

BRENDA GAIL ANDERSON

Brenda Gail Anderson

Wilson Anderson attended adult night classes at the age of sixty to learn how to read and write. His daughter, Brenda, said he was taught by Mr. Willie Wilson, who was also her teacher at that time. She recalled sitting at the table with her father and doing their assignments together. We were both so excited when he first wrote his name and read a new sentence without anyone's help. It opened up a new way of life for our whole family.

I was filled with joy knowing I could help my father because he had always been there for me and my brothers and sisters. He worked hard taking care of his family. He grew vegetables and sold his goods throughout the area where we lived. My sister Betty Sue and I followed in his footsteps – we started a business selling strawberries when we were in elementary school with the help of our father. We sold our produce to friends and teachers. We would take orders and hurry home after school to gather the berries from our patch. When the teachers came by after school to retrieve their orders, my father would have an opportunity to talk with them about our education. He knew how important it was because of what he had gone through as a young man.

I will never forget my years at Kirkland Elementary School. I loved all my teachers and friends and I want to thank Mr. Wilson for being there for each of his students. I would also like to express my appreciation to Ms. Cora Sue Sawyer for teaching me my multiplication skills and being so patient. I will always carry fond memories of my years at Kirkland Elementary.

Wilson Anderson   Willie Wilson   Cora Sue Sawyers

Kirkland Elementary Tigers

Kirkland Elementary School was built in 1954 after the old wooden-framed building burned, and sits on a hill overlooking Horton Highway. The scene above shows their May Day Festival, a much-enjoyed tradition.

Kirkland School Girls: Wanda Johnson, Brenda Norris, Faye Biggers, Verleen Hatcher, Robin Thompson, Sarah Burns, and Deborah Claybrooks.

Kirkland School, circa 1912. This is one of the earliest photographs of Kirkland Elementary School. Professor Fred Jordan, shown in doorway, taught there for many years. The siding on the school building is board and batten, indicating an early schoolhouse.

The students are: First Row Left: 1. Irma Jordan? 2. Will Allen Wray, 3. Tom Ewing, 5. Edgar Jordan? 6. Bessie Scales, 7. Louise Wray; Second Row: none identified; Third Row Left: 1. Will Harris Webb, 7. Alma Wray Thompson, 8. William Thompson, Sr. (father of Jimmy Thompson, Sr.), 12. Lewis Jones.

Students of Kirkland in the same schoolhouse. Sadly, identification of students is unknown.

Kirkland School, 1st Row: Ed McClain, Judge Webb, Jr., James McClain, Charles Norris, C. Shelton, John Scales, Huck Scales, and Earl Scales;

2nd Row: Sadie Jones, Willeva Scales, Eula Pearl Rucker, Fannnie Lou Jones, unknown, Sadie Pearl Jones, Annie May Jordan, Sina Mai Ellison, Mai Scales, Sadie B. Thompson, Aneva Dobson, Palmar Woods, Lillie Mai Rucker, Polly Mai Covington, Evelena Ellison, Rosie Bell Jordan, Bertha Oglesby, Annie Bell Rucker, Sweet Woods, Elizabeth Jones, Climmie Oglesby, and Pauline Woods;

3rd Row: Hobert Bedford, unknown, unknown, Oscar Thompson, Joe Ellis Scales, Powell Anderson, Bessie Scales, Emma D. Scales, Tommie Covington, Nellie Jane Scales, unknown, Betty Covington, Tish Webb, Mamie Lou Redmond, unknown, unknown, and Mrs. Walker, teacher;

4th Row: Julius Shelton, John Frank Anderson, unknown, Frank Scales, Joe Thompson, Hazel Scales, and Rena Dobson.

COMING OUT OF THE DARK INTO THE LIGHT

Kirkland School Mr. W.B. Covington and Mrs. Lucinda Rucker, Teacher

Front Row Left: William B. Covington, Jr., Lawrence Burns, and Bobby Scales; 2nd Row Left: Leon Oglesby, Odie Lee Anderson, Joe Ernest Strawther, Hurley Lanier, Jr., Felix Scales, and Jerome David Covington; 3rd Row Left: Edward Anderson, William Strawther, Eugene McClain, and Tom Lee; 4th Row Left: Arthur Floyd, Jr., O'Neal Vaughn, Charlie B. Covington, and Raymond Burns;

Seated on step: Charles Vaughn; 2nd row right: Pearlie May Covington, Mary Lean Oglesby, Earlene Lanier, and unknown; 3rd Row Right: Aggie J. Covington, Addie B. Strawther, Margaret McClain, and Theresa Lanier; 4th Row Right: Virginia McClain, Buelah Jones, and Izella Covington; 5th Row Right: Willie B. Ewing, Sarah Oglesby, and Eula Jones;

6th Row: Jesse Covington, Principal W.B. Covington, Mrs. Lucinda Rucker, Eula Pearl Lee, and Maime Rene Lanier.

Kirkland Elementary School, 1948, Grades 1-4, Mrs. Rucker, Teacher

1st Row: unknown, unknown, Jesse Anderson, Howard Eugene Anderson, Felix Scales, William B. Covington, Jr., George Edward Covington, unknown, and Mary Elizabeth Bedford Pennington;

2nd Row: unknown, unknown, Leon Oglesby, unknown, Tom Allen Ewing, Willie Frank Ewing, Joe Ernest Strawther, unknown, unknown, Mary Lena Oglesby, Earlene Lanier, and Willie Clarence Covington;

3rd Row: Mrs. Lucinda Rucker, unknown, unknown, Odie Lee Anderson, Willie Starnes, Jesse William Covington, Eugene Russell, unknown, Sadie Pearl Covington, Annie Mary Anderson, Theresa Lanier, James Boleyjack, Bertha Mary Edwards, and unknown.

Kirkland School, Grades 5 through 8, abt. 1948

1st Row: Albert Boleyjack, Jerome Covington, Sarah Oglesby, Mamie McClain, Mamie Covington, Margaret Jean McClain, Aggie Jane Covington, unknown, and Virginia McClain;

2nd Row: Willie B. Glenn, unknown, Mildred Covington, Eula Lee Jones, Edward Anderson, Beulah Lee Jones Polk, Sadie Frances Bowen, Izella Covington, and Cora Ann (last name unknown);

3rd Row: unknown, Herbert Hardeman (?), unknown, Tommy Lee, Alberta Scales, George Boleyjack, Hurley Lanier, Jr., Eula Pearl Lee, unknown, and Professor William B. Covington.

Kirkland School 8th Grade Graduating Class of 1964. Front row: Mary Ann Dotson, Bertha Howse, Robbie Scales, and Sadie Haley; Back Row: Nannie Lanier, teacher; O.W. Vaughn, Jr., Wayne Shelton, Edward Lee Patton, Charles Patton, Robert Preston Scales, Nathaniel Hatcher, and Prof. William B. Covington.

Kirkland School 8th Grade, 1966. Front Row: Delores Thompson, John Russell, Buford Hatcher, Katherine Harris, Reginald Johnson, and Lonnie B. Anderson; 2nd Row: Theodore Thompson, Tim Demonbreun, Delores Claybrooks, Martha Ridley (Anderson), Delores Patton, and Marie Ridley (Ogilvie); 3rd Row: Annie M. Johnson, Ernestine

Covington, Margaret Burns, Thomas Boleyjack, and Ewellyn Claybrooks; 4th Row: Paul Sawyers, Margaret Oglesby, Annie M. Ridley, Lonnie S. Anderson, Clarence Esmond, Prof. W.B. Covington, and Bernard Jordan.

Nannie Lanier's 8th Grade Class, Kirkland School

1st Row: Mattie Ruth Anderson, Ovie Elaine Boleyjack, Barbara Ann Carney, Geraldine Webb, and Annie Mildred Oglesby;

2nd Row: Mary Louise Dodson, Etta M. Ridley, Betty Ann Esmond, Lillia P. Rucker, Hayes Anderson, and Thomas Oglesby;

3rd Row: Mrs. Nannie Lanier – teacher, Jimmy Johnson, Thomas Mayberry, Larry Covington, and Berry Hardin.

Mrs. Lanier's 6th Grade Class, Kirkland School, 1966

1st Row: Eugene Cunningham, Robert House, Sereta McCord, Robin Thompson, and Ella Anderson.

2nd Row: James Harris, Jerry Esmond, James Ridley, Brenda Norris, Wanda Johnson, Deborah Claybrooks, and Verleen Biggers;

3rd Row: Clarence McCord, Eugene McClain, Barbara Biggers, Sarah Burns, Barnell Patton, Herbert Russell, Michael Jordan, Sally Davis, Hazel Anderson, and Mrs. Nannie Lanier.

COMING OUT OF THE DARK INTO THE LIGHT

Kirkland Elementary School Second Grade Class with teacher, Annie Hunter Patton. 1960s.

[1]

1. Battle, Thelma. *Thelma Battle African American Photographic Collection*, 1999 Black History Month Exhibit. Williamson County Public Library.

Maudell Parrish Dotson's Class

Front Row: Michael Strawther, Jessie Covington, Dexter Norris, Herbert Russell, Bernis Ewing, David DeWayne Covington, Vincent Hatcher, and Jimmy Russell; Back Row: Jackie Strawther, Juanita Anderson, Regina Anderson, Mary Davis, Beverly Williams, Jesse Anderson, Jr., Mary Norris, Theresa Carney, and Sarah Norris.

COMING OUT OF THE DARK INTO THE LIGHT

KIRKLAND SCHOOL FACULTY AND STAFF

Professor W.B. Covington, beloved principal, teacher, and friend.

Center front to right: Hazel Scales Covington, wife of W.B. Covington, Tish Webb and Geneva Thompson; back left: Carolyn Wray.

Faculty: Vella Moody, Dorothy North, Jessie Thompson Covington, Nannie Lanier, Willie Wilson, William B. Covington, and Edward Johnson.

Faculty and aides listed left to right: Principal William B. Covington, Nannie Lanier, Willie Wilson, Jessie Thompson Covington, Edward Johnson, Earlene Lanier, Maudell Dotson, Annie Patton, and Cora Sawyers.

Pattie Davis Taylor

Maudell Dotson

Vella Moody

Dorothy North

Lucinda Campbell Rucker

Annie Patton

Edward Johnson, Kirkland

Willie Wilson

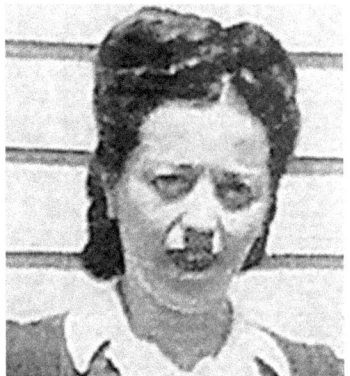
Colleen Williams

Hattie Reams

Earlene Lanier, Aide

Jessie Thompson Covington, Aide

Winnnie Vaughn, Cook

Tish Webb, Cook

Annie Well Scales, Cook

Cora Sawyers, Secretary

Jimmy Green Thompson, Bus Driver

Herbert Patton, Bus Driver

COMING OUT OF THE DARK INTO THE LIGHT

Ebb Starnes

John L. Jordan, Bus Driver

Preston Scales, Bus Driver

Judge Webb, Custodian

Kirkland School Students

Ella Anderson

Hayes Anderson

Hazel Anderson

Howard Anderson

Joe Anderson

Josie Anderson

Lonnie Anderson

Mattie Ruth Anderson

COMING OUT OF THE DARK INTO THE LIGHT

Powell Anderson, Jr   Sue Anderson   Barbara Biggers   Alma Boleyjack

Howard Boleyjack   Larry Boleyjack   Thomas Boleyjack   Carol Ann Britton

Jesse Britton   Patsy Britton   Sarah Burns   Betty Lou Carney

 Jo Ester Carney
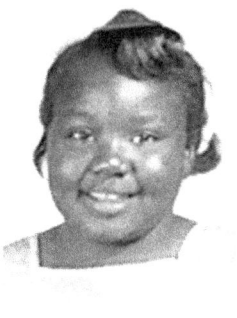 Theresa Carney
 Charles Claybrooks
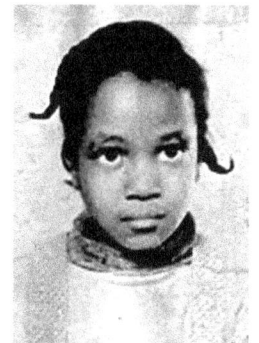 Delores Claybrooks

 Eulyn Claybrooks
 Lamont Claybrooks
 Linda Claybrooks
 Shirley Claybrooks

 Aretha Covington
 Bernice Covington
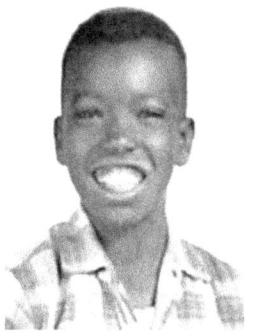 Charles Covington
 Clarence Covington

COMING OUT OF THE DARK INTO THE LIGHT

Greg Covington Henrietta Covington Jesse Covington Mattie Mai Covington

Mike Covington Theresa Covington Veronica Covington Mary Crowder

Carol Cunningham Eugene Cunningham Mildred Cunningham Earline Davis

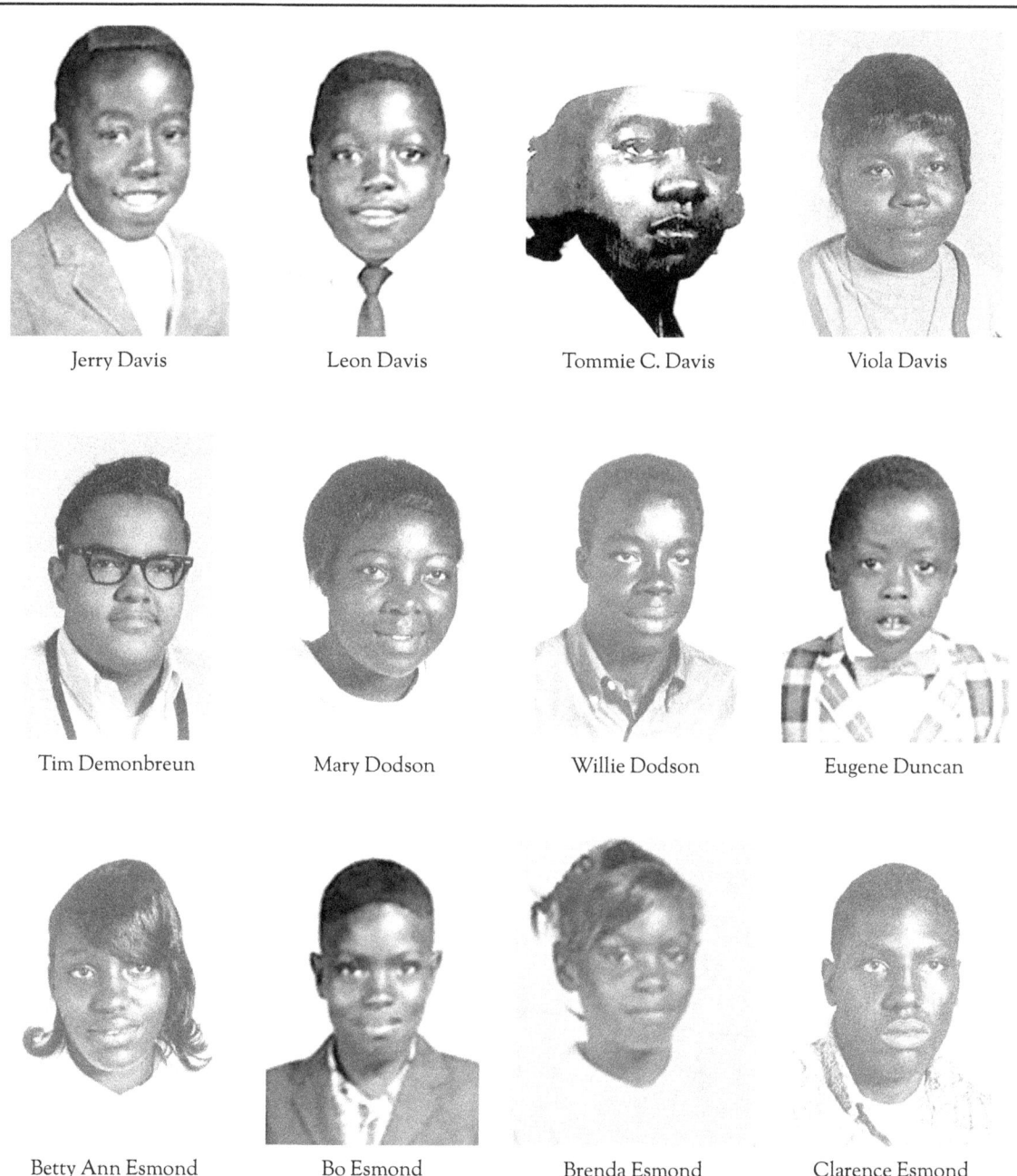

COMING OUT OF THE DARK INTO THE LIGHT

Jerry Esmond

Robert Esmond

Diane Ewing

Thomas Ewing, Jr.

James Oscar Garrett

Charles Glenn, Jr.

Sadie Haley

Alan Tyrone Hatcher

Gail Hatcher

Gwen Hatcher

Jackie Hatcher

Marvin Hatcher

Kirkland

 Nathaniel Hatcher
 Vincent Hatcher
 Bertha Howse
 Loretta Howse

 Robert Howse
 James Hughes
 Frank Johnson
 Peggy Johnson

 Reginald Johnson
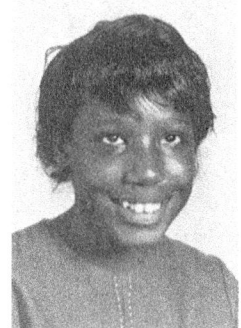 Wanda Johnson
 Houston Jones
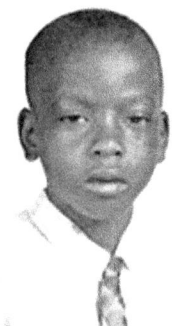 Jerry Jones

COMING OUT OF THE DARK INTO THE LIGHT

Martha L. Jones	William D. Jones	Bernard Jordan	Fannie Mai Jordan
Jerry Wayne Jordan, Sr.	Randall Jordan	John Leach	Robbie Leach
Patricia Lee	Christine Mayberry	Claude McClain	William McClain

COMING OUT OF THE DARK INTO THE LIGHT

Janice Norris · John Norris · Marie Norris · Robert Norris

Frank Ogilvie, Jr. · Anna Oglesby · Larry Oglesby · Robbie Oglesby

Thomas Oglesby · Ernest Oliver · Nancy Oliver · Larry Patton

 Robert Russell

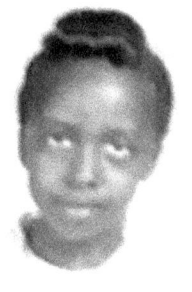 Sharon Russell

 Dorothy Sawyers

 Paul Sawyers

 John Kirkland Scales

 Robbie Scales

 Robert Scales

 Hattie Floyd Smith

 Derrick L. Smithson

 Terrence A. Smithson

 Timothy Scott Smithson

 Jesse Starnes

COMING OUT OF THE DARK INTO THE LIGHT

Jackie Strawer

Mike Strawer

Cindy Thompson

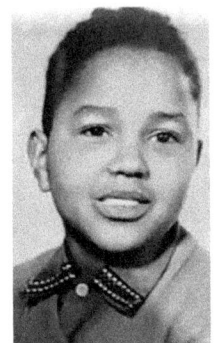
Hubert Thompson

James "Pete" Thompson

Robin Thompson

Sherrdon Thompson

William Thompson

Charles Vaughn

James T. Vaughn

Juanita Vaughn

Richard Vaughn, Jr.

 Sherry Vaughn
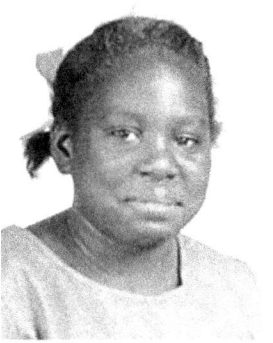 Vera Vaughn
 Donzetta Webb
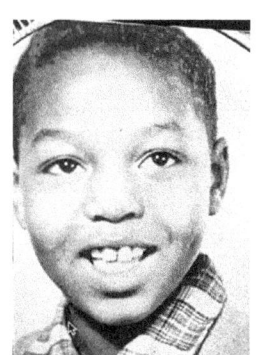 Elliot Webb

 Geraldine Webb
 Judy Webb
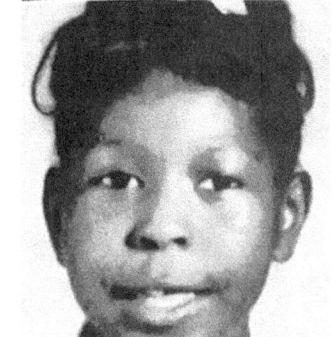 Zennia Webb
 Beverly Williams

 Larry Williams
 ? Williams
 Unknown
 Unknown

Wesley and Gloria Vaughn

Jessie Johnson, Richard Johnson, and James Ridley

The Daltons: Michael, Charley, Doyle, and Bobby

The Majorettes

At Franklin Training School and Natchez High School

Eloise "Ella" Boleyjack (Sowell)

Alma Boleyjack

Hattie Boleyjack (Lane)

Patricia Lee (Wheeler)

Young majorettes at Kirkland School: Front Row: Barbara Faye Biggers, Margaret Jean Burnes, Carolyn Wray, and Aletha Thompson; Back Row: Brenda Demonbreun and Mary Ann Floyd.

Kirkland School Pageantry: Josie Ann Scales, Robbie Scales, Rosemary Buchanan, Patricia Lee, Aletha Thompson, Clara Leach, Mary Ann Claybrooks, and Pattie Johnson.

Gone Too Soon

William B. Covington, Jr. | John Kirkland Scales | Larry Herbert Patton

You were with us for such a short time yet left a lasting impression in our hearts and minds. You will never be forgotten and your loving memory will be with us always.

William B. Covington Jr. (1942-1956)
John Kirkland Scales (1954-1971)
Larry H. Patton (1954-1969).

COMING OUT OF THE DARK INTO THE LIGHT

Obituaries for William B. Covington Jr.,[1] John Kirkland Scales,[2] and Larry H. Patton.[3]

Colored Out-of-Town
College Grove, Tenn.
COVINGTON—At a local infirmary, 6:45 p.m. William B. Covington Jr. Survived by mother, Mrs. Hazel Covington; father, W. B. Covington; three sisters, Inella, Beirnice M., and Ernestine Covington; one brother, Jerome D. Covington; seven aunts; 10 uncles; two great aunts; four great uncles; grandparents, Mr. and Mrs. Risdon Woods of College Grove, Tenn.; a host of other relatives and friends. The body will lie in state at his home from 6 p.m. Friday until funeral services Saturday at 11 a.m. from Mount Pleasant Missionary Baptist church, conducted by the pastor, Rev. E. E. Thomas Jr. Interment Scales cemetery. H. Preston Scales and Sons, in charge.

William B. Covington,
Tennessean, April 27. 1956

College Grove, Tenn.
SCALES, John Kirkland — Age 17, suddenly Saturday morning, Nov. 13, 1971 at Vanderbilt Hospital. Survived by mother, Mrs. Annie Scales; one brother, Robert Preston Scales; two sisters, Miss Josie Annie Scales, College Grove, and Mrs. Robbie Moore, Nashville; grandparents, Mr. and Mrs. Preston Scales Sr., and Mr. Joe Frank Pinkerton; brother-in-law, Milton Moore, Nashville; seven aunts; five uncles; 12 great aunts; 10 great uncles. Remains are at the Scales & Sons Funeral Home, Murfreesboro, Tenn. Friends may visit with the family this Sunday evening from 7 to 10 p.m. at Mt. Pleasant Missionary Baptist Church, Kirkland, Tenn. Funeral service Monday, at 1 p.m. from the above church conducted by the pastor, Rev. Edwin Thomas Jr. Interment Scales Cemetery. H. PRESTON SCALES & SONS FUNERAL HOME, Directors, Murfreesboro, Tenn.

John Kirkland Scales,
Tennessean, Nov. 14, 1971

PATTON, Larry H. — Of College Grove, Tenn. Sunday, November 2, 1969. Survived by mother: Mrs. Ella Mai Patton; brothers: Edward, Barnell, and J. D. Patton, Jr.; sisters: Stephane and Dolly Patton; grandparents: Mr. and Mrs. John H. Patton; Mr. Baxter Hardiman; devoted cousin: Mrs. Ollie Scales; nephew: Master Rodney Patton; uncles: Mr. John H. Patton, Herbert Hardiman, Edward Hardiman, Chicago, Ill.; Joe Anderson; aunts: Mesdames Mary Claybrooks, Annie Anderson, Alice Patton and Jane Hardiman; sister-in-law: Mrs. Annie Mai Patton; great-uncles: Mr. Sam, Henry and Robert Russell; great-aunts: Mrs. Frances Johnson, Mrs. Myrtle McCord; dear friends: Harold McClain and Mr. and Mrs. G. P. Linebaugh & Daughter; other relatives and friends. Remains are at Wright's funeral Home where family will receive friends this Tuesday from 8 to 10 p.m. Funeral Wednesday 1:00 p.m. from Beech Grove Methodist Church conducted by the Pastor Rev. G. T. Jobe assisted by Elder Lowery Mooney. Flowergirls and Pallbearers selected from Cousins and Friends. Interment Beech Grove Cemetery. WRIGHT'S FUNERAL HOME, 255-8735.

Larry H. Patton,
Tennessean, Nov. 5, 1969

1. William B. Covington Obituary. April 27, 1956 (page 55 of 61). (1956, Apr 27). Nashville Tennessean. Retrieved from https://www.proquest.com/historical-newspapers/april-27-1956-page-55-61/docview/1900054590/se-2
2. John Kirkland Scales Obituary. November 14, 1971 (page 31 of 204). (1971, Nov 14). Nashville Tennessean. Retrieved from https://www.proquest.com/historical-newspapers/november-14-1971-page-31-204/docview/1906088908/se-2
3. Larry H. Patton Obituary. November 5, 1969 (page 43 of 51). (1969, Nov 05). Nashville Tennessean. Retrieved from https://www.proquest.com/historical-newspapers/november-5-1969-page-43-51/docview/1905835353/se-2

New Beginnings

LINDA BOLEYJACK WILLIAMS

Linda Boleyjack

When I entered Kirkland Elementary in 1955, it was a time of many new "firsts" for me. It was my first time riding a bus. I stepped on the bus with help before taking my seat beside two others. There were many students from high school to first grade. It was crowded! However, I was thrilled to be with them and hear their conversations.

My sister, Ella, walked me to my classroom when I arrived at school. Before she left me, she said, "Don't cry." I must have looked scared. I became fascinated with the water fountain as I looked around the classroom. I could not wait to drink from it for the first time. I had to learn to turn and hold the handle to get a drink. I went thirsty, had water splashed on my face, and got wet clothes, all in the process of learning how to use the water fountain. Once I got the hang of it, I would use it at the wrong time, which led to my first and last spanking at school. I learned to obey the teacher early to avoid embarrassment in front of my peers.

My next first was eating lunch in the cafeteria with my classmates. Mrs. Scales had the entire school ready for lunch, with the aroma coming from there. The rolls smelled and tasted so good. We had tasty desserts each day.

Recess was an exciting time to be with friends. It was not organized. We created our own games, and many brought equipment to use, such as jump ropes, hula hoops, softballs, gloves, and even boxing gloves. We were very competitive and occasionally had some squabbles. Despite that, Kirkland students remain close to this day. We are always happy to see each other.

After completing college, I returned to teach in Williamson County, where I retired after 30 years of service. When I reflected on how I could have had a successful career, I knew where it all began. I deeply appreciate the principal, teachers, bus drivers, and all the staff at Kirkland for giving me a good first start. How did they do it in such a woefully under-resourced, segregated school system?

Linda Boleyjack Williams' Kindergarten Class at Lipscomb Elementary School, 1982

They taught us, despite limited materials and ill-prepared students, who lacked life experiences to prepare them for learning. They were dedicated educators who did their best to help us. Kirkland did not have specialists for struggling students. The high achievers, who finished work early, were encouraged to help others without ridicule. We enjoyed the opportunity to help others.

These teachers taught more than the Three Rs. They also taught us many valuable moral lessons. I recall Mrs. Lanier always encouraging us to tell the truth. She said, "If you lie, you will steal; both are forms of cheating." This helped me. I would lie occasionally to get out of trouble, but I thought it to be terrible for someone to think of me as a thief. I wonder what Mrs. Lanier would think of today's politicians, with their alternative facts.

Oh, I always remember the things we learned and the relationships we formed to help us become the people we are today! The experiences we had were our first but not our last. The students went on to become soldiers, preachers, church leaders, college graduates, teachers, college professors, owners of businesses, healthcare workers, insurance agents, office workers, food service managers, artists, lawyers, salesmen, bus drivers, working in large factories, property owners, wonderful parents, and good citizens.

All Williamson County Chorus 1965-66, David Kannon, Director

1st row: Serrila Hartley, Sue Whidby, Jerre Stinson, Shirley Maxwell, Lillian Scruggs, Sandra Tomlin, Nora Jordan, Carolyn Wray, Lau Carol Dobson, Jane Fitzgerald, Deloris Coe, Della Harper, and Linda Boleyjack; 2nd row: Jane Ryan, Elaine Givens, Barbara Mangrum, Cynthia Owens, Vickie Lampley, Carolyn Bright, Brenda Jones, Gail Rollins, Connie Ivery, Faye Powers, Janice Spann, Eva Haynes, Jennie Mangrum, and Peggy Warren; 3rd row: Mary Nance, Mary Jane Ray, Donzetta Webb, Dorothy Sawyers, Jo Clary, Willie Spencer, Vicki York, Patricia Spencer, Janice Barnhill, Joyce Hamm, Juanita Barnhill, Claudia Gosey, Evelyn Gosey, Norma Burns, Mary Peters, and Annette Scruggs; 4th row: Don Esmon, Paul Sewell, Tommy Ryan, Leonard Lee, Bill Mangrum, John Easley, Howard Kelton, George Ridley, Philip Brown, and Charles Hamilton.

Looking Back at Kirkland School

OVIE ELAINE BOLEYJACK BELL

Looking back on yesterday, I realize it has transformed my mind over the years that have passed. When I view my life from a child's perspective. I wonder how I became the person I am today, living during the time of Jim Crow laws and segregation. I'm so proud of my parents for sheltering us from as many harmful elements of life as they could. I was given time to expand my mind and venture into life free from the chaos. I can't remember seeing a sign that said:

WHITES ONLY

But I do recall the way that I felt when they would gaze at me as if I had done something wrong, which brought about a feeling of uncertainty.

Attending Kirkland Elementary School helped alleviate the feeling of being alone in a world where I felt unwanted. There were children who looked like me and understood what I was going through. The microcosm atmosphere surrounding us made us feel whole when we were told we were inferior. Our teachers were like our parents; while in school, we knew to show them respect because if we didn't, our parents would be notified. They were strict but caring, especially when it came to our education. They did the very best they could with limited supplies, including hand-me-down books with torn-out pages, but somehow, we made it through. Maybe it was the devotional program on Monday morning. All the students would come to the cafeteria, Professor Covington would say a prayer, and a student would recite a Bible verse. Then we would sing a gospel song, which brought about a sense of serenity. After the devotional, we returned to our classrooms and began our day.

We had a lot of fun playing together during recess; some of the games we played included jacks, pick-up sticks, jump rope, softball, and tag. As we grew older, in the 7th and 8th grades, we became interested in music. My friends, Barbara Ann, Juanita, and I, wanted to sing like the Supremes, and we would rehearse songs during recess. Our minds were filled with dreams of the future, and we thought we could become whatever we wanted to be. Those were the good old days.

It was both a happy and a sad day when it was time for us to graduate from eighth grade. We were leaving a life and a place where we felt safe and secure, and it was like leaving home for the first time. Our surroundings changed as we took a bus to Natchez High School in Franklin; we would now be the little fish in the big pond. While we were in the eighth grade, the younger kids looked up to us for guidance, and now we will be the new kids in a big school, trying to navigate our way around. Our teachers had prepared us for what was about to come. All we had to do was trust our abilities and move forward, one step at a time. Life goes on.

John L. and Clatie Lytle Jordan

THELMA JORDAN WALDEN

Clatie Lytle and John L. Jordan

John L. and Clatie Lytle Jordan were two of the few business owners in their area. They moved to the Kirkland community in 1951. Soon after moving to the area, they built a triplex in 1958. The triplex consisted of a grocery store, a dance hall for local teenagers on weekends, and a small beauty shop on the back side of the triplex, as Clatie was a licensed beautician. The grocery store was very popular among the students, especially after school. They would go to the store to get treats like cookies, gum, candies, and anything else they could afford while waiting for the school buses to take them home.

The teenagers enjoyed going to the dance hall, which had a jukebox filled with the current R&B hits (45s). They could also buy hot (fried) or cold bologna sandwiches, hot dog sandwiches, ice cream cones, and those all-time favorite sugar cookies. This is only a short list of the menu items they favored.

John L. was a businessman who believed education was the key to success. Even though he only had an eighth-grade education, he continued to learn through every available resource. He served his country in the U.S. Army for three years. He had an opportunity to travel to Europe while in the army. That kindled his desire to learn more. He had a long career as an insurance agent who went door-to-door selling and collecting health, life, and disability policies. He encouraged young people to always strive to be the best at whatever they choose to do in life.

Thelma Jordan

John L. and Clatie shared the same desire to impact the lives of young black people positively. They opened the only night spot for teenagers in that area. They believed that nothing good went on after midnight, so they closed the night spot at 11:30 p.m., allowing the teenagers to get home before the midnight curfew. John L. and Clatie employed several teenage girls to work in the dance hall on weekends and perform bookkeeping duties for the insurance business and the grocery store.

The triplex business was closed in 1967, but they continued to live in the Kirkland community. They truly enjoyed it when the young folks came back to visit and told them how much they enjoyed the long talks and the wisdom they shared. John L. passed away in 2005, and Clatie passed away in 2008. They spent 54 and 57 years in the community they loved.

The John L. Jordan Store, Beauty Shop, and Teen Center

Those Were the Days

At Kirkland School

ANNIE MAI JOHNSON

Maggie Bess Johnson   Eugene Johnson   Annie Mai Johnson

I grew up in the Arrington, Tennessee, area. My parents were Eugene and Maggie Johnson, and eight children were born into the family. My sisters and brother, Bessie, Martha, Jimmie, Paulene, Annie Mai Johnson (Patton), and I attended Kirkland Elementary School in the 1960s, and we loved it.

At that time, Mr. Preston Scales was the bus driver, and his wife, Mrs. Annie Well Scales, was the cook in the cafeteria. She was the best cook ever. I couldn't always buy my lunch, and sometimes she needed help after lunch. When that happened, I would volunteer to help. *Those were the days!*

I also remember some of the teachers who taught us: Mrs. Moody, Mrs. Lanier, and Mr. William B. Covington, who was both the principal and a teacher. Mr. Covington took his job seriously, and now and then, he would pull that paddle out, especially if you were acting up. Most of the time, my brother Jimmie would be on the other end of that paddle, but sometimes it was me on the other end! I would say to myself, "Poor Jimmie."

Many other family members attended Kirkland Elementary School, including the Ruckers, Jordans, Covingtons, Harrises, Burns, Ridleys, Esmonds, Vaughns, Boleyjacks, and Claybrooks. We were all going through the same things, trying to endure tough times. All our parents were hard workers trying to provide for their families. I will never forget those wonderful times and precious moments we spent with family and friends at Kirkland Elementary School. *Those were the days.*

Our hairstylist, Mrs. Clatie Mai Jordan, I tell you, she was the best. I know she did lots of hair because, during those times, there were not many Black hairstylists close by, and she was in the right spot to take care of most of our hair needs. Even though we lived a few miles away, my mother would get Daddy to take her there to get her hair done. Mama always looked good when she came out of Mrs. Clatie Mai's shop. I will never forget the good and bad times. *After all, those were the days.*

Aggie Jane Norris

Aggie Jane Norris

Aggie Jane Norris was born to Elder A. M. Bedford and his wife, Bettie Lewis, on February 16, 1936. Her stepfather was Ken Lewis. Aggie was a member of Shady Grove Primitive Baptist Church. She cherished her church family and was a dedicated Mother of the church and the Cumberland Association.

She attended Kirkland School and Franklin Training School. She worked for the Joseph May Welch family and at Tennessee Poultry throughout her career.

Aggie was married to John C. Norris for fifty-seven years. Together, they had five children: Brenda Janice, Marie, John, Robert, and Antonio Norris.

Aggie passed away on July 28, 2010.[1]

Those we love don't go away; they walk beside us daily.

1. Aggie Jane Norris Obituary. *The Thelma Battle African American Funeral Program Collection.* Williamson County Public Library. Accessed online on June 9, 2025.

Charles Lee and Nettie Mae Jones

Charles Lee and Nettie Mae Jones

Nettie Mae Burns was born to George W. and Rosa L. Burns on August 16, 1918, in the 20th Civil District of Williamson County, Tennessee. She married Charles Lee Jones on April 21, 1938, and died on August 25, 1995. She is buried in Locust Ridge Cemetery.

Charles Lee Burns was born on December 27, 1921, in Williamson County, Tennessee. He died on March 14, 1970, and is buried in Locust Ridge Cemetery.

The children of Charles Lee and Nettie Mai Burns Jones are: Mary "Mai" Emma Roberts, Charlie Frank Jones, Bessie Lee Floyd, Bettie Jean Turner, Marvin Henry Jones, William Jones, Thomas Jones, Melvin Eugene Jones, Marcus Jones, and Robert Blackman.

> **JONES, Mother Nettie Mae Burns**— Fri., August 25, 1995. Age 77. Survived by daughters, Mai Emma (Willie) Roberts & Bettie Jean Turner (who cared for her); sons, Charlie (Robbie), Marvin (Carolyn), William (Esther), Thomas E., Melvin & Marcus Jones; two foster children; 35 grandchildren; 66 great grandchildren; one great great grandchild; sisters, Annie Pearl Bowens, Mildred Rodgers, Thelma Pendergrass, Bessie Jenkins & Wilma Burns; brothers, George Jr. & William Burns; mother-in-law, Elsie Mai Coleman; four sisters-in-law; five brothers-in-law; six aunts; two uncles; a host of nieces, nephews, cousins, relatives and friends. Family Visitation Wednesday, August 30, 1995 from 11am-12noon at Locust Ridge P.B. Church, College Grove, Tn. Funeral to follow. Elder Jasper Hatcher officiating. Interment Locust Ridge Cemetery. SMITH BROTHERS FUNERAL DIRECTORS, 706 Monroe St., 726-1476, Henry L. & Melvin J. Smith, Directors

(ESSEAN — Tuesday, August 29/1995 • 5B)

Nettie Mae Jones Obit, The Tennessean, August 29, 1995.

> **Arrington, Tenn.**
> **JONES, Mr. Charlie** — of Rt. 1, Arrington, Tenn. Saturday, March 14, 1970 at a Nashville Hospital. Survived by wife, Mrs. Nettie Jones; three daughters, Mrs. Mai E. Roberts, Bessie L. Floyd and Betty J. Turner; seven sons, Charlie F., Marvin H., William C., Thomas E., Melvin E. and Marcus E. Jones, Robert Blackman; Mother, Mrs. Elsie M. Johnson; two sisters, Mrs. Ida M. Blackman, Mrs. Hattie P. Buchanan; brother, Mr. John L. Jones. 20 grandchildren, mother-in-law, Mrs Rosie L. Burns, a host of nieces and nephews and other relatives and friends. Remains will be conveyed to Locust Ridge P.B. Church, this Wednesday for visitation with family from 7 until 10 p.m. Funeral Thursday 1 p.m. from the above church, conducted by his Pastor, Rev. Frank Brown. Interment Locust Ridge Cemetery. WRIGHT'S FUNERAL HOME, 255-8735.

Charlie Jones Obit, The Tennessean, March 18, 1970.

1. "March 18, 1970 (Page 35 of 64)." Nashville Tennessean (1923-1972), 18 Mar., 1970, pp. 35. ProQuest, https://www.proquest.com/historical-newspapers/march-18-1970-page-35-64/docview/1905860388/se-2.
2. "August 29, 1995 (Page 13 of 54)." The Tennessean (1972-), 29 Aug., 1995, pp. 13. ProQuest, https://www.proquest.com/historical-newspapers/august-29-1995-page-13-54/docview/1912554636/se-2.

Annette, Dwight, and Yvonne, children of Bessie Lee Floyd

Bessie Lee Jones Floyd

Thomas Edward Jones, Sr.

Carolyn Gray, daughter of Bessie Lee Floyd

Ella Virginia Anderson McClain

Edwin E. and Ella Virginia McClain

Minnie Anderson Ogilvie and Ella Virginia McClain

Mrs. Ella Virginia Anderson McClain was born August 26, 1920, and died September 1, 1979. Her parents were Lytle R. Anderson and Annie Claybrooks. On February 4th, 1939, she married Edwin E. McClain, and one child was born to this union, Margaret J. McClain Coleman. Mrs. McClain was a member of Shady Grove Primitive Baptist Church and served faithfully on the Mother's Board for many years.

Margaret Jean McClain Coleman

Mrs. Margaret Jean Coleman was born on October 9, 1937, and died on May 8, 2005. She married Robert M. Coleman on August 8, 1957. To this union, five daughters were born: Donna M. Esmond (Clarence), Stephanie L. Coleman, Virginia D. Coleman, Melanie J. Coleman, and Cynthia E. (Tim) Coleman-Lackey. She had six grandchildren. Margaret attended Kirkland School. Mrs. Coleman is buried in the Scales Cemetery in Kirkland.

Margaret Jean Coleman

Robert Coleman

COMING OUT OF THE DARK INTO THE LIGHT

Donna Esmond, Stephanie Coleman, Virginia Coleman, Melanie Coleman, and Cynthia Coleman-Lackey

George Coleman, father of Robert Coleman

Kirkland's Roadside Businesses

ROBBIE D. JONES

Located north of the Harpeth River and College Grove in rural Williamson County, the Kirkland community once featured several African American roadside businesses catering to automobile travelers. The community grew up at the split of U.S 31A (State Route 11) and U.S. 41A (State Route 16), with U.S. 31A connecting Pulaski with Nashville via Columbia and Lewisburg and U.S. 41A connecting Monteagle with Clarksville via Shelbyville, Tullahoma, and Nashville.

Originally known as the Nashville and Chapel Hill Pike, U.S. 31A was an eastern alternate route for U.S. 31 between Pulaski and Nashville. Dating from the mid-nineteenth century, the turnpike was a popular farm-to-market road radiating out from the state capital at Nashville. It was improved into a state highway in the 1910s and later designated a federal highway. By 1940, the route was renamed the Horton Memorial Highway. U.S. 41A was a western alternative route for travelers along the Dixie Highway (U.S. 41), a popular intrastate highway that connected the Midwest with Florida. U.S. 41A was also known as Nolensville Pike, a nineteenth-century turnpike that connected to Nolensville and Nashville.

Serving travelers going south to Georgia, Alabama, and Florida or north to Kentucky and points beyond, the split at Kirkland became a popular location for roadside commercial businesses such as service stations, cafes, general stores, markets, boarding houses, tourist court motels, lounges, and nightclubs. Throughout the twentieth century, the Kirkland community was notorious for unlicensed and underaged alcohol sales by business owners and operators, resulting in many arrests publicized by local newspapers.

At Kirkland, many of the roadside businesses were owned and operated by members of the Scales families – one Black and one White. The Black business owners were descendants of enslaved persons who once lived on adjoining plantations owned by the Scales and Webb families that settled in the area in the early nineteenth century and intermarried. Joseph Griffin Scales (1798- 1870) and Dr. William Smith Webb (1776-1866) were both wealthy planters, owning from 35 to 40 enslaved persons each. The circa 1845 Joseph G. Scales House (WM-212) was NRHP [National Register of Historic Places]-listed but has been demolished. The adjoining "Sylvan Retreat" (WM-261) plantation, built around 1850 by James Webb, still stands and is listed on the NRHP (it was later renamed "Kirkview" due to its hilltop view of Kirkland). At least five other members of the Scales and Webb families at Kirkland also owned from 10 to 20 enslaved persons each. The farmhouse (WM-221) of his brother Absalom Gollehugh Scales (1821-1887), who owned 16 enslaved persons, still stands.

An 1860s map shows a plantation on the west side of Nolensville Pike at Kirkland as owned by Dr. Sam Scales, most likely referring to Dr. Samuel Webb Scales (1834-1868), a local physician who attended medical school in Nashville and Philadelphia from 1855 to 1857 and served as a military surgeon for the Confederate Army during the Civil War. Members of the Scales and Webb families are buried at the Webb Family Cemetery at Kirkland, and other farmhouses at Kirkland owned by the family members are NRHP-listed, including the circa 1864-1872 William Felix Webb House (WM-213) and the circa 1887 James Scales House (WM-224).

After the Civil War, many of these freed enslaved persons stayed at Kirkland, establishing their own farms carved from the former Scales and Webb plantations. Black members of the Scales and Webb families established a Black cemetery on land that was formerly part of the William Smith Webb plantation. Slave descendants also established the Mt. Pleasant Baptist Church and Kirkland School. One of the freed enslaved persons was Jerry Scales (b.1835) and his wife Louisa Scales (1839-1877), who raised nine children, including Cora and Delora, who moved to Murfreesboro where they became community leaders (see *In The Footsteps of Notable Women: A Self-Guided Tour of Rutherford County*), and Thomas Ellis Scales.

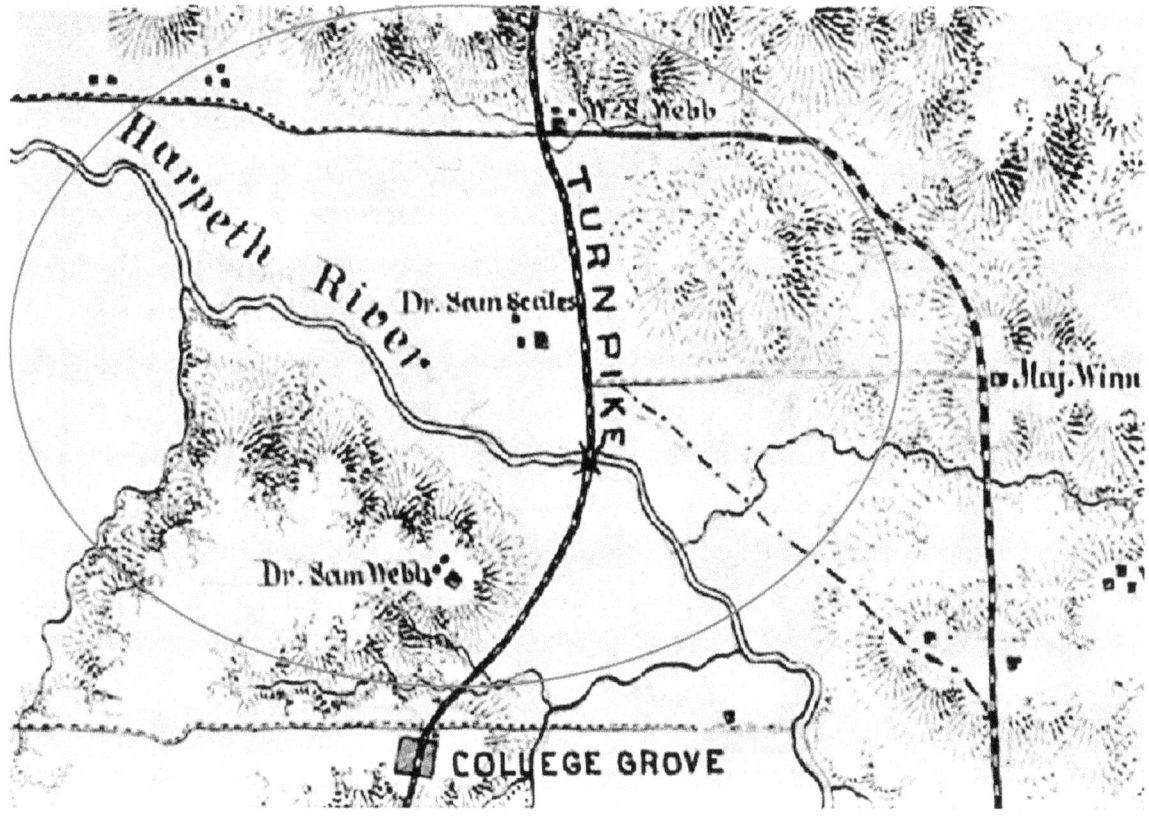

Map showing the Scles and Webb Plantations at Kirkland, circa 1861-1865. Source: The National Archives and Records Administration.

THOMAS ELLIS SCALES, SR.

At Kirkland, several of the roadside business owners were African Americans, including Thomas Ellis Scales, Sr. (1867-1943), a local farmer and blacksmith. In the late 1880s, he started a commercial business along the east side of the Nolensville Pike. This two-story complex contained a blacksmith shop, general store, and funeral home. By 1930, the business also included a boarding house, most likely operated by his wife Jennie "Jane" Cardwell King Scales (1865-1958), a native of Haywood County. In 1930, the boarding house had 13 lodgers, all African American men working as highway laborers on the Horton Highway. In 1940, the boarding house had one lodger,

COMING OUT OF THE DARK INTO THE LIGHT

an African American schoolteacher. Scales also added a service station that sold Esso brand fuel.

Married in 1882, Thomas Ellis and Jane raised 11 children, who helped run the business enterprise. One son, Perse "Percy" Scales (1887-1949), became a blacksmith, and another, Earl Scales (1884- 1954), became a house carpenter at Murfreesboro (see *In The Footsteps of Notable Women: A Self-Guided Tour of Rutherford County*). Their son, Thomas Ellis Scales, Jr. (1897-1971), assisted in running the family grocery store. At some point, the business was operated by their son Hettley Carter Scales (1899-1963). The business was known as Hettley's Tavern and Grocery and Hettley's Store and Gas Station during his tenure. Thomas Ellis Scales, Sr. died in 1943, and his wife Jane died in 1958; both are buried in the Scales Cemetery. Some of their children moved to Chicago and Detroit, while others stayed in the local College Grove community. According to aerial photographs, this entire complex of buildings was demolished between 1981 and 1997.

A.G. Scales sits in front of his home located southwest of Kirkland near the intersection of Horton Highway and the road to Eagleville. Many of his slave family resided in the Kirkland community.

176

Historic Photograph of Hetley's Tavern and Grocery

Hetley's Store, owned by Ellis Scales, a prominent Black businessman.

T.E. Scales, Jr., is standing behind the car.

THOMAS ELLIS SCALES, JR.

In the late 1930s, Thomas Ellis "Little Ellis" Scales, Jr. (1897-1971) and his wife Robbie Lee McClain Scales (1909-1986) opened their own café in a dwelling located just north of his father's roadside business in the west side of the highway. They had married on December 24, 1936, and raised one son, William Flem Herbert (1930-1973), from her previous marriage. In 1961, the "Negro Green Book" advertised the T.E. Scales, Jr. Service Station & Café at Kirkland. This indicates that Little Ellis Scales continued to operate the service station after his father died in 1943. Little Ellis and Robbie are also buried in the Scales Cemetery at Kirkland. The former café still stands but is in derelict condition.

Former Ellis's Cafe in Kirkland. Photo by Laura Holder, MTSU.

SCALES' ROADSIDE INN / OASIS RESTAURANT AND MOTEL

In the 1940s, the Scales family opened a roadside inn and restaurant on the west side of the highway across from the service station and just south of Ellis's Café. Around 1956, the facility was replaced with an L-shaped stone tourist court featuring drive-up motel rooms and a small stone office building alongside the road. The Oasis Court and Café featured an eight-unit motel with a restaurant and nightclub/lounge on an eight-acre parcel. The Oasis was owned and managed by F.A. Coleman and his wife, Cora Coleman. In 1962, Mrs. Coleman was arrested during a weekend raid for selling beer to minors at the Oasis nightclub. According to a newspaper article, in 1964, a tractor-trailer crashed into their cabin after rolling down the hill from the neighboring hilltop restaurant, which was undoubtedly Ellis's Café. The Oasis was sold in 1972 by Mrs. Cora Lee Coleman (1902–1976), who had been recently widowed. According to a newspaper article, she had operated the facility for many years and lived in a house four miles south in College Grove. In 1980, the facility was sold at a public auction. At that time, several of the rooms had been converted into efficiency apartments. Located at 8327 Horton Highway, this facility still stands. At this time, research does not indicate that this 1950s roadside motel and restaurant facility was owned or operated by Blacks.

Oasis Restaurant. Photo by Laura Holder, MTSU.

Oasis Motel. Photo by Laura Holder, MTSU.

URBAN SCALES SERVICE STATION

In the 1950s, Urban Samuel Scales (1931-2018) constructed the Kirkland Service Center, a large roadside service station with a repair garage at 8351-8353 Horton Highway in front of the Absalom Gollehugh Scales House (WM-221), his grandfather's farmstead. His son, Joe Kelley Scales (1960-2016), later operated this facility as Joe Kelley's Market and Steve's Auto Repair. The masonry building features four garage bays and an open canopy covering the fuel bays. Urban S. Scales operated the facility for over 50 years and was known locally as the "Mayor of Kirkland." This facility still stands.

Urban Scales, undated. Source: Findagrave.com

25425 Urban Scales Service Station in Kirkland

C.L. SCALES DAIRY DAR

The C.L. Scales Dairy Bar is located adjacent to the Urban Scales Service Station, a small masonry drive-up dairy bar located at 8355 Horton Highway. This business was apparently operated by Charlie Lavender Scales (b.1940), the brother of Urban Scales and grandson of Absalom G. Scales.

Urban Scales Dairy Bar (left) and Service Station in Kirkland: Source: Google Streetview, 2018.

CONCLUSION

The Kirkland community in rural Williamson County retains a significant number of roadside businesses associated with automobile tourism in the early to mid-twentieth century. Descendants of the local enslaved community owned and operated a number of these businesses, including a funeral home, boarding house, service station, and two cafes. One of the cafes, operated by Thomas Ellis Scales, Jr. and his wife, Robbie Scales, is extant but in deteriorated and significantly altered condition. The primary Black roadside business, the T.E Scales Esso Service Station and Café complex, and a boarding house and associated residence are no longer extant. This service station and café was listed in the 1961 edition of the "Negro Motorist Green Book."

Although in deteriorated condition, Ellis's Café is a very rare surviving Black roadside business in rural Tennessee, and further research, documentation, and preservation strategies should be pursued. Likewise, the site of the circa 1880s T.E. Scales Esso Service Station and Café should be interpreted with a roadside historical marker and perhaps documented with archaeological survey investigations.

Additionally, available research and preservation planning documentation for the Kirkland community focus nearly entirely on nineteenth-century white plantations and farmsteads. With an over 200-year-old Black history, the Kirkland community includes at least one Black church, a Black cemetery, a former Black school, and farmsteads and dwellings that have not been surveyed, documented, or evaluated for NRHP eligibility. There may even be additional roadside businesses that have yet to be identified.[1]

---

1. Jones, Robbie D. *Roadside Businesses of Kirkland, Tennessee*, MTSU student paper for fulfillment of Historic Preservation course requirements, abt. 2005

Kirkland Masonic Lodge

The 1930 Report of the Kirkland Masonic Lodge provides the names of members and officers. Many descendants of these members may not be aware that the lodge played a crucial role in the Black community.[1]

COLLECTION OF DUES, ENDOWMENT, ETC. AND DISBURSEMENTS.

COLLECTIONS	DISBURSEMENTS
June 21 — $27.90	$ 6.55
July 5 — 22.35	187.50
July 19 — 37.75	23.85
Aug. 2 — 9.45	1.85
Aug. 16 — 45.05	3.00
Sep. 6 — 52.05	15.00
Sep. 20 — 21.65	11.60
Oct. 4 — 33.65	197.50
Oct. 18 — 42.65	3.10
Nov. 1 — 32.20	
Nov. 15 — 48.05	6.00
Dec. 6 — 31.95	4.95
Total — $404.70	Total — $460.90

And same was turned over to the M. of E.

FINANCIAL MEMBERS

George T. Herbert	James Webb
A. B. Scales	John W. Sheffield
W. D. Ewing	Marvin Hatcher
J. T. Gentry	Joe F. Pankerton
E. V. Starnes	William Thompson
John Smithson	Palmer Woods
Jerry Rodgers	Charley Crowder
John H. Sawyers	E. V. Starnes
Clarence Thompson	J. H. Shelton
Alfort Lee	Will H. Webb
J. G. Webb	John Beal
Risbon Woods	Steave Woods
Lane Crite	

MEMBERS WHO OWE BACK TAXES

Robert Bostick — $1.85	Will Tucker — $15.—
Joe Herbert — 5.05	Will Owens — 2.—
George Rodgers — 3.85	Jesse Andrewson — 3.—
Willie Crowder — 14.75	H. E. Starnes — 9.—
A. M. Bedford — 10.70	George Ogilvie — 3.—
Harrison Colwell — 1.15	Brice Starnes — 2.—
Grant Luster, Sr. — 1.15	Henry House — 5.—
Grant Luster, Jr. — 1.10	Lewis Jones — 5.—
Milkih Starnes — 1.15	Richard Covington — 5.—
Walter Claybrooks — 5.25	Charley Bostic — .—
Grundy Claybrooks — 1.15	Jeff Russell — 1.—
Jim Ridley — 1.15	John Morris — 2.—
S. S. Johnson — 3.85	John Andrewson — 1.—
Ollie Hutton — 2.95	Will Russell — 2.—
George Ferguson — 5.25	Edd Sutton — 5.—
Nick Andrewson — 5.25	John Fulton — 6.—
Odelia Crowder — 6.60	Steve Jones — 7.—
Harrison Andrewson — 17.85	Wm. M. Doubson — 1.—
	James M. Gentry — 3.—
Henry B. McClain — 2.50	Izar Dolton — 10.—
James A. Hatcher — .50	John Bracket — 9.—
William Shelton — 2.50	Dale Merry — 8.—
Felix Patton — 2.90	Oscar Thompson — 5.—
Bogal Merry — 8.00	John Bostick — 1.—
Mitchell Sawyers — 7.55	
Total due $232.10	Cash on hand $153.22

I beg to remain yours in F. C. & B.,
GEO. T. HERBERT, M. of F. No. 204

Semi-Annual Report of Kirkland Masonic Lodge No. 204, June through December, 1930.

---

1. Herbert, George T., M. of F., Kirkland Lodge No. 204. Semi-Annual Report, College Grove, Tennessee, 1930.

Familiar Faces Remembered

Odie Lee Anderson and Daisy Floyd

COMING OUT OF THE DARK INTO THE LIGHT

Willie Gene and Dorothy Mayes

Hazel and Charles Tucker

Emma and Pete Tuloss

Dorothy Jean Esmond

Bishop Waymon Biggers

Susie Mae Russell (1914-1995)

George, Barbara, and Betty Ogilvie

Sadie Frances Burnes

James Oscar Garrett

James Ben Claybrooks

Irene Claybrooks

Lilly Mae Scales

Mary Ann Floyd

Jonas "Pop" Morton

John Willie Bostick

Daisy Floyd

Juanita Claybrooks

Bertha Boyd

Sara and Hewitt Sawyers

Annie Well Scales

Louie Jones, Jr. and Texarue Jones

Hewitt Sawyers and James Alfred Williams

Ada Mae, Lillian, Robert, John Leslie, and O'Neal Vaughn

Viola Davis

Jerome and Jessie Covington

David DeWayne, Gregory, Michael, and Darrell Covington

William Covington

Delores Vaughn with her grandson, Nicholas Samuel German

Earleen Lanier (center) and Dolores Vaughn (right)

Jessie James Anderson and Wesley Anderson

Sam Williams, Jr., Tommie C. Davis, Lillie Williams, and Sam Williams III

Louise Hughes and Rose Cunningham

Clara Ann Ogilvie and Patricia Lee

Mary and Joanne Jones

Joe and Hazel Anderson

COMING OUT OF THE DARK INTO THE LIGHT

Lonnie Anderson and Juanita Johnson Anderson

Josie L. Ewing Murray

Elder Richard Lloyd, Bertha Lloyd, Annette Lloyd

Richard, Beatrice, and Jesse Johnson

Mary Elizabeth Cunningham, Nancy Jones, Marie Ridley, Hattie Rucker, and Millie Hardin

Wesley Anderson and Joe Billy Russell

Anita L. Carter Jones and Frank Carter

Anna Ridley

Valerie Scales McClain
and Eugene McClain

Gwen, Regina, Verleen, and Gail Hatcher

Mary Elizabeth Patton Claybrooks and Millard Claybrooks

Delores Claybrooks

COMING OUT OF THE DARK INTO THE LIGHT

Dorothy Sawyers

Josie Anderson

Christine Mayberry

Cora Sawyers

Bertha Boyd

Willie "Junior" Dalton

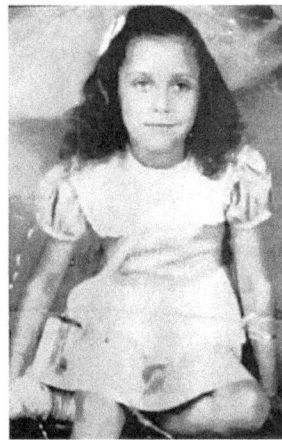
Brenda Demonbreun

Betty Ogilvie

Juanita Ridley

Ramona Norris

James and Henry Perkins

Willie Gene Mays

Joe Billy Russell, Juanita Vaughn, and Wannetta

Mary Jones

Charles Hyde and Bertha Boyd

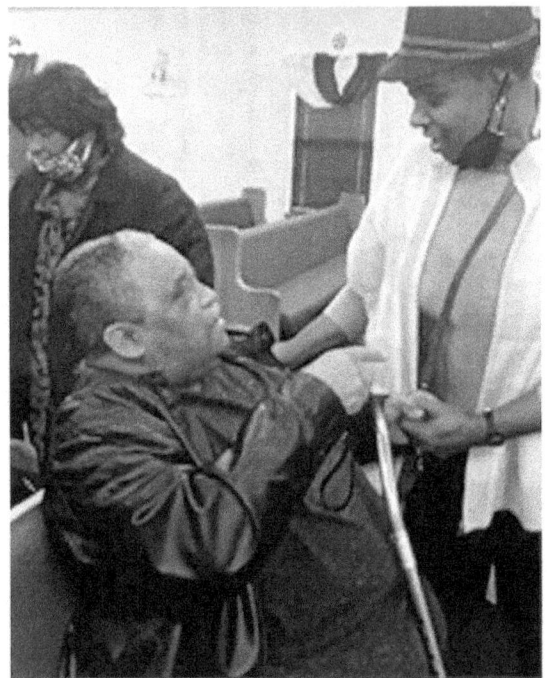
Ramona Norris, John Russell, and Thelma Jordan

Vivian Claybrooks and Myra Ann Wray

Christine Mayberry and Annie Ruth Yeargins

James Wilson Anderson

The George and Dorothy Sawyers Acklin Family

The Scales Family; from left: Robbie Scales, Mrs. Annie Well Scales, Josie Ann Scales, and children

COMING OUT OF THE DARK INTO THE LIGHT

College Grove

Wealth, Education, and Business Community

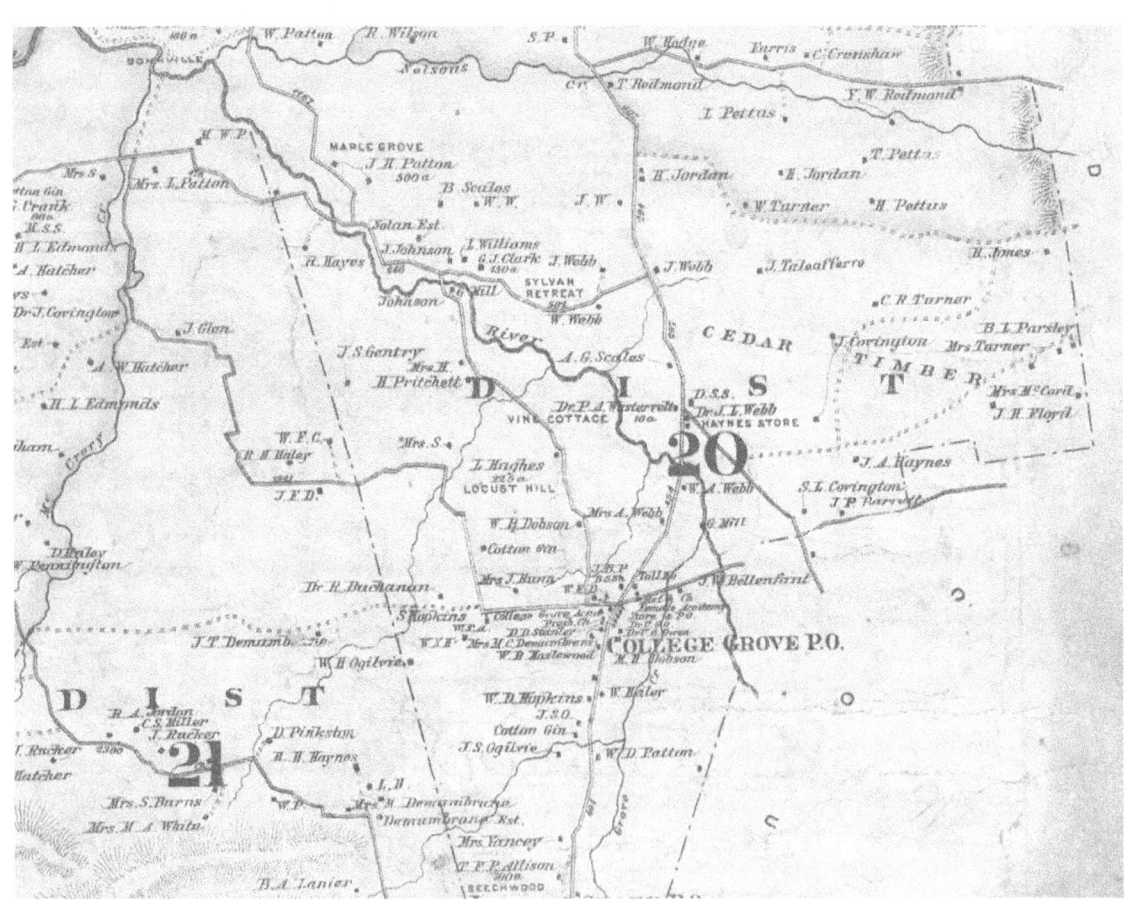

1878 Beers Map of College Grove

The First

OVIE ELAINE BOLEYJACK BELL

When Williamson County was forced to integrate schools in 1966, some white families were devastated by the change that was taking place in their lives. They found it necessary to ask the black families that worked for them to relocate because they didn't want blacks to go to school with their white children. This brought about an upheaval in the College Grove community that lasted for many years.

THE PIONEER STUDENTS WHO INTEGRATED COLLEGE GROVE HIGH SCHOOL IN 1966

Frances Kay Jones   Peggy Jones   Ramona Jones   Jo Ann Jones   Theodore Thompson

The first five students to attend College Grove High School in the 1966-67 school year were Theodore Thompson and the Jones sisters: Peggy, Frances Kay, Jo Ann, and Ramona. Only two of the students are still living. I don't know what it felt like when they walked into the building that day, but I can capture the emotions when all eyes are upon you, without a smile on your face, as you move through the crowd of students and parents. That is what I experienced the following year, on my first day, and often during the next two years. It was hard trying to find the person deep down inside, with that outgoing personality, when the pain had replaced the joy in my soul. Having classmates from my old school, Natchez High, helped me stay focused and look forward to graduation.

Things became less challenging during my senior year with most of my classmates. We were ready to enter the world and see what it had to offer. We learned many things during this time. First and foremost, we were resilient, which enabled us to recover and leave the residue behind.

Betty Esmond and the College Grove Varsity Cheerleaders, 1967-68

Robert Norris, Ovie Boleyjack. and Barbara Biggers were the first Black members of the College Grove High School Student Council in 1969-70.

John and Pauline Rucker Cunningham

MARY ELIZABETH CUNNINGHAM ANDERSON

John and Pauline Cunningham

John and Pauline Rucker Cunningham moved to College Grove in the 1950s and lived on the W.B. (Bill) Dobson farm. They had a daughter, Rosie Cunningham, and two grandchildren, James Andrew Cunningham and Mary Elizabeth Cunningham, who lived with them. They raised crops and did housework. Pauline and Rosie worked in homes in College Grove and Nashville. John raised crops, pigs, and a garden. They also bought groceries at the store. If they didn't have the money to pay for it, they would charge it until they had it. There was always plenty of food since Pauline canned all kinds of vegetables and some meats, since they didn't have a freezer. A wood stove was used to cook meals.

Mary Elizabeth and James went to school at Kirkland and had to walk in all kinds of weather. They walked to school or stayed at home. College Grove School was about a quarter of a mile from their house, but they had to pass that school because it was not integrated.

James graduated from Franklin Training School in 1964 and went to work for Genesco. Later, he joined the Army and served in Vietnam for two years as a medic. He was killed on March 22, 1967. His body was shipped home, and his funeral and burial were at Shady Grove P.B. Church.

At the time of his death, he was in Pleiku, South Vietnam, and was ambushed by North Vietnamese near Polei Duc in the Valley of Tears. You can find his name on the Wall; if you visit, it is located on Panel 17E, Row 017. For more information on James, see www.VirtualWall.org/dc/CunninghamJAO1b.htm.

Mary graduated from Franklin Training School and is married to Jesse Anderson. They live on Covington Road in Eagleville, TN. They have three children: Jesse Anderson Jr., Loretha Lynn Anderson, and John Abe Anderson, five grandchildren, and one great-grandchild.

Jesse Anderson Jr. lives on Covington Road, Eagleville. He is married to Fredia Diane Fulton Anderson of Chapel Hill, Tennessee, and they have no children.

Loretha Beach lives in Nashville and has three children: Pierre Murphy, Johnetha Beach, and Damon Beach. She attended Page High School and later got her GED.

John Anderson lives in College Grove and has two children: Zachery Anderson and Leah Anderson. He is a graduate of Page High School.

Rosie's younger children are Gene Cunningham, Mildred Cunningham, and Carol Cunningham.

Gene Cunningham lives in Smyrna and has one son, Marcus Cunningham. Gene attends church at Locust Ridge Primitive Baptist Church.

Mildred Cunningham Jordan lives in Nashville and has three children: Toni Cunningham Wetzel, Jason Jordan, and Jasmine Jordan. She also has three grandchildren: Jaylan Wetzel, Lauryn Wetzel, and Joe Siah Jordan. She graduated from College Grove High School.

Carol Cunningham Adkinson lives in Franklin. She has two children, Reketta Adkinson and Tyson Adkinson, and one grandchild. She graduated from Page High School.

John and Pauline Cunningham

Gene, Mildred, and Carol Cunningham

"Big Mama"

MARY ELIZABETH CUNNINGHAM ANDERSON

Pauline "Big Mama" Cunningham

One day, my grandmother, Pauline Cunningham, whom we called "Big Mama," was sweeping the porch, as she often did, and we saw Mr. Malachi Pollard driving up. He was the owner of the property that we lived on. My brother James was working for him on that day. Mr. Pollard got out of his vehicle and walked toward Big Mama. He told her he had hired out James to Dr. George Hatcher for the day.

Big Mama started to sweep faster and faster, and I had seen that look on her face before when she was angry. I stepped back halfway into the doorway, and I heard her say, "YOU DID WHAT?" Mr. Pollard had his head turned because he couldn't see well from one of his eyes. Big Mama raised her broom and hit him across his head at least four times. He grabbed his head in pain as he shouted at her to stop. She told him loudly that you don't have a son named James and can't hire him out, as if he belonged to you. Then she told him to go and get him and bring him home.

When he left, she waited on the porch with the broom until he arrived home. She told Mr. Pollard that James would never work for him again, and that put an end to that. We cannot sweep this under the rug.

Mary Elizabeth Cunningham   Walter Malachi Pollard

The humble home of Pauline Cunningham

COMING OUT OF THE DARK INTO THE LIGHT

Maudell Parrish Dotson

Maudell Parrish Dotson

Maudell Dotson was born Maudell Laura Parrish on Feb. 16, 1914, to Minerva and Dee Parrish in Allisona, TN. She was the youngest of the children born to this union. Her sisters, Eliza Holford and Lucy Mae Reeves, and her brother, John Dee Parrish, preceded her in death. While residing in Allisona, TN, she was a member of Beech Grove Methodist Church.

Maudell attended school in College Grove, TN, and became an elementary school teacher. Her first teaching assignment was at Allisona Chapel Elementary, a one-room school, where she taught grades 1-8. She influenced the lives of countless youngsters during a career that spanned almost 50 years.

After she retired from teaching in College Grove, she became an active volunteer in the senior citizen community. Maudell also liked to travel and went on a cruise to Hawaii with her sister, Lucy Mae, and to Venezuela with her cousin, Mary Elizabeth.

Luther Dotson, her husband of more than 50 years, preceded her in death. Soon after he passed away, she relocated to Detroit, MI, to be near her remaining family. She adapted well to a new environment and remained blessed with a joyful spirit. Despite declining health and mobility, she never complained. Her response was always the same when questioned about her day: "I had a wonderful day."

She lived to the blessed age of 90 when she answered the master's call at Sinai-Grace Hospital in Detroit, Michigan, on the afternoon of June 4, 2004.

Copied from her funeral program.

Della Wilson Scales

Sallie Ezell Wilson is pictured holding her grandson, William Wilson Thompson (Ovie Thompson's baby), alongside two of her children, Della Wilson Scales and William M. "Buddy" Wilson. ca.1909.

Della Wilson was born about 1898 in Williamson County, Tennessee, the fourth child of Thomas Jefferson Wilson and Sallie Ezell Wilson.

Della married Joe Abb Scales March 17, 1915, and to that union they had twelve children: Joe Frank Scales, William James Scales, Thomas Houston Scales, Irene K. Scales Lyons, Buela S. Scales Peacock, Eula D. Scales Coolidge, Christine Scales Green, John L. Scales, Addie B. Scales, and George E. Scales

Della died on May 24, 1933, at the age of 34. Sadly, the family didn't have any life stories to tell about her since she died so young.

The Sawyers, Howse, and Parrish Family

William Sawyers with Bertha, Loretta, and Rob

Will Amos Sawyers (1906-1985) and Bertha Mae Caldwell (1910-1940) were the parents of Clara Belle Sawyers, born in 1932 at College Grove, and died in 2021. Clara was born on Owen Hill Road at the location marked with a historical marker. Clara's brothers and sisters included Arthur Lee Sawyers (a half-brother), Will Amos Sawyers Jr., Caroline Walden Sawyers, James O'Neal Sawyers, and a stepbrother, Charles Lawrence Johnson, son of Annie Lou Howse Johnson, Will Sawyers' second wife.

Annie Lou Sawyers was also the aunt of Robert E. Howse (1928-1997), who married Clara Sawyers (1933-2021) in 1949. Robert and Clara Howse had four children: Bertha Lou Howse, Loretta Howse, Robert William Howse, and Daniel O'Neal Howse. Each of her children married, and between them gave Clara ten grandchildren.

Clara started school at Allison Chapel School on Owen Hill Road, attended Queen's Chapel School on Possum Trot and Locust Ridge School, and finished her education at Franklin Training School. The family attended Locust Ridge Primitive Baptist Church.

Clara always worked. She did housework for nine years, then was employed by Georgia Boot (later Durango Boot) for more than 23 years until they closed in January 1991.

In 1965, Clara married Noble Parrish. Noble had two daughters, Mildred Marie Jordan and Marguerite Adkinson. Together, they have 16 grandchildren and 13 great-grandchildren.

Sawyers-Smithson

Clifton Sawyers was one of five children, including John Henry Sawyers, Ruth Ann Sawyers, Emma Sawyers, and Mamie Sawyers. Clifton married Lena Pearl Claybrooks, whose brothers and sisters were Millard, Emmett, Bessie, and Georgia Mae. Clifton farmed and worked for the railroad.

Sara Sawyers married Clarence Smithson and had four children: Terrence Smithson, Derrick Smithson, Jennifer Smithson, and Timothy Scott Smithson. Sara and Clarence Smithson built a brick home on part of the farm where they raised their children, and continue to live.

Willie Amos Sawyers, Sr., Mamie Cliffe, Clifton Sawyers, and Ruth Christmon

Lena and Sara Sawyers

Clifton Sawyers

Clarence and Sara Smithson

Terrence A. Smithson

Timothy Scott Smithson

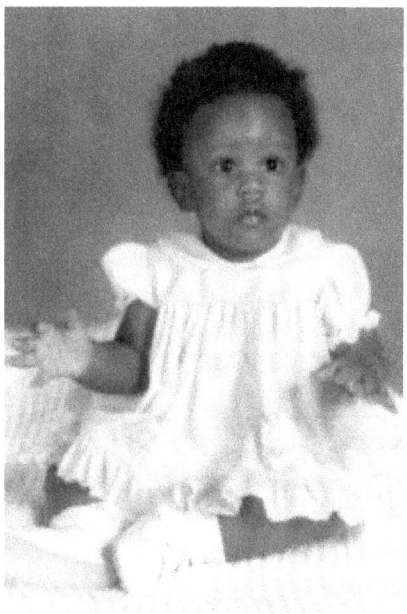

Jennifer D. Smithson

Derrick L. Smithson

The Thompsons

ROBIN THOMPSON

William Wilson Thompson (1908-1994) and Geneva "Sis" Oglesby Thompson (1926-2019)

THE CHILDREN OF WILSON AND GENEVA THOMPSON

William Wilson Thompson, Jr.
Clarence Alexander Thompson
Thomas Theodore Thompson
Delores Thompson Griffey
Robin Thompson
James Thompson
Anita Thompson Coley

College Grove

William Wilson Thompson and Geneva Oglesby Thompson were God fearing people who worked hard and loved the Lord. Wilson worked at the Battery plant in College Grove, Tennessee, and Geneva, better known as Sis, worked as a nanny. She also worked at Mays Hosiery Mill and R.H. Boyd Publishing in Nashville.

I went to school at Kirkland Elementary. My teachers were Ms. Moody, Ms. Patton, Ms. Dalton, Ms. Lanier, Mr. William B., and Mr. Wilson. We used whatever books we had which were old and torn. There were not enough books, so we had to share. But life went on. Our playground was a hill of clay. We played with bats, ball, a jump rope, jacks, and pick up sticks. Years later, they finally gave us a black top to play basketball. Then they gave us monkey bars, a swing and a merry go round.

I also remember nurses coming to the school to give us smallpox vaccinations, which left a round scar on everyone's arm. They also gave us an oral polio vaccine which was given as liquid drops on a sugar cube.

Before going to College Grove High School, they sent one black boy and four black girls before allowing other blacks to attend. Those children were Theodore Thompson and the four Jones sisters – Peggy, Frances Kay, JoAnn, and Ramona. Theodore was in the 10th grade when he first went to College Grove High School. The following year we all went to College Grove High School.

My first year at College Grove High School was rough. I remember in first period, Tandy King didn't want to sit in front of me, so he moved his seat away from mine. We were so far behind the other students in education because we did not have the books that the white kids had. I became vice president of the Freshman class and Tandy King was president.

With a student body almost equally divided between black and white students, I remember the time that Delores Thompson received more votes for the title of Miss College Grove. A white girl was in second place, and Delores' win was not to be. To placate the whites, a new vote was taken, and the crown and title went to the white girl.

The nicest teachers were Ms. Lee, Mr. King, Mr. Mayfield, Mr. Greathouse, and Ms. Drone.

Things momma and daddy told me: "Respect other people; Always help the needy;

and be careful going through Lawrenceburg, Lewisburg, Pulaski, Chapel Hill, and Franklin."

College Grove High School Freshman Class Officers: Robin Thompson, V.P., back right, and Tandy King, back end

Left: Robin Thompson, Center: Robin Thompson and Sereta McCord; Right: Delores Thompson

Biracial Families in Southeastern Williamson County

RICK WARWICK

Lucy Redmond, mother of three biracial sons, was the daughter of an ex-slave named Peggy Jane Redmond and T.J. Redmond. Photo courtesy of Thelma Battle.

It has been described earlier in this volume; the straining effect visited on the Thomas H. Perkins family when his son, W.O.N. Perkins, openly cohabited with a slave and recognized her children as his own. Biracial children were not uncommon in Williamson County, as the term mulatto is often noted in the U.S. census and local newspaper reports.

T.E. Redmond, a well-to-do College Grove farmer and businessman, shocked the county's citizens when he died in 1901, and his brother, Young Redmond, contested the will. On April 21, 1904, *The Review-Appeal* reported that the jury had sustained the will, which gave Young Redmond and a niece only $8,500, and the balance of the estate, valued at over $40,000 to Lucy Redmond, colored, and her three sons. The Redmond farm on Murfreesboro Road remained in the family until it was sold by Will Redmond, a grandson of T.E. Redmond, for the present-day Sturbridge Point.

COMING OUT OF THE DARK INTO THE LIGHT

The College Grove area was more tolerant of biracial families than any other section of the county. Homer Demonbreun and Joe Billy Bellenfant, both from prominent College Grove families, openly lived with women of color. Demonbreun sent some of his children north to further their education and assimilate into white society. Today, the families of Covington, Patton, Scales, and Webb recognize their biracial kinships.[1]

---

[1]. Warwick, Rick. *Williamson County in Black and White*. Williamson County Historical Society Journal, Vol. 31, 2000.

College Grove

Just the Two of Us

OVIE ELAINE BOLEYJACK BELL

WITH TIMOTHY DEMONBREUN AND JUANITA VAUGHN BATEY

The Homer Maurice Demonbreun Family. Maurice is the son of Homer W. Demonbreun and Willie B. Haley. Left to Right: Brenda, Sadie B., Homer, Sr. "Rooster," Homer, Jr., and Carmack Demonbreun, in front.

I read an article in a book compiled by Rick Warwick and the Williamson County Historical Society entitled *Williamson County in Black and White*. The topic was biracial families. That piqued my curiosity since this subject has lingered in the shadows since the early 1900s, and no one wants to have a conversation about it, even to this day.

COMING OUT OF THE DARK INTO THE LIGHT

There were many people of mixed race in the rural areas of Triune, Kirkland, and College Grove, Tennessee. The two men featured in the story are well-known: Homer Waldorf Demonbreun and Joe Billy (William) Bellenfant. The time has come to provide illumination and bring clarity. I often wondered why they chose women of color, knowing that it was a felony punishable by imprisonment.

I ponder deeply when I look at my great-great aunt, Ella D. Thompson, and Willie B. Haley, both of mixed race. Were they afraid of being with these two white men, or was that the norm? Did they just say they were the cook to deflect all eyes from themselves?

During slavery, it was pretty standard. President Thomas Jefferson had children with enslaved women and looked the other way when the resemblance was undeniable. The more things change, the more they stay the same.

Life wasn't easy for families of mixed race in the South. They were looked down upon as if they didn't belong anywhere. They were called vulgar names and frowned on with displeasure, but for some reason, Joe Billy Bellenfant and Homer Demonbreun felt that it was worth the risk of being shunned.

Or, did they know being white and affluent would shield them from harm and had no regard for the women they lived with? We will never know the answer to that question.

Looking at my aunt, I can see why he wanted to be with her; she was beautiful, carried herself with high regard, and had a generous spirit. I'm sure no one would have ever known that she was black if Joe had taken her places other than College Grove. A different environment would have made their relationship a little less complicated. Racism was unrestrained in this area of the country. Please understand, I am not here to judge; I want to bring them out of the dark and into the light. Biracial families will always be a part of America's fabric.

Ella D. Thompson's son, William, wasn't the child of Joe W. Bellenfant, but he was of mixed race. Homer Demonbreun's children were born to Willie B. Haley. The Thompson and Demonbreun families have continued growing and some still live in College Grove and have prospered, leaving a legacy for the next generations.

Willie B. Haley and Ella D. Thompson were never allowed to marry the men they lived with for many years. They were never called Mrs. Joe W. Bellenfant and Mrs. Homer W. Demonbreun. They will be forever known as their cooks when you view the census, but there is more to this story than meets the eye if you dig deep. I found Joe William Bellenfant's will; he named Ella and gave her money and household goods from the estate. I also found deeds to two parcels of land, with her name, William and Alma Wray Thompson. They couldn't have bought the land independently as a farmer and a cook. Some things are best done in the dark so that you can bring forth a ray of sunlight.

Homer W. Demonbreun passed away on December 15, 1947, and surprised everyone that he left everything he owned to Willie B. Haley and his children. He even made her executrix in his will. What he could not do in life, he did in death, showing the community how much he loved his family.

We have never lived in a perfect world with perfect people. We face what is in front of us, and we move forward, seeking God's help through it all.

Joe Billy Bellenfant   Ella Thompson   Homer W. Demonbreun

The handwritten and signed Last Will and Testament of Homer W. Demonbreun (or Demumbrane) is shown on the next page. It is dated March 6, 1923. The same will was filed for probate on December 27, 1947. Homer Demonbreun was born about 1871, and his wife, Willie B. Haley (1890-1965) lived eighteen more years after Homer died.

FILED Dec 27, 1947
ENTERED
D. L. JONES
County Court Clerk

I, Torrus W. Demumbrane, a citizen of the County of Williamson, State of Tennessee, being of sound and disposing mind, do hereby make and publish this my last Will and Testament, and hereby revoke all previous Wills made by me:

Item 1 — I Will to Willie B. Haley and her 2 children Morris W. Haley and Edward Allen Haley (64) Sixty-four acres of land, known as the Mrs. M. C. Demumbrane Dower the same lying and being in the 21st Civil District of Williamson County Tennessee the same being set out as the Dower of my Mother, as shown by the Records of the County Court of Williamson Co. to which Record reference is made.

Item 2 — I Will to Willie B. Haley all of my Personal Property of every description. The said Willie B. Haley shall have the right under this Will to select and keep for her own use any of said

220

> ...sonal property and such as she may not need, my Executor is hereby ordered and empowered to sell the same at Public Sale on Terms that he or she may think best and all the proceeds shall be paid over to said Willie B. Haley.
>
> Item 3. I will that in the event the 64 acres of land devised in Item 1 is ever sold that Proceeds be re-invested in Real Estate.
>
> Item 4. I hereby appoint Willie B. Haley as Executrix to this my last Will and Testament, without Bond.
>
> This 6 day of March, Nineteen hundred and Twenty-three = 1923.
>
> Witnesses: Homer W. Demumbrane
> W. J. M. Covington
> x E. C. Bizzell

Homer W. Demumbrane Last Will and Testament

---

1. *Tennessee County Court (Williamson County)*, Will Books Vols. 30-31, 1943-1954. Accessed in digital format at Williamson County Archives, Franklin, Tennessee on July 3, 2025.

The Wilson Anderson Family

ELIZABETH OGILVIE BATTLE

Wilson Anderson

As a child growing up in College Grove, Wilson Anderson was told by his grandparents that he was a descendant of slaves. It is believed that his great-grandparents, Mary Jane Anderson and Crockett Anderson, were the children of enslaved people belonging to the Allison and/or Ogilvie families in College Grove. Both of these pioneer families brought enslaved people with them from North Carolina to Tennessee.

It was noted in Williamson County Deed Books that in 1885 J.S. Ogilvie sold 20 acres of land to Crockett Anderson for $500. This was the hill overlooking the New Town part of College Grove. This 20-acres would have given Crockett land for a garden and possibly, pasture for a cow, hogs, chickens, etc. All of these were necessary for feeding a family in those times. The house was already built there. This writer believes that Crockett and Mary Jane then continued to work for the Ogilvies to help pay off the $500 cost of the 20 acres.

It was written into the deed that in exchange for Crockett Anderson building and maintaining a good fence, he could have a lane 10 feet wide as an outlet from his tract along W.T. Allison's land, now 6648 New Town Road. Today, the same place only measures 6 acres, instead of 20.

College Grove

Nick Anderson, son of Crockett and Mary Jane, would have been 15 years old at the time. It is not known if there were other children. Nick began working as a child for J.S. Ogilvie and continued until his death. He brought his wife, Sinthy, (Cynthia) to live there in the house of his parents. She worked for the Ogilvies, doing laundry, cooking, and housekeeping for as long as her health permitted.

Nick and Sinthy Anderson's daughter, Rachel Anderson, was born within a few days time of the birth of Rachel Webb Ogilvie to Anna and Samuel Ogilvie (on the farm adjoining J.S. Ogilvie). Sinthy's body was producing no milk for her baby, while Anna Ogilvie had more than enough milk for her baby, Rachel. Anna then breast fed Sinthy's baby, as well as her own baby, thereby saving her life. Sinthy then named her baby Rachel also.

It was this Rachel Anderson who gave birth to Woodrow Wilson Anderson on January 13, 1915, there at the homeplace. In 1925, Rachel died, leaving the care of ten year-old Wilson to his grandparents. Wilson learned to work hard at an early age, always living there and taking care of his grandparents until their deaths.

Florine Rucker Anderson

Wilson first married Florine Rucker, daughter of David and Nettie Rucker. Living in the house of his ancestors, they became parents to six daughters and two sons. Their children are: May Clara, Annie Kate, James Wilson, Lonnie, Mattie Ruth, Ella Catherine, Betty Sue, and Brenda Gail Anderson. They attended College Grove schools. Brenda now lives in Eagleville and is a member of College Grove Senior Citizens. Brenda's children are Genita and Samuel McCord Jr., and Joe Anderson. Sam Jr. and his wife Tonia have a daughter, Shila. Genita's children are Chevalier and Shakiya McCord.

Florine died on April 28, 1957. For two years, with the help of the older girls, Wilson was able to care for his children. He was then married to Eula Pearl Sheffield. She was a good helpmate for him and his children until her death. After Eula Pearl's death, he married Betty Lou Johnson. She and Wilson were parents of Devon Anderson. Betty Lou continues to live in the home following Wilson's death in 1995.

Wilson was a hard worker throughout his years, starting as a young boy with his grandfather, Nick. He worked as a farmer/sharecropper with many of the farmers in this community. As new methods of farming became available, he was quick to learn them all – from mules to tractors and modern farm equipment.

Wilson's schooling was limited, as the only school for him was at Allison Chapel, or later at Kirkland. Both of these were several miles away, and he was needed at home for working. At the age of sixty years, he attended an adult class at Kirkland Elementary School, where he learned to read and write.

As a lifetime member of Beech Grove Methodist Church in Allisona, he took his family there for worship and was an usher there each week. When he died in 1995, he was buried there.

One of his great pleasures each summer was the job of frying the fish for the "Jim Johnson Picnic" at Allisona. This was done for many years until he could no longer work. But he remained cheerful and "upbeat" until the end of his 80 years, always enjoying his children, grandchildren and great-grandchildren.

Jock Anderson, Shila McCord. Brenda Anderson holding Shakiya McCord, Chevalier McCord, Genita McCord, and Samuel McCord, Jr.

Wilson and Betty Anderson

Back: Lonnie Anderson; Middle: Brenda Gail, Ella Catherine, May Clara; Front: Betty Sue and Annie Kate Anderson

The John Frank Anderson Family

MARY ELIZABETH CUNNINGHAM ANDERSON

The Powell Anderson family. Seated: Hazel Tucker, Josie Allen, Mary Gertrude Starnes Anderson, Powell Anderson, Sr., Minnie Kathryn Howse, and Jane Anderson; Standing: Haze Anderson, Jimmy Anderson, Joe Anderson, Lonnie Anderson, Powell Anderson, Jr., and Calvin Anderson.

John Frank Anderson (1912-1976) was the son of Lytle Webster Anderson (1879-1960) and his wife, Annie Bellenfant Claybrooks (1887- 1926), who was the daughter of Grundy Claybrooks Sr. and Mandy Bellenfant. In 1932, John Frank Anderson married Elizabeth Lavender (1910-1959), who was the daughter of Richard and Mary Lavender. John Frank and Elizabeth Anderson lived on the knob off McDaniel Road for several years, then moved to Forrest Home, and eventually purchased a home on Cox Road, where they spent the rest of their lives.

Annie Bellenfant Claybrooks, wife of Lytle Anderson

John and Pauline Cunningham

- **Jesse Anderson** married Mary Cunningham. They have three children – two boys and one girl – and live in Eagleville, Tennessee.
- **Lytle Anderson**, son of **Frank Anderson** and Bettie Crafton, was born in 1879. Lytle and Annie B. Claybrooks were the parents of **Powell Edward Anderson**, who married Gertrude Starnes; **Virginia Anderson**, who married Edwin McClain; **Betty Anderson**, who married Henry Russell; **Webb Anderson**, who married Rosie; and **Minnie Anderson**, who married Frank Ogilvie.
- **Howard Anderson** married Dorothy Floyd. They have six children – two girls and four boys. He was also a preacher and a member of Westwood Baptist Church. Howard is deceased.
- **Annie Mary Anderson** married Houston Norris. They have seven children, six boys and one girl. Annie and Houston live in Murfreesboro, Tennessee.
- **John and Elizabeth Anderson** had seven children and one stepson. The children were educated in the Williamson County school system at Kirkland Elementary and Franklin Training School (later, Natchez High School)

- **Elizabeth Lavender Anderson** was a homemaker and never worked outside the home. John worked as a farmer and later worked in Nashville as a warehouse worker, maintenance worker, and horse trainer.
- The first son was **Edward Anderson**, who married Dorothy Braden. They have six children, two girls and four boys. He later married Shelia Wright, and they had no children. Edward is a minister and pastors Westwood Baptist Church.
- **Wesley Anderson** married Ruby Mayes, and they had no children but raised several. Wesley had one daughter.
- **Richard B. Anderson** married Francis K., and they had one son. Later, he married Lucille Bradley and they had two daughters. Richard is now married to Ethel Evans, and they have one son and one daughter.
- **Nick Anderson**, son of **Crockett and Mary Jane Anderson**, would have been 15 years old at this time. It is unknown if there were any other children. Nick began working as a child for J. S. Ogilvie and continued until his death. He brought his wife, Sinthy, (Cynthia) to live there in the house of his parents. She worked for the Ogilvies, doing laundry, cooking, and housekeeping for as long as her health permitted.
- John Anderson's stepson, **Willie Wray Jr.**, married Minnie Gooch and had no children.
- **John F. Anderson** and his family, along with his father, Lytle Anderson, lived on Cox Road for many years.
- After the death of Elizabeth, **John F. Anderson** married Bertha Floyd (1926-1990). They had no children, but Bertha already had a son, James Shaw. Fire destroyed their home, so they had another house moved on John Anderson's land. They stayed there until his death. He was a member of Shady Grove Primitive Baptist Church. In a time when black students had to provide their own transportation to Franklin in order to attend high school, it is a mark of accomplishment that three of the children of John F. Anderson graduated from high school.

Jesse, Sr., Jesse, Jr., John, Loretha, and Mary Anderson

Frank Oglvie, Sr.

Minnie Anderson Ogilvie

Edwin and Virginia McClain

Lillian and Christine

The people we hold most dear never truly leave us. They live on in the kindness we shared and the love they brought into our lives. We love you.

LILLIAN FLOYD COVINGTON

Lillian Floyd Covington was born on January 17, 1917, in College Grove, Tennessee, to Isaac Floyd and Pearl Yeargins. She had a son, Charlie B. Covington, and a daughter, Pearly Mae Claybrooks. Lillian passed away on August 20, 2011.

Her family includes Pastor Barton Harris of Westwood Baptist Church in Nashville, Tennessee, and her sister, Geneva Thompson. Her grandchildren also survive her: Rita, Veronica, Mattie Mae, Henrietta, Rebecca, Robbie, Mike, Teresa, and Marilyn. Additionally, her nephew is Clifton E. Duncan.

CHRISTINE LAWRENCE RUSSELL

Christine was born on November 28, 1903, and died on December 27, 1996. She was the daughter of Will Russell and Pasty Rosa Lee Jones Russell, and she grew up in Williamson County. Christine had four children: Tom Howse, Willie Dalton, Felix Lawrence, and her daughter Savanah Floyd. She also had one stepdaughter, Mary Whitehead, and a sister, Addie Frances Jordan.

She was a member of Shady Grove Primitive Baptist Church, where Elder Zema W. Hill served as the pastor. Known affectionately as "Big Mama," she was a person who never met a stranger and consistently reached out to help others, striving to make the world a better place. Those who knew her loved her dearly. Christine is laid to rest at Jones Cemetery in Kirkland, Tennessee.

College Grove

The Wray Sisters

The Wray Sisters: Willie Jean, Ella Louise, and Carolyn

One of a kind! That's the Wray sisters – Ella Louise Wray Batts, Myra Ann Wray, Carolyn Wray Mason, and Willie Jean Wray Lee. It must have been in their genes. Having a father like Will Allen Wray and a mother like Lucile McClain Wray, a powerful couple in the College Grove Community, who instilled in their daughters and son, James, the love of music and Christian service. Faith without works is dead. Whenever there is a need, all we have to do is pick up the phone and call Ella Louise, Willie Jean, and Carolyn.

The Wray family always stepped up, especially the girls, because they have the gift of song, a God given gift, and they don't hide it under a bush. They share it with all who call upon them, and when they sing, the doors of Heaven open to hear their angelic voices.

Whenever there was a program at church, they were there. When there was a funeral, they were there, even if they weren't on the program. All we had to say was, "We need your help." We knew the whole family could sing – mother, father, and brother, but how many times can you call on someone who never lets you down? That is the Wray family.

To illustrate, Marie Ridley Ogilvie shared this story: Her choir at Green Grove Church in Triune was having a problem organizing their songs. They called Willie Jean and she stepped in and worked with their choir, at home and at church, until they felt comfortable being on their own. We thank them for all that they have done, and for all that they continue to do, in the name of Our Lord and Savior, Jesus Christ.

Carolyn Wray

Lucille and Will Allen Wray

Willie Jean Ray

William B. Covington

Friend to All

ERNESTINE COVINGTON BARNETT

William B. and Hazel Scales Covington

William B. Covington was born in Williamson County on January 8, 1910, to Risdon Woods and Beulah Covington. He departed this life on Saturday, February 1, 2003.

He received his early education in the Williamson County School System and graduated from the High School Department of Tennessee State. In 1934, he received his bachelor's degree with high honors from Tennessee A & I State College, presently Tennessee State University., William B. Covington believed God and education were the keys to success. He was no stranger to hard work and overcoming obstacles. While attending classes at Tennessee A & I, he did farm work, worked in the science lab, played on the basketball team, and was a member of the Kappa Alpha Psi Fraternity, Inc.

After graduating from college, he served as a teacher and principal in the Williamson County School System for more than 36 years. He was affectionately called "Professor Covington" or "Mr. William B."

At an early age, Mr. Covington professed his faith in Jesus Christ and united with Mount Pleasant Missionary Baptist Church in Kirkland. He served as Sunday School teacher, superintendent of the Sunday School, church treasurer, and chairman of the Board of Deacons. He loved his church and his church family. Even with failing health, he continued to be a faithful and devoted member.

On January 25, 1936, he united in holy matrimony with Hazel Scales. To this, union five children were born, two of whom preceded him in death, Jerome D. Covington and William B. Covington, Jr. The remaining children are: Izella Covington Baugh, Bernice Covington Goodwin, and Ernestine Covington Barnett.

Izella Covington

Ernestine Covington Barnett

Remembering William B. Covington

ERNESTINE COVINGTON BARNETT

Professor W.B. Covington, beloved principal, teacher, and friend.

My father, William B. Covington (1910-2003), served as principal of Kirkland School in Williamson County. My father loved his family and cherished his roles as a teacher and principal. He loved his students' school, the people he worked with, and the community. These are some of my memories of those years.

In 1967, the principalship was taken away from black principals due to desegregation and a campaign promise made by a man who later became Superintendent of Schools in Williamson County. My father was placed at College Grove High School teaching math.

We found out years later from one of his former white students that my father endured profanity and paper balls thrown at him while teaching in his classroom. It was doubly hurtful because she still thought it was funny. A year or so later, my father was placed in charge of the textbooks for Williamson County Schools and was relegated to a basement. A year or so later, he retired.

Did he favor his own children at school? No. In fact, he once took the side of one of my best friends, and I got paddled. Was he right? Yes. It happened a couple of times more, and his judgement was right every time.

During his principalship at Kirkland Elementary School there were two students, Jerry Jordan and Hubert Thompson, who scored the highest score on the an achievement test. The Williamson County Board of Education sent a supervisor to the school to transport the students to Franklin to retake the test, because they thought my father had helped the boys cheat. He called their parents, who gave their consent, and he appointed a teacher to go with them. The boys scored higher on the retake test. Thank God the supervisor was honest. He brought both test scores to the school to show the first and the second test scores and he gave copies to the school and parents.

Williamson County Board of Education voted not to give Kirkland School back to the Community like they did the white schools, the old all white schools became community centers. Kirkland School was sold to a boating company. Are we perfect? No human is perfect, but everyone should be treated with respect regardless of skin color.

Have things changed from Kirkland School days? Some things are better, some are the same, but operate on a different level. There is good and bad in every race, and situations. I'm praying that good outweighs the bad.

There are many great stories of the good times we had at Kirkland School, we had devotional service before going to classrooms, learned to be respectful, plays, fashion shows, fund raising activities, lasting friendships, played baseball, softball, basketball and other games, programs at Franklin Training School (later named Natchez High School), delicious lunches, and community activities for local churches and educational programs for adults.

Good memories and bad ones, too, make us wiser. The good memories linger longer than the bad, and for that I am thankful.

Let's Weigh In

JIMMY GREEN THOMPSON, JR.

Harry and Mildred Taylor

Here's a little-known fact about the Harry Taylor store in College Grove: Reaching back into my memory, I recalled a conversation that I had with Mr. Taylor. He told me that Ovie Jane Thompson was his first customer when he opened his store. He also told me that when babies were born in the community, mothers would bring them to his store to be weighed on his scale. I was one of the kids brought there by my mother. I wonder how many babies there are in College Grove that shared this experience?

Harry Taylor also gave out tickets for a raffle when people shopped at his store. He would have a drawing, and on Saturday night you would need to be there at 7:00 p.m. with your ticket to win. The prize was $25 worth of groceries.

If people would just take the time to talk, and listen we could learn so much about the past and view the future with clear eyes.

Inside Taylor's Store

Baxter Herbert Hardemon, Sr.

Baxter Herbert Hardemon

A long life filled with memories of the past that linger in the minds of friends and family.

Mr. Baxter Herbert Hardemon, Sr., of Kirkland, was born in the year 1909, to Oscar Hardemon Sr. and Mattie Hughes Hardemon. He was the second of ten children. Baxter had no formal education, but lived his life by his wit and common sense.

Baxter married Minnie Mai Bostic and to this union two daughters, Ella Mai Patton and Annie Blackman, and two sons, Baxter Herbert Hardemon, Jr. and Edward L. Hardemon were born.

Baxter was employed for several years at Werthan Bag Company in Nashville, Tennessee. He later returned to farming and raising dairy cattle for most of his life, among other trades. He was a member of Mt. Pleasant Missionary Baptist Church of Kirkland, Tennessee, from the 1960s until his death in 2010.

Baxter Herbert Hardemon, Jr.

Ella Mai Patton

Edward Hardemon

Ann Hardemon Anderson

History of the Esmond Family

The Jimmy D. and Willie Mai Esmond Family. First Row: Jimmy, Charles, **Willie Mai**, **Jimmy D.**, Betty Ann, and Mary; Second Row: Thomas, Jerry, Clarence, Brenda, Louise, Dorothy Jean, Rosie, and Willie.

The twelve Esmond children: Mary | Rosie* | Dorothy Jean | Betty Ann* | Brenda | Louise | Jimmy* | Willie* | Clarence | Jerry | Thomas | Charles | *Deceased*

COMING OUT OF THE DARK INTO THE LIGHT

Willie Mai Esmond	Jimmy D. Esmond
March 22, 1921 to May 21, 1996	May 24-1917 to October 28, 2011
Parents (Arrington):	Parents (College Grove):
Willie B. Patton	Zack Esmond
Martha Hendricks-Patton	Emma McCord-Esmond

Some of the Esmond children started school at Westwood Community School on Crowder Road in a big classroom under Mrs. Jimmy Gentry. When we left there, we went to Kirkland Elementary School in College Grove. Mr. William B. Covington was the principal and sometimes taught classes. Mrs. Annie Well Scales worked in the lunchroom. Some of the teachers were Mrs. Moody, Mrs. Patton, Mrs. Dotson, and Mrs. Lanier. The grades went from 1st to 8th grade. On certain days we would have field day and play ball and everyone enjoyed themselves. We also used to travel to places to play ball and sometimes other schools would come to Kirkland.

After leaving Kirkland School some of us went to Natchez High School in Franklin during segregation. This school went to the 12th grade. After segregation ended my other siblings went to College Grove High School where Betty Ann was the first Black cheerleader. The siblings who graduated from CGHS were Clarence, Jerry, Charles, Thomas and Betty Ann. Out of 12 children, eight graduated from high school.

We were sharecroppers because we didn't own land. We lived on the Jordan farm. The older boys along with my father would primarily milk cows, work in the tobacco fields and whatever else that needed to be done. The cows had to be milked before and after school and the milk was sold for spending money.

During the summer months we would take orders for blackberries and would sell to buy school clothes. We didn't have a lot of conveniences such as running water and a bathroom. Instead, we had to use an outhouse. At times, three or four of us slept on one bed. We also raised our own garden and chickens for food.

During the winter months we chopped our own wood just to stay warm. After the older boys grew up, they all got public jobs and in their spare time they worked for Harry Lillard doing farm work. We had to work hard because we did not have the opportunities that people have today. Some of the work ethic that we had back then is still instilled in us today.

To God Be The Glory

The Hatcher Family

Roots From Owen Hill Road

THELMA BATTLE

The Meredith and Mariah Hatcher family. In front: Marvin P., Meredith holding Clarence, Rosa holding Sam, Charlie, and Jimmy; In Back: Andrew, James Ewing, and Johnny.

The Hatcher family of African American lineage from Williamson County, Tennessee, has roots that are deeply embodied within the College Grove and Arno communities. The Hatcher family lived in the 21st District between Allisona and Arno on Owen Hill Road. This remarkable family is traced to slaves Ned/Ed Hatcher, born in 1810, and his spouse, Mariah. These two slaves were owned by a white slave owner named John R. Hatcher (1818-1857), son of William and Lucy Rucker Hatcher of Bedford County, Virginia.

Ex-slaves Ned and Mariah Hatcher remained in the 21st District after slavery. Ned and Mariah were the parents of nine children: Martha Jane, Almeda, Sam, Winnie, Meredith, Isham, Alice, Jacob, and Susan.

The most widely known of Ned and Mariah's descendants are the children of their son, Meredith Hatcher, and his wife, Rosa Moss Hatcher. Their children were Charlie, Andrew, John, James Marvin, Sr., Clarence, Simon, Susan, Jane, and Sam. Meredith Hatcher's second wife was Vinnie Starnes Reams Hatcher. His two-step children were Manervie Reams, and her brother, Jessie Reams.

Elder Jasper G. Hatcher

Meredith Hatcher's grandson, Elder Jasper G. Hatcher, Sr. related these memories of his grandfather: "He was a good-hearted man. He was a hardworking man, and he was…if he had a dollar, he would save half of that dollar. He was very tight, but he was a man, though, that you could love and could work with. And he always had good advice to give you. He always talked about being productive and saving and putting up things for the rainy day, as he would call it."

To grasp the true story of Meredith Hatcher and his clan, elder Jasper Hatcher, Sr., shared the following details: "I was born May 6, 1929. My parents were Marvin, Sr., and Era Emma Odell ("Sadie") Kinnard Hatcher. My parents owned the farm where I was born and had thirteen children: 1. James, 2. Laeunia, 3. Winnie, 4. Jessie Mary, 5. Willie Ewing, 6. Earleen, 7. Jasper, 8., Maudine, 9. Ester Lee, 10. Lawrence Buford, 11. Elliot, 12. Lorenzo, and 13. Marvin, Jr. I was born on a one-hundred-and-eighty eighty-three-acre farm…a family farm that three brothers, Marvin, Sr. (my father), Charles, and Jimmy Hatcher owned."

When my grandfather, Meredith Hatcher, bought the farm, it was unusual for

Blacks to own their own farm. Many Blacks had bought farms, but at the time this farm was bought, it was rare. Because at the time this farm was bought, there were one hundred and eighty-three acres on the farm. And back in the 1920s, the price of it was twenty-five thousand ($25,000) dollars. So, it was unusual for a Black man to be able to purchase that much land and borrow that much money to purchase a farm. The Hatcher family represents a strong, industrious alliance that continuously maintained family land, values, love, and service to their community, state, and country.[1]

The Marvin P. Hatcher Family. Seated: Laeunia Thompson, Maudene McCord, Jessie Rodgers Vaughn, Era "Sadie" Kinnard Hatcher, Marvin P. Hatcher, Sr., and Earleen Biggers; Standing: Ester lee Hatcher, Elder Jasper Hatcher, Lorenzo Hatcher, Willie E. Hatcher, and Winnie M. Vaughn

---

1. Battle, Thelma. "Roots from Owen Hill Road," *The Thelma Battle African American Photographic Exhibit and Collection*. Williamson County Public Library, Franklin, Tennessee, 2023.

Elder Jasper G. Hatcher

A Legacy of Love

DR. MARQUINTA HARVEY AND BRANDON HARVEY

Elder Jasper Hatcher, Sr.
(1929-2020)

Jasper G. Hatcher, Sr. was born May 6, 1929, to the late Marvin and Sadie Hatcher and lived all of his life on the same land purchased in the 1920s by his grandfather and three brothers. Jasper was reared in a family with a strong Christian foundation and was the seventh of thirteen children, all of whom preceded him in death. His siblings were James Hatcher, Laeunia Thompson, Jessie Vaughn, Willie Hatcher, Earleen Biggers, Ester Hatcher, Winnie Vaughn, Lorenzo Hatcher, and Elder Marvin P. Hatcher, Jr. (Eli Hugh Hatcher and Lawrence Hatcher both passed at an early age). He received his education at Allison Chapel, a one-room log cabin with one teacher in rural Williamson County. During his childhood, Jasper spent time doing chores and working outside. His family grew their own food, specifically wheat, corn, tobacco, and cotton, and tended to hogs and dairy cattle.

At the age of 17, Jasper met his wife-to-be, Thressa Thomas, at a fish fry. He decided to approach her and, playing hard-to-get, she tossed orange peels at him. After his unyielding persistence and Thressa running out of orange peels, she gave in and started a conversation that turned from friendship to true love. They were united in holy matrimony on July 2, 1948, when Jasper was 19 and Thressa was a tender age of

15-years old. They shared a beautiful marriage of 67 years. Through this union, eight children were born, four boys and four girls. Thressa was truly the love of Jasper's life, and in her own words, "he was the head, and she was the neck that turns the head."

Jasper worked in Nashville for 37 years, first working for MP Brothers as a truck driver. Believing in justice for all, he organized a union at MP Brothers, ultimately costing him his job but leaving a legacy of fairness for those who followed. He then worked and retired from Kroger Warehouse after 28 years of service. He would come home from Nashville each night, sleeping just a few hours only to rise and tend to his farm and family.

On May 8, 1962, Jasper G. Hatcher, Sr. was converted and joined Locust Ridge Primitive Baptist Church under the leadership of Pastor Walter Amos. On February 17, 1963, he was ordained a Deacon, and on the fourth Sunday in September of 1969, he accepted his calling to the ministry.

Elder Jasper Hatcher, Sr., and Thelma Thressa Thomas Hatcher

On October 12, 1969, he preached his first sermon at Locust Ridge Primitive Baptist Church. The text came from Isaiah 6:8, and his subject was "The World is Sick, and it Needs a Doctor." On March 15, 1970, he was ordained as a minister and served as Pastor of Beech Grove Primitive Baptist Church in Franklin, and Watson Tabernacle Primitive Baptist Church in Pulaski, TN. He culminated his pastorship at Locust Ridge Primitive Baptist Church, retiring after 33 years of dedicated service. Elder Jasper G. Hatcher, Sr., was a forward-thinking visionary, and at the age of 81, he passed the mantle to his successor, 21-year-old Pastor Brandon L. Mason.

Elder Jasper G. Hatcher, Sr. was a giant in ministry with impacts that spread throughout the local communities. Under his guidance and leadership, he counseled many sons and daughters, several went on to pastor their own churches.

To know Jasper G. Hatcher was to love him. His love was not just a word; it was an action. He demonstrated humility and God-fearing love, which was shared not only

COMING OUT OF THE DARK INTO THE LIGHT

within his family but with anyone who encountered him. His love lives on through the very many lives he touched.

On Friday, September 25, 2020, Elder Jasper G. Hatcher, Sr., transitioned from this life to be with our Lord and Savior, Jesus Christ. He was preceded in death by his loving wife, Thelma Thressa Hatcher; his grandson, Kadafi N. Hatcher; and great-grandson, Kenneth Xavier Hatcher (son of Kadafi).

Jasper and Thressa Hatcher's grands and greats

Elder Jasper Hatcher in the pulpit at Locust Ridge P.B. Church

Jasper Hatcher highway marker on Murfreesboro Road

Elder Jasper Hatcher, Sr, Jasper "Jay" Hatcher, III, Jasper Hatcher, Jr., and Jasper Hatcher IV

Rev. Judge Webb, Jr.

Rev. Judge Webb, Jr.

Reverend Judge Webb, Jr., was born in Arrington, Tennessee, to the late Judge Webb, Sr., and Gertrude Woods Webb. Reverend Webb accepted Christ at an early age at Mount Pleasant Missionary Baptist Church in Kirkland, Tennessee. He served as the superintendent of Sunday School, president of the choir, and chairman of the Deacon Board. He was later called to the ministry and became pastor of the church he grew up in.

Reverend Webb received his early education in Williamson County Schools and later moved to Nashville, where he attended Pearl High School. After graduation, he attended Tennessee A&I State University until he was called into the Armed Forces. He was a World War II Veteran, seeing action in the South Pacific and the occupation of Japan.

In September 1946, he married Mildred Lee Patton Webb of Alabama, the daughter of Jack Patton and Lily Jordan Patton. She was a lovely lady who was always there for her husband and children. She was often seen at Kirkland School, where her children attended during their elementary years. Their six children are Elliott, Donzetta, Geraldine, Judy, Zennia, and Tony.

Reverend Webb was employed and retired from the Beechcraft Flying Service, where he worked for over 25 years. He was also an avid gardener and farmer.

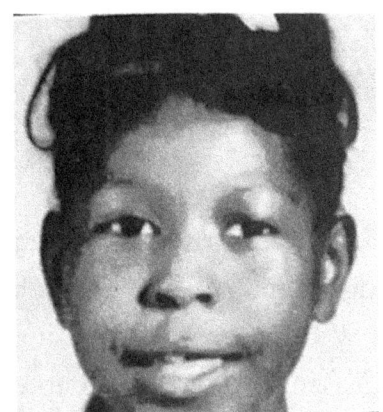
Zennia Webb

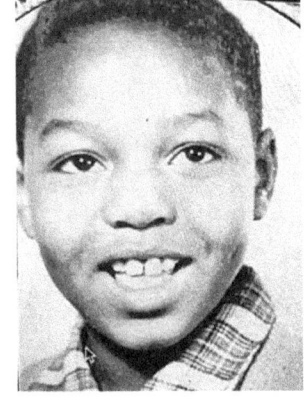
Elliot Webb

Judy Webb

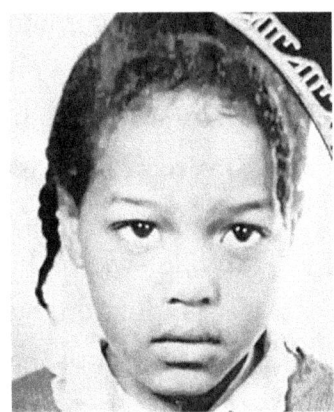
Geraldine Webb

Donzetta Webb

"Aunt Tish"

Tishie Webb

Tish Webb

Tishie Webb was born in Arrington, located in Williamson County Tennessee. Her parents were Judge Webb Sr. and Gertrude Woods Webb.

Tisha was a Mount Pleasant Missionary Baptist Church member in Kirkland, Tennessee. She served on the Usher Board and Mother's Board for many years.

She received her education in the public schools of Williamson County and was also employed for many years with the Williamson County School System. "Miss Tish," as the students called her, was one of the cooks at Kirkland Elementary School. The students who helped in the cafeteria early in the morning, before school started, told of how she would always encourage them to do their best and follow their dreams. She later worked at the Holiday Inn.

Ms. Webb loved nature and working in her flower and vegetable gardens. Her most precious possessions were her nieces and nephews. She loved them as if they were her own children.

– *Elliott, Tony, Donzetta, Geraldine, Judy, and Zennia*

Life Goes On

FRED NORRIS

William Norris, father of Fred Norris

Fred Norris is one of twelve children born to William (Bill) and Elizabeth Floyd Norris of Kirkland, Tennessee. He is the grandson of William Norris, Sr. (1861-1931), and Martha Demunbreun Norris (1867-1908), and is now 86 years old.

His father and mother were sharecroppers on two different farms while he was growing up – the farms of Bruce and Jane Covington and George Hatcher. Jane Covington was a teacher at College Grove High School and George Abram Hatcher lived on Arno Road. The Norris family worked in tobacco, corn, and cotton.

Fred went to Locust Ridge in elementary school, then transferred to Kirkland Elementary School when all the black schools in the area consolidated. Mr. William B. Covington was his teacher, and he said he remembered Mr. Covington's paddle. He got spanked on the hand and the bottom. That is something he will never forget. Years at Kirkland school also introduced him to many of his friends, like O'Neal and Charles Vaughn, and they had a lot of fun together.

When he became a young man, he would go to Ellis Scales's place on the hill in Kirkland. He was hoping to find some girls to talk to. He said the place was jumping and full of laughter. He talked about the alligator that Ellis kept in the back. People would throw quarters at the alligator. Ellis never thought about the money being stolen.

College Grove

Fred and Joyce Norris

Fred married twice; his first wife was Mamie Robertson. To that union, five children were born: Dexter, Travis, Shanita, Cordell, and Ramona. They all attended Kirkland Elementary. Travis and Shanita also served their country in the military. Fred worked at the Battery Plant in College Grove for many years.

Fred later married Joyce Norris, the light of his life. She loved taking care of her yard, which had gorgeous flowers that beautified God's green earth. She was a loving, caring person filled with joy. Fred still lives in their home in College Grove. Life goes on.

Dexter Norris

Travis Norris

Shanita Norris

Cordell Norris

Ramona Norris

Jane and Bruce Covington

George Abram Hatcher

My Thrill Upon the Hill

ANITA CARTER JONES

Anita Carter Jones

My first connection with College Grove, Tennessee, and Kirkland School began in 1810 with two ex-slaves, Ned and Mariah Hatcher, who were owned by a white slave owner named John R. Hatcher (1818-1857), son of William and Lucy Rucker Hatcher of Bedford County, Virginia. Ned and Mariah are the grandparents of my grandfather, Jimmy Hatcher, and the father of my mother, Mary Eunice Hatcher Carter. She was born on the farm owned by her father, Jimmy, on Owen Hill Road in College Grove. This property remains in the family today.

In 1960, I had the privilege of attending third grade at Kirkland School. I later called it "My Thrill Upon the Hill." This was the most fun, most memorable year of my 14 years of school. We had the coolest principal, William B. Covington, who was also the 8th-grade teacher. Mrs. Nannie Lanier taught 7th grade, Mrs. Maudell Dotson taught 5th and 6th grade, Mrs. Ann Elizabeth Patton taught 3rd and 4th grade, Mrs. Pattie Davis Taylor taught 2nd grade, and last, but not least, perhaps most memorable was 1st grade, taught by Mrs. Vella Moody. My brother, Frank Carter, was in Mrs. Lanier's class. We thought she was so pretty.

I had one, if not two, relatives in every classroom. I never felt alone. Being the new girl in town from Nashville, I got much attention. Mr. William B. thought I was the cutest thing and could do no wrong. The school's water supply was from a sulfur spring. I tried to drink it but could not, so daily, around 2 P.M., I was allowed to go to the cafeteria to get a bottle of the best cold milk I have ever tasted. I don't know, but there is a good chance that milk came from the Hatcher Diary on Arno Road, the same family that once owned my great, great grandparents, Ned and Mariah Hatcher. It would be like them to produce the best milk I have ever tasted.

Mrs. Vella Moody, "My most memorable teacher."

When the school day ended, we had approximately one to one and a half hours to wait for the school bus to come from Franklin High School, where it picked up the high school students first, then picked us up and took us home. While waiting, during good weather, we would play softball for many of those days. Jackie Hatcher and one of the Boleyjack boys would be team captains, being the oldest and best players. If you wanted to play, everyone got picked. Our team captains made it so much fun. Sometimes, we would sneak down the hill to a small store and buy candy. During bad weather, many would hang out in Mr. William B.'s room. The location of his room allowed us to immediately see the school bus come up the hill, and because there was a radio in his room, we would listen to the radio station out of Nashville, WVOL. Every day around the same time, they played the Pop song by Hank Ballard, *There's A Thrill Upon the Hill, Let's Go, Let's Go, Let's Go*. We would dance and have fun until the bus picked up and took us home. That 1960 school year at Kirkland was my "Thrill Upon the Hill."

Kudos to all the wonderful teachers, cafeteria workers, custodians, and bus drivers; ours was Mr. Pete Thompson. They all gave us a happy and safe learning experience.

"They Called Me Mr. Carney"

MARGARET LOUISE "PEE WEE" OGLESBY

Margaret Louise "Pee Wee" Oglesby and grandson, Montrell Pointer, Jr.

Named Margaret Louise Oglesby, I am the daughter of Margaret Elaine Carney Oglesby and Risdon Oglesby. I was born on October 25, 1950, and was called "Pee Wee." I lived with my grandparents from the first day I came home from the hospital because they obtained custody of me. My grandfather's name was Joe Henry Carney, but he went by Claude. My step-grandmother was Maggie Lou Carney. My parents divorced when I was four years old, and I lived with my grandparents until adulthood.

Mr. Carney is the name that all the neighbors call him, Black and White, but I call him Papa. Papa was a strong man, over six feet tall and very calm-spoken. My grandmother was forceful but nice and couldn't read or write. When she was a child, she had to babysit the White children that her mother worked for because they stayed on their property. She was the same age as the children, but she had to watch over them. I was also told that she had to drag the boy around on a blanket because he was too heavy to carry and wanted to be picked up. The Black children had to work like their parents to stay on the White man's property. They couldn't go to school, so that is why she was unable to write her name or read a book.

My grandfather had an eighth-grade education. He was born in Eagleville, Tennessee. His father owned the land and the home where they lived, and a schoolhouse was on the property. His great-aunt was also the teacher. The property is in the family's name to this day, and it is located in an area called "The Cedars."

My grandfather was a hard-working man who read the Bible every night. He loved his land and kept a beautiful yard. He constantly told me that I needed to own property because that is where my wealth would grow. I was always told that my money was just as valuable as the White man's.

When he was growing up, Mr. Carney (Papa) was not allowed to go to restaurants that didn't serve Black people. He was also not allowed to go to the movies in Franklin because he had to sit in the balcony due to the color of his skin.

Papa taught me never to go anywhere I was not wanted and treated with respect. So, the first time I went to a movie, I was a senior in high school. I went to a theater in Nashville with my date, Lawrence B. Hatcher, and we sat on the lower level with the White people.

My grandfather was well off for a Black man, financially, during the 1960s and 1970s. He was well known at the College Grove Bank. He helped me secure a loan to purchase my first car. When I received the title to my car after it was paid off, I was told this is how you establish good credit. Papa was a man of great character, and he was smart.

Mr. Carney had entrepreneurial skills when it came to business. He worked very hard on his farm, with crops of tobacco, which he sold at the warehouse in Franklin. He had cows, sold milk, and was an avid gardener. He loved growing vegetables and shared his produce with his neighbors and friends throughout the Arrington area. There were a few Black families that also lived on Cox Road in Arrington: Mr. Patton, Mr. Eugene McClain, Joe Carney, his wife Rosie, and their children. They all owned their property during that time of our lives. I'm so proud of my grandparents for being there for me and my family. They were truly a Godsend.

Ebony and Ivory

MARGARET LOUISE "PEE WEE" OGLESBY

Margaret Louise Oglesby

My neighbor Maxie and I played together for years, then, when it was time for us to attend school for the first time in our lives, everything changed.

Maxie and I were waiting for the bus to come. Maxie got on the bus with all the White students and drove away. I felt a little traumatized until I was told my bus was coming. Mr. Preston Scales was driving the bus that I got on with all Black students. I was a little confused as to why Maxie and I were not going to the same school. I found out later that she went to Trinity Elementary School, and I was now enrolled in Kirkland Elementary. I would stay at Kirkland from the first grade through the eighth.

This is when I realized I was different from Maxie. We stopped playing together and being friends. But that didn't stop her mother from coming over to ask for vegetables from our garden.

The best years of my young life were those I spent at Kirkland School. They are memories that I will always take with me. I will never forget my principal, Mr. William B. Covington, my teachers, and my friends.

After eighth grade, I went to Natchez High School in Franklin, an all-Black school, for two years. When I started my junior year, I was forced to go to College Grove High School. It was a nightmare because the White kids didn't want us there, and the teachers felt the same way. There were fights daily, name-calling, and spitball throwing, it was a bad experience all around, until we realized we had the same number of Black and White students.

When it came to electing students in our class, they could not outvote us, so we ended up with two students for the same office. It became a little less intimidating my senior year because they knew we would not back down. To this day, I will never tell anyone what school I graduated from, and I will just say I went to Natchez High in Franklin.

Preston Scales

Margaret Louise Oglesby

Mammy and Pap

Gone But Not Forgotten

THE BOLEYJACK GRANDCHILDREN

William Clarence Thompson and Ovie Jane Wilson Thompson with sons Oscar and William Wilson Thompson

She called her husband, Mr. Clarence, and he called his wife, Ms. Ovie. We never really knew why, but maybe it was out of respect—something they very seldom received during this time of their lives.

William Clarence Thompson (1887-1954) was born in Marshall County, Tennessee, to Lizzy Murphy Thompson and a man of European descent in 1887. He married Ovie Jane Wilson (1890-1952) in 1907. William Clarence and Ovie Jane Thompson resided in various locations throughout Williamson County, including Triune, Kirkland, and College Grove. They had five children: three boys and two girls, named Wilson, Oscar, Joe, Annie Lizzy, and Ella Mae.

He worked on different farms throughout the area as a sharecropper, and he took great care of everything he touched. Everyone he knew marveled at his beautiful gardens. He would share his vegetables but never let anyone in his garden. His grandsons, Joe and John, still walk in his footsteps when it comes to caring for the garden.

He was also great with math, which came in handy when he needed to help his children and grandchildren with their homework. This gentle, soft-spoken man gave from his heart, leaving a lasting memory for his family. He passed away in 1954.

Ovie Jane Wilson Thompson

Ovie Jane Wilson Thompson was born to Thomas Jefferson Wilson and Sallie Ezell Wilson in 1890. They were a very close-knit family. She had three sisters and one brother. Ovie had an unwavering, steadfast spirit whenever she took on a task. She was a strong, Christian woman who believed in having her say. She attended church and was an active member at Mount Pleasant Missionary Baptist Church in Kirkland.

Ovie will always be remembered for her excellent cooking. She cooked many meals at the Burgess Cafe in College Grove. Robert (Blue) Windrow, the principal at College Grove High School, once said that she cooked the best biscuits and chicken that he had ever tasted.

Ovie was always there for her children and grandchildren. When she came to visit, she came with a purpose. She would travel on the bus from College Grove to Triune, then walk for a few miles to reach our home. Her grandchildren would always run to meet her. She would often bring two bags filled with things for the family. She loved her grandchildren enough to discipline them when needed, never asking for permission if it was necessary.

Our grandmother was full of life and was ready to help in any way she could for Black or White families and friends. She delivered many babies and took care of White ones until they were old enough to take care of themselves. She did everything that was needed of her in order to sustain her way of life during difficult times. She passed away in 1952.

Albert holding baby Ovie Boleyjack with Ella and Hattie behind

Alma Burgess, owner of the Burgess Cafe

Ovie Jane Wilson Thompson on right with unknown lady in front of the Burgess Cafe in College Grove.

Linda, Joe, Thomas, and John Boleyjack

John and Joe Boleyjack, grandsons of William C. Thompson

William Wilson Thompson

Right: Ovie Jane Thompson holding unknown child in her care; Left: unknown lady and child in her care.

Astonished!

OVIE ELAINE BOLEYJACK BELL

Mr. Bob Greathouse, College Grove HIgh School Principal

During my senior year of high school at College Grove, 1969 – 1970. Things had calmed down somewhat in the school. Everyone had gotten over the shock of our presence, yet there were times when nostalgia for what used to be crept in. I could see it on my classmates' faces whenever we had to vote for anything in our class. They would start to look at each other with unspoken words: "Help me out." "Let's stick together." "You vote for me, and I will vote for you next time."

To my surprise, a few of us were called to the office one day. I was confused about why I was there. As we walked into the room, the principal said we must pick the student council members for your class. We started with the president, and he was picked with no problem. Then Mr. Greathouse said let's skip the vice president for now. When all the offices were filled, Mr. Greathouse pointed at me and said, "You're the vice president." I didn't know what to say, so we just all walked out of the room.

To this day, I still wonder why he made me vice president. Did he see what was going on around the school? I guess I will never know, but I would like to thank him for allowing me to see the good through all the chaos that took place during that time of my life.

Planting a Seed

OVIE ELAINE BOLEYJACK BELL

Cathy Walter

Cathy Walter was a new teacher at College Grove High School, and she was like a breath of fresh air. She dressed differently and carried herself with confidence and vitality. She taught English literature for our senior class from 1969 to 1970.

One day, she entered the room, placed her belongings on the desk, and distributed sheets of paper to all the students. To my surprise, I saw the name *Langston Hughes* and that he was black, which sparked my curiosity. She said, "It's time to learn about different authors." I can't remember how she taught the class, but I never forgot Langston Hughes.

I have some of his poetry books, and my favorite poem by him is "I, Too." It opened up my mind to a world I had never seen before. I had only gone to black schools when it came to my education, and I wondered if I would ever be taught about anyone black in a white environment. Mrs. Walter gave me that one spark that lit a flame in my soul for black authors. I could hear the voices of my people ringing in my ears, and what a beautiful sound it was.

So, thank you, Mrs. Cathy Walter, for that one moment of clarity in my life. Most teachers will never know if they have reached a student and made an impact. I want you to know that you did.

Imagine

OVIE ELAINE BOLEYJACK BELL

Ovie Elaine Boleyjack Bell

I'd like to share a story with you about something I heard during the Democratic Convention. If you watched it, you may recall when Joe Biden's daughter spoke. She said, "My father told me, 'You're not any better than anyone else, and no one is any better than you.'" Those were the exact words my father told me in 1967 when I was going to College Grove High School. I had lived a life of segregation, and now things were about to change. You can imagine how surprised I was to hear those words, knowing that they came from the president of the United States and my father, who was just a farmer. Yet, knowing the impact that it had on both of us, we would

College Grove

never forget what they said. My father also said to "Keep your head high," because he knew it wasn't going to be easy, and it wasn't.

Attending an all-white school in the area where I lived for most of my early childhood was something that never entered my mind. During that time, black people were considered to be inferior. However, as the years went by, I began viewing my place in this environment as an experiment. As my mind took notes of all my surroundings and evaluated my inner thoughts, I concluded that what my father had said was true. No one was any better than me, and I just needed to believe it.

I often wondered why we were so disliked, When white people would come to our home, they were so nice to us. The men that my father knew showed us respect when they came for a visit. I never thought that their children would be so unhappy that we were attending their school. I think they would be surprised to know we didn't want to be there because we came from a better school, Natchez High School in Franklin. I pondered why they would force us to attend this rundown school. They didn't have a football or track team, something I desperately wanted to be on, so my dream was taken away. I felt like I was living in a different world. I was informed that things were going to be better for us academically, but it never happened. Due to the environment we were placed in, it was a stifling experience for our minds.

We just learned to adapt as we always did. Now that I'm grown, I realize that most people have two faces: the one they show you and the one they hide. The difference that I see today is that I can choose my friends and try to know the true person inside and out. Maybe I'm a little bit naive when it comes to relationships with other races. We all see life differently because of how we were brought up, but love and kindness should be universal. I have forgiven the people who treated me unfairly, and I hope they will forgive themselves.

I shared this story with you because we need to have a dialogue about the past. It's almost impossible to move forward while still waiting for the next shoe to drop. We live in a wonderful country with wonderful people. If we could talk and tell the truth without being angry. It may hurt, but it is refreshing when we can breathe and take in the pleasure of knowing we're on our way to something beautiful.

Highlights and Challenges

ADDIE MARIE RIDLEY OGILVIE

Addie Marie Ridley Ogilvie

I attended Green Grove school for the first grade, and then we were transferred to the new Kirkland Elementary. I was put back into the first grade when I arrived there, for reasons unknown, but I adapted fast to my new surroundings and my classmates. The teachers were very helpful in my adjustment. I had so much fun at Kirkland, and the years flew by.

    I loved working in the cafeteria, helping with the food service when needed. I felt close to my teachers and had great respect for all of them. During that time, I would watch for the teachers to drive up and run outside to help them with the things they were carrying. We were like a family at our school, I'm still in contact and have a loving relationship with many of my former classmates. We talk about the good old days, playing ball, jump rope, the May Day activities, and other things. Many of us still go to church together. We had a great foundation to stand on, because of the devotional program on Monday mornings, the singing and the praying kept us grounded. Those days have long passed but will never be forgotten.

After my eighth-grade graduation, it was time for a new adventure – going to high school. For my freshman and sophomore years, I attended Natchez high school in Franklin, an all-Black school. It was so exciting when we were riding the bus from Kirkland to Natchez. I was able to listen to the other students talk about the school and fill me in on what was to be expected. As I arrived, I felt that this was going to be quite different for me. I was now in a large school with many students, some old some new. It was a quick awakening and I fell in love with all the possibilities that were about to come my way.

Martha Ridley Anderson

My homeroom teacher was Ms. Grisham and, she was also my gym teacher. Mrs. Grisham was a big help getting me adjusted to the school, and its activities. We had a basketball team, football team, track, and a band with majorettes. On Fridays we would go to the gym and have a pep rally. I would go to the games, with my sister Martha and help Ms. Grisham in the concession stand. By my sophomore year, I was thriving. I felt comfortable enough to think about my future, and the person I wanted to become.

Then the shock came when the year was almost over, I was told that we had to go to College Grove High School the next year due to integration. I didn't want to go, just the thought of leaving Natchez made me sick. I had never gone to school with white children before, and I was a little afraid of what was about to come.

On my first day at College Grove High, I felt out of place, but nothing could have prepared me for what I encountered. The actions of the students and the teachers made it clear that they didn't want us there. I tried to look past their expressions, and the rolling of their eyes. But the more I held back, I felt that I couldn't breathe and had to speak up. The black students were at a boiling point. They called us names, threw spit balls at us, and we protested by saying we didn't want to be at this school, any more than you want us here. They told us to go back where we came from. This would go on day after day, which brought the principal Mr. Windrow into this mess. He told us it is time to stop fussing and fighting, but it didn't stop.

R.L. Windrow

When it was time to elect class officers, we realized we had as many black students as whites, and we decided to vote for our own people. Most of the time we would have two people for the same office. Every once and a while a white classmate would tell us to vote for them, and they would vote for us to a lower position. That rarely happened. My junior year was pure misery, because all I could think about was what I was missing, and wondering why I was here.

One day in study hall, Karen Hosford, brought a poster of a painting of a black boy, with little knots on his head for hair, and all the white students were laughing. I often heard about things like this happening to black people, but not to me. I guess we had to go through this to come out stronger on the other side.

Karen Hosford

The next year was a little better. We were talking with each other and trying to get along. I was once bitter about what took place with me, then I took it to the Lord. He made me understand, I can't change anyone else, I can only change my thoughts, and forgive, because if I carry it with me, I can't be of any service to others. I still see some of my white classmates and we talk as if nothing ever happened and move on.

College Grove

Ministers and Evangelists

JASPER HATCHER	MARVIN HATCHER
FRANK J. OGILVIE	GEORGE RIDLEY
HEWITT SAWYERS	EULYN CLAYBROOKS
HOWARD ANDERSON	EDWARD ANDERSON
HOWARD RUCKER	FELIX SCALES
GEORGE OGILVIE	BESSIE JOHNSON
ANNIE MARY RIDLEY	MARGARET J. BURNS
CHARLES H. TUCKER	JOE BOLEYJACK
PAUL SAWYERS	HATTIE BOLEYJACK
JUDGE WEBB, JR.	ELLIOTT G. WEBB, SR.

Green Grove Primitive Baptist Church

7816 Nolensville Road, Nolensville

MOTHER ELIZABETH DALTON, IRENE PARKS, AND DELORES CLAYBROOKS

Green Grove Primitive Baptist Church, built in 2001 on the site of the old church.

Shortly after the Civil War, there were no Black preachers for Black Christians in the Triune community. It was learned that a little church in Franklin, Tennessee, held regular service. Brother D.K. Bostic, who lived in Triune, walked to Franklin, located the church, and connected with it. The church's name and pastor are unknown, but it was a United Primitive Baptist Church.

Elder Robert Howse, First Pastor

After Brother Bostic joined that church in Franklin, it was learned that a young minister from Rutherford County named Elder Robert Howse was going around preaching. He came to Triune, preached a sermon, and was received with much enthusiasm. From then on, he held regular meetings once a month under a tree and in homes.

Soon, a church was organized and named Green Grove United Primitive Baptist Church with Brother D.K. Bostic, Gus Bostic, and Brother Webb as deacons. The names of the other deacons or the enrolled number are unknown. After becoming an organized church, these dedicated people began planning to build a church to hold their meetings. The first order of business was to find a suitable spot to build. They were badly in need of both a church and a school. They wanted the place to be convenient to all concerned. They wanted their children to have the proper training and be brought up the way they should go.

A spot was decided on, high on a hill overlooking the Horton Highway, which was called the Old Nolensville Turnpike at the time. This land belonged to Deacon D.K. Bostic. When a satisfactory agreement was made, all able-bodied men and women, young and old alike, and members of the community gave their service to build the combined church and school. The men went to the forest and cut down the trees for the building.

Green Grove U.P.B. Church, showing the timber-framed construction of 1870.

The women went about finding something to cook for the workers. The work was done at night because the men had to work from sunup to sundown for fifty cents a day. The women held the oil lamps and lanterns so the men could see how to drive the nails. As they were called, Mr. Nash and Mr. Pete Hyde made the benches. The front benches were made with aprons, and no one was allowed to sit on them but mothers and deacons.

COMING OUT OF THE DARK INTO THE LIGHT

At long last, the church was completed and given the Name "Green Grove United Primitive Baptist Church," with Elder Robert Howse as Founder and Pastor. It is not known to date, but it was in the year of Our Lord 1870. It is thought that when the Black Primitive Baptists came out from the White Primitive Baptists, some came out with a different understanding of the resurrection of the dead. They were known as the United Primitive Baptist Church, but Green Grove was set up in the old London Profession of Faith, its orthodox, its fundamental principles, and its practices.

Green Grove U.P.B. Church, built in 1870 and demolished in 2000.

ELDER A. M. BEDFORD
Second Pastor

ELDER R. A. WRIGHT
Third Pastor

ELDER HENRY DOZIER
Fourth Pastor

ELDER JOHNNIE E. TAYLOR
Fifth Pastor

ELDER RICHARD LLOYD
Sixth and Present Pastor

Green Grove Primitive Baptist Church has had only seven pastors throughout the ages. Elder Robert Howse, the first pastor, served the church and community for many years. Elder Howse grew weak and feeble after many years of going from place to place and spreading the gospel. Elder A.M. Bedford (1900-1952) became the second pastor at Green Grove, serving 52 years. Elder R.A. Wright (1953-1966) became the third pastor, followed by Elder Henry Dozier (1967-1972), Elder J.F. Taylor (1972-1979), Elder Richard Lloyd (1980-2022), and presently, Elder Charles Claybrooks (2024-   ).[1]

Elder Charles Claybrooks, seventh and current pastor

---

1. Dalton, Mother Elizabeth, and others, "Green Grove Primitive Baptist Church," 1982, *History of Green Grove Primitive Baptist Church Anniversary Program*, 1982. Republished in *Triune, An African American Review: We've Come This Far By Faith*, by Thelma Battle, 2003. Updated by Valerie Ogilvie in 2025.

Shady Grove Primitive Baptist Church

8220 Shady Grove Trail, Eagleville

FRANCES GREATHOUSE AND MARY ANDERSON

Shady Grove Primitive Baptist Church is located just off Taliaferro Road.

Shady Grove Primitive Baptist Church was founded in 1921 in Eagleville, TN, near the Little Harpeth River, by Bob House and a group of fellow Christians. Elder Zema Hill became the pastor and served from 1922 until 1939.

Deacon Gus Russell gave the church a gift of land on a plot known as Jones Hill in the nearby Kirkland community so that a building could be built for worship. In preparation for the move, Deacon Lewis Jones worked with other church members to tear down the building in Eagleville. The materials were then transported by wagon to the new site as the new building was being constructed. Some of those who worked

College Grove

during the 27 months it took to rebuild the new site were Lewis Jones, Anderson Jones, Tom Covington, and Betty Lewis. During the construction period, church services were held at the Kirkland Church. Shady Grove members had a thankful and joyous worship in the new building on the first Sunday in May, 1939. The new location is now known as Shady Grove Trail, located just off Taliaferro Road, approximately one mile from Horton Highway heading eastward.

Elder Robert Bostic began serving the church as pastor in its new building and served until the 1950s when his health began to fail. Elder John Thomas Lee from Little Harpeth Church in Franklin came to serve as assistant to Elder Bostic. In 1961, Elder Lee sent his young minister, Elder Willie Fisher, to replace himself as assistant to Elder Bostic. After 24 years of faithful service to Shady Grove, Elder Bostic passed into eternity in February 1963. Elder Willie B. Fisher was called to be a pastor and had served as Mildred Hardin Rucker. Before Pastor Robert Bostic, elders who remained pastor of Shady Grove, six elders were ordained to serve other churches as pastors. These were Elder Odie Anderson, now deceased, who served at White Chapel Primitive Baptist Church and St. Peter's Primitive Baptist Church; Elder George Ogilvie, pastor of Pleasant Valley; Elder Gerald Ogilvie, pastor of Mt. Zion Primitive Baptist Church; Elder Clarence Esmond, pastor of St. Peter's Church; and Elder Tommy Greenlee, who has moved out of the area.

With a vision for the future, members of Shady Grove saw the need for a new church building, and in 1997, a new building was erected on the same site. During the rebuilding, the church was privileged to worship in the College Grove Community Center. Shady Grove members were made to feel so blessed because other churches offered to use their building for worship or invited those from Shady Grove to worship with them. Members have expressed thankfulness for all the

Christian fellowship extended to them. The move into the new building occurred on the fifth Sunday of August 1997. Elder Richard Lloyd, pastor of Green Grove Primitive Baptist Church, served as host for the special occasion.

Ladies who have served the church as Mothers in the past include Gertrude Anderson, Alene Bowens, Margaret Coleman, Pauline Cunningham, Eula Johnson, Alice Jones, Virginia McClain, Minnie Ogilvie, Sarah Oglesby, Lillie Russell, Annie Sawyers, Annie Shannon, and Ivory Yeargins. Currently serving are Daisy Anderson,

COMING OUT OF THE DARK INTO THE LIGHT

Mary Anderson, Vickie Anderson, Jessie Barnes, Mary Davis, Aggie Norris, Mildred Rucker, and Hattie Smith.

Daisy Anderson, Jesse Anderson, Mary Anderson, Willie Jordan, Aggie Norris, Bertha Oglesby, and Sadie Pearl Scales are among those with current membership at Shady Grove who have worshipped there between 40 and 50 years.

Sunday morning worship is at 11 a.m., with attendance averaging around 600. Bible study is scheduled each Wednesday night at 6 p.m. Though small in number, the church family is active and has a big heart for all who will work with them to serve the Lord with gladness.[1]

Shady Grove – Left to Right: Howard Rucker, Jessie Bonds, Louise Norris, Tina Jones, Mamie Perkins, Thomas Rucker, Mary Ogilvie, Jerry Russell, Kristle Jones, Henry Perkins, Frank Rucker, Carolyn Jones, Miesha Roberts, Elder George Ogilvie, Wanda Ogilvie, J.D. Perkins, Joey Thompson, Elder Tommy Greenlee, Elder Willie B. Fisher (pastor), Renae Roberts, Fred Roberts, Whitney Perkins, Darius Roberts, Marquia Pickens. Sharon Rucker, Clifton Johnson, Elder Gerald Ogilvie, Donna Coleman, Tyrika Perkins, Elder Odie Anderson, Ashley Jones, Chasity Jones, Mattie Ransom, Holly Norris, Belinda Perkins, Vickie Anderson, Tiffany Norris, Bryan Greenlee, Mary Anderson, Jackie Perkins, Daisy Anderson, Zachary Anderson, Eula Johnson, Margaret Coleman, Aggie Norris, Jessie Anderson, Jennie Norris, Bill Smith, Pierre Murphy.

1. Greathouse, Frances, Carolyn Smotherman, and others. *College Grove: Williamson County, Tennessee, History and Families,* "Shady Grove Primitive Baptist Church." Williamson County Historical Society, 2011.

Seated: Jesse Anderson, Frank Rucker, Henry Perkins, Howard Rucker, Robert Coleman, and Willie Jones; Standing: Margaret Coleman, Daisy Anderson, George Ogilvie, Willie B. Fisher, Odie Anderson, Mary Anderson, Eula Johnson, and Aggie Norris; Back: Gerald Ogilvie and Tommy Greenlee.

First Row: Mattie Ransom, Trent Wright, Miesha Roberts in front of Aggie Norris, Eula Johnson holding Frederick Roberts, Mary Anderson holding Zachary Anderson, Darius Roberts, Margaret Coleman, Holly Norris, and Daisy Anderson; ***Second Row:***

COMING OUT OF THE DARK INTO THE LIGHT

Joey Thompson, Dontae Brown, Marquia Pickens, Zachary Brown, Ashley Jones, Chasity Jones, and Bryan Greenlee; **Third Row:** Willie Jones, Clifton Johnson, Elder George Ogilvie, Elder Gerald Ogilvie, Elder Willie B. Fisher (pastor), Elder Odie Lee Anderson, Jerry Russell, Howard Rucker, Darnell Jones, and Jesse Anderson; **Fourth Row:** Malik Bradford held by Tina Ridley, Juanita Anderson, Donna Coleman, Stephanie Coleman, Wanda Ogilvie, Della Greenlee, and Regina Thompson; **Fifth Row:** Jessie Bonds, Louise Norris, Donna Sparkman, Janice Norris, Renae Roberts, Jessica Rucker, Ladunia Anderson, and Baby Wright held by Annie Ridley; **Sixth Row:** Chris Thompson held by Cynthia Coleman, Darian Coleman held by Jenny Coleman, Vickie Anderson, Andy Perkins, Wesley Wright, Loletha Rucker, Hattie Smith, Jennie Norris, and Elizabeth Patton.

Mount Pleasant Missionary Baptist Church

8318 Horton Highway, College Grove

JOSIE ANN SCALES

Mount Pleasant Missionary Baptist Church

The Mount Pleasant Missionary Baptist Church stands on a hill on the east of Horton Highway in the Kirkland community. The church cornerstone proudly proclaims, "Organized in 1880." Before having a building to worship, devout people often gathered under trees for prayer meetings or religious services on the Lord's Day. The community was sparsely populated in the earliest years, with families widely scattered. Rev. Balim Manier came declaring God's Word and worked tirelessly so that a church could be formally established to meet in a building used for a school and a place for worship.

Traditional lore handed down through church members relates that Absalom Scales, a slave owner prior to the Civil War, had provided a place for his slaves and their families to use for worship and a school. Its location was on the west side of the road near the area of the former Oasis Motel and was known as Scales Chapel. The church continued to grow in number, and the people bought land on the hill across the road from Abb Scales and Will D. Ewing for about $25 an acre, upon which a church building was erected during the pastorate of Rev. Tom A. Brown. By the members' vote, the church's name was changed to Mount Pleasant Missionary Baptist. The date on the cornerstone reflects the change in name and location.

When Rev. Brown died, Rev. Gary became pastor and served until his death. These early pastors were followed by Reverends Watkins, Frierson, Parnell, A. F. Murray, Roy Lee Brown, Leroy Crinell, and Moore, who served for several years. Rev. Edwin E. Thomas became pastor in 1954, and during his tactful leadership and strong instructive gospel preaching, a new atmosphere of confidence was born among the members. Church activities were reorganized, and auxiliaries were formed. During the tenure of Rev. Thomas, a new modern building was erected and furnished with new pews. Upon the passing of Rev. Thomas in 1983, Rev. Anderson served as interim pastor.

On Oct. 7, 1984, Judge Webb was elected pastor. Rev. Webb served the church without compensation for two years. After the church mortgage was fully paid, he began receiving a monthly salary. Membership grew during his service. In 1991, Rev. Webb became ill and could not pastor for most of the year. Realizing the church needed spiritual leadership to function as a spiritual body of Christ, members felt prayers were answered when Rev. Claude McCathern came to them to pastor the church in March 1991. He was officially called to pastor in January 1992. Rev. McCathern was a young man and was well-received by the congregation. He gave new life to the church with his inspiring messages. Under his leadership, membership grew, attendance increased, and knowledge of scripture became evident. Rev. McCathern resigned as pastor due to illness in June 2004. On Dec. 12, 2004, Rev. Adlai S. Coffee was elected pastor and began his pastoral ministry on Jan. 2, 2005.

Currently singing in the choir are Brenda Coffee, Lindsey Easley, Lauren Easley, Paula Murray, Ernestine Covington-Barnett, Carolyn Wray-Mason, Robert Batts, Michelle Collier, and DiAnne Ewing, pianist. Members of the male choir are Jimmy Thompson Sr., Jimmy Thompson Jr., Carl Patton, Tony Vaughn, Rev. Claude

McCathern, and Rev. James Russell. A junior choir also includes Lauren Easley, Lesley Easley, Lindsey Easley, Larry Easley, Jr., Milton Murray, and Thomas Murray.

Annie Well Scales and Ella Louise Wray-Batts are ladies who serve as deaconesses or Mothers. Those who served well but are now deceased are Hazel Covington, Charlotte Drew, Johnny Ewing-Covington, Willie Eve Johnson, Daisy Owens, Emma D. Lanier, Gladys Scales, Willa Scales, Eddie B. Thomas, Ella Thompson, Willie B. Thompson, Sadie B. Demonbreun, Essie Ewing, Lena Ewing-Beal, Josie Ewing Murray, Martha Johnson, Lizzie Jones-Ewing, Erma Norris, Ella Scales, Ernestine Solomon, Alma Thompson, and Gertrude Webb.

The current ushers are Deborah Thompson-Easley and Linda Patton. Deceased ushers include Cora Shelton, Alma Thompson, Tisha Webb, Sadie B. Demonbreun, Robbie Scales, Lucille Wray, Martha Blue, and Jerome Covington. A memorial list of deacons who served includes John Beal, W.B. Covington Sr., Larry D. Easley Sr., Will D. Ewing, Tom Ewing Sr., Ben Haley, and J. B. Haley.

Under the guidance of Pastor Adlai S. Coffee, new energy permeates the congregation. New members have been added, volunteer work within the community is being done, the parking lot has been paved, a new keyboard and amplifier has been purchased, the Wednesday night Bible class has been reactivated, a member has been added to the Mother's Ministry and to the Deacon's Ministry, and a Deacon Ministry class has begun. Members feel they are blessed to be co-laborers in Christ.[1]

---

1. Smotherman, Carolyn, Frances Greathouse, and others, ed., *College Grove: Williamson County, Tennessee History and Families*, "Mount Pleasant Missionary Baptist Church," Williamson County Historical Society. 2011.

Locust Ridge Primitive Baptist Church

4991 Murfreesboro Road, Arrington

Locust Ridge Primitive Baptist Church

In the year 2000, Pastor Jasper G. Hatcher, Sr. revealed to Locust Ridge his Vision from the Lord to build a new sanctuary. A Kingdom Building Committee was established, and Pastor Hatcher appointed members. In 2004, we purchased one acre of land adjacent to the church. We also purchased 10 acres of land at 4991 Murfreesboro Road, Arrington, Tennessee, in Williamson County. On the 5th

Sunday in May 2005, a groundbreaking ceremony was held at the future site of the Locust Ridge Primitive Baptist Church. The church building at 6490 Arno-College Grove Road, College Grove, Tennessee, was sold. Our last service at that location was held on the 4th Sunday in September 2005. Our Church Sunday School, Morning Worship Service, and Communion and Feet Washing services began at the College Grove Community Center with prayer meetings, bible study, choir rehearsals, business meetings, baptisms, and funerals held at our sister churches. We thank God for our sister churches.

On July 10, 2008, the Williamson County Planning Commission approved construction documents and drawings by TLP Architects for our new church edifice. On August 27, 2008, Pastor Jasper Hatcher, Trustees John Dodson, Sandra Hunt, and Thomas Jarrett signed the construction contract with Baron and Dowdle Construction Company. On October 1, 2008, Pastor Jasper Hatcher, Trustees Ronnie Brown, John Dodson, Sandra Hunt, Thomas Jarrett, Andrew Jones, Yvonne Scott, and Clarence Smithson signed loan documents with Pinnacle Bank and construction began on October 2, 2008. In May 2009, Minister Brandon L. Mason was appointed as Youth Minister. On the 5th Sunday in November 2009, we held our last service at the College Grove Auditorium.

We thank God for another blessing. On December 3, 2009, construction was completed. On December 6, 2009, our first worship service was held in our new edifice. On December 9, 2009, we began our dedication celebration. On December 13, 2009, we celebrated our official opening and dedicatory ceremony. On May 14, 2011, Elder Brandon Mason was appointed Assistant Pastor. On the 1st Sunday in July 2011, Pastor Jasper Hatcher announced his retirement after 33 years of hard work and dedicated service to the Locust Ridge Church. On October 2, 2011, the church cornerstone was laid. On the 1st Sunday in October 2011, Elder Jasper Hatcher preached his last sermon as Pastor.

On October 8th, 2011, The Locust Ridge Church held a business meeting and elected a spirit-filled man, in the person of Elder Brandon L. Mason, and on October 30th, 2011, he was installed as the eighth pastor. Under Pastor Mason's leadership, the church has grown phenomenally in membership and attendance, reaching the Locust Ridge Church to the largest Primitive Baptist Church in the state of Tennessee.

During the Pastorate of Elder Mason, God blessed the Locust Ridge Church financially, including eliminating a substantial amount of debt. Numerous ministries have been added to the church, including the expansion of a youth ministry, which provides youth an opportunity to worship in their own creative space during morning worship under the leadership of a Youth Pastor. Pastor Brandon Mason also launched a Media Ministry, which reaches a weekly attendance of over 1000 viewers on social media platforms. Additionally, many capital improvements, enhancements, and investments in the community have been made.

With this acquisition, the church is well-positioned for expansion and kingdom-building opportunities. The church welcomes those in Metro Nashville and beyond to worship God, share the gospel of Jesus Christ with others, and execute the business of the Kingdom with excellence.[1]

---

1. Smotherman, Carolyn, and others, ed., updated by Yvonne Scott. *College Grove: Williamson County, Tennessee History and Families*, "Locust Ridge Church." Williamson County Historical Society, 2011.

College Grove

Our Service Men and Women

Jimmy Anderson ··· Joe Anderson ··· Lonnie Anderson
Powell Anderson, Jr. ··· Hobert Bedford, Jr. ··· James A. Cunningham

Carmack Demonbreun ··· Edward Allen Demonbreun
Homer Maurice Demonbreun ··· Diane Ewing ··· Joe B. Ewing

Tom Allen Ewing, Jr. ··· Willie Frank Ewing ··· Charles Floyd

Thomas Floyd ··· Marvin Hatcher, Jr. ··· Marvin Hatcher, Sr.
Lorenzo Hatcher ··· Vincent Hatcher ··· Daniel Howse ··· Robert Howse

William B. Jordan, Jr. ··· Larry Luster ··· Alvin McCord ··· Jackie McCord

Evan Norris ··· Tony Norris ··· Shanita Norris ··· Frank J. Ogilvie, Jr.
Jerry Perkins ··· James Ridley ··· Marshall Rodgers

Clifton Sawyers ··· Paul Sawyers ··· James "Pete" Thompson

Jimmy Green Thompson, Sr. ··· Oscar Lee Thompson
Theodore Thompson ··· William Wilson Thompson, Jr.

Charles H. Tucker ··· John Henry Walden ··· Elliott G. Webb, Sr.
Judge Webb, Jr. ··· Judge Webb, Sr.

COMING OUT OF THE DARK INTO THE LIGHT

Jimmy Anderson

Joe Anderson

Lonnie Anderson

Powell Anderson, Jr.

Michael Covington

Carmack Demonbreun

James A. Cunningham

H. Maurice Demonbreun

Diane Ewing

College Grove

Tom Ewing

Lorenzo Hatcher

Marvin Hatcher, Jr.

Marvin Hatcher, Sr.

Vincent Hatcher

Daniel Howse

Robert Howse

Shanita Norris

Frank James Ogilvie, Jr.

COMING OUT OF THE DARK INTO THE LIGHT

James Ridley

Clifton Sawyers

Paul David Sawyers

Jimmy Green Thompson

Oscar Lee Thompson

Charles H. Tucker

John Henry Walden

Elliott Webb

Judge Webb, Jr.

Brothers: Theodore, James Pete, and William Wilson Thompson

Edward Allen Haley Demonbreun

Acknowledgements

We want to thank everyone who joined us on this fantastic journey to discover and uncover the untold stories of the past. We have traveled many miles, talked to people in their homes and on the streets, and spent untold hours on the phone.

If you shared your stories with us, we want you to know that they will stay in our hearts forever. If you didn't share your story, please consider sharing it with your family and friends. Never keep your history in the shadows. Give it wings to fly as high as the open sky, because we're free to tell the truth.

God bless every one of you.

Love always,

Ovie Elaine Boleyjack Bell and Addie Marie Ridley Ogilvie

Ovie Elaine   Marie

A Hopeful King

OVIE ELAINE BOLEYJACK BELL

"Let us all hope that the dark clouds of racial prejudice will soon pass away and the deep fog of misunderstanding will be lifted from our fear-drenched communities; and in some not-too-distant tomorrow, the radiant stars of love and brotherhood will shine over our great nation with all their scintillating beauty."
Dr. Martin Luther King Jr.
"Letter from Birmingham Jail, April 16, 1963"

Looking through the eyes of Dr. Martin Luther King Jr., during his time in jail, fighting for our civil rights. Did he make the sacrifices in vain, because we have placed a veil over our subconscious. The light has been eclipsed, and we have lost sight of what we have overcome. We're drifting back in time, when we should be moving forward. We must never let anything or anyone stand in our way, when it comes to our rights. Dr. King would say …

"Injustice anywhere is a threat to justice everywhere."
— *Dr. Martin Luther King, Jr.*

So, pick up that fallen banner, shake off the dust, and view it with new enthusiasm. Remember the people who came before us, who couldn't vote, who sat in the back of the bus, and were stripped of their human rights. Eyes are upon us now, and we must meet the challenge without hesitation.

COMING OUT OF THE DARK INTO THE LIGHT

Take

OVIE ELAINE BOLEYJACK BELL

This chapter is dedicated to President Barack Obama and First Lady Michelle Obama (2008-2016), our nation's first presidential couple of color. We also pay tribute to Vice President Kamala Harris (2020-2024), the first United States vice president of color. You may have been the first, but you will not be the last. Thank you for your service to our country. You served with the utmost dignity, honor, and grace at a time when it was needed. God bless America.

Take, take, take. Take everything that one holds so dear: family, land, comfort, peace of mind, joy of heart, and faith in oneself. When you plunder and take away that which is not yours, what do you call yourself? A thief, a poacher? As you move around in such an unforgiving way, do you think you have a right to all that you have taken?

Someone once told me, if you continue to let a person control you, you will never be free. Freedom has always come with a price, but we must never give up or give in.

As we tear the scab off the open wound from time to time, we know that it will bring pain, but we must never allow the wound to heal completely, because if we did, we would become complacent and feel satisfied with ourselves or our achievements. It will take our people back to when we were "willing to please." We must never try to fit into the mold that has been put before us. It is a trap that we may never escape.

God didn't make everyone the same, so that He could use us for all He needed us to do. Stop trying to be someone that you are not and be who you are. We know where we came from and who brought us here. Our history has been passed down from generation to generation. It is up to us to continue the struggle. We must tell of the sadness and the brief moments of joy. This is how we go on, with love in our hearts and a will to fight in our souls. We're of African American heritage, and proud of it.

Take

Take, take, take. Take what you must, but when you do, know that we will never be silenced. We will shout from the mountain top, because no one will ever control our spirit.

"Free at last, free at last, thank God Almighty, we're free at last!"

President Barack Obama and First Lady, Michelle Obama, 2008-2016

Kamala Harris, Vice President of the United States, 2020-2024.

COMING OUT OF THE DARK INTO THE LIGHT

Inaugural Address of President Barack Obama

January 20, 2009

My fellow citizens:

I stand here today humbled by the task before us, grateful for the trust you have bestowed, mindful of the sacrifices borne by our ancestors. I thank President Bush for his service to our nation, as well as the generosity and cooperation he has shown throughout this transition.

Forty-four Americans have now taken the presidential oath. The words have been spoken during rising tides of prosperity and the still waters of peace. Yet, every so often the oath is taken amidst gathering clouds and raging storms. At these moments, America has carried on not simply because of the skill or vision of those in high office, but because We the People have remained faithful to the ideals of our forbearers, and true to our founding documents.

So it has been. So it must be with this generation of Americans. That we are in the midst of crisis is now well understood. Our nation is at war, against a far-reaching network of violence and hatred. Our economy is badly weakened, a consequence of greed and irresponsibility on the part of some, but also our collective failure to make hard choices and prepare the nation for a new age. Homes have been lost; jobs shed; businesses shuttered. Our healthcare is too costly; our schools fail too many; and each day brings further evidence that the ways we use energy strengthen our adversaries and threaten our planet.

These are the indicators of crisis, subject to data and statistics. Less measurable but no less profound is a sapping of confidence across our land; a nagging fear that America's decline is inevitable, and that the next generation must lower its sights.

Today I say to you that the challenges we face are real. They are serious and they are many. They will not be met easily or in a short span of time. But know this, America: they will be met.

On this day, we gather because we have chosen hope over fear, unity of purpose over conflict and discord.

On this day, we come to proclaim an end to the petty grievances and false promises, the recriminations and worn out dogmas, that for far too long have strangled our politics.

We remain a young nation, but in the words of Scripture, the time has come to set aside childish things. The time has come to reaffirm our enduring spirit; to choose our better history; to carry forward that precious gift, that noble idea, passed on from generation to generation: the God-given promise that all are equal, all are free, and all deserve a chance to pursue their full measure of happiness.

In reaffirming the greatness of our nation, we understand that greatness is never a given. It must be earned. Our journey has never been one of shortcuts or settling for less. It has not been the path for the faint-hearted, for those who prefer leisure over work, or seek only the pleasures of riches and fame. Rather, it has been the risk-takers, the doers, the makers of things – some celebrated, but more often men and women obscure in their labor, who have carried us up the long, rugged path towards prosperity and freedom.

For us, they packed up their few worldly possessions and traveled across oceans in search of a new life.

For us, they toiled in sweatshops and settled the West; endured the lash of the whip and plowed the hard earth.

For us, they fought and died, in places like Concord and Gettysburg; Normandy and Khe Sahn.

Time and again these men and women struggled and sacrificed and worked till their hands were raw so that we might live a better life. They saw America as bigger than the sum of our individual ambitions; greater than all the differences of birth or wealth or faction.

This is the journey we continue today. We remain the most prosperous, powerful nation on Earth. Our workers are no less productive than when this crisis began. Our minds are no less inventive, our goods and services no less needed than they were last week or last month or last year. Our capacity remains undiminished. But our time of standing pat, of protecting narrow interests and putting off unpleasant decisions — that time has surely passed. Starting today, we must pick ourselves up, dust ourselves off, and begin again the work of remaking America.

For everywhere we look, there is work to be done. The state of the economy calls for action, bold and swift, and we will act not only to create new jobs, but to lay a new foundation for growth. We will build the roads and bridges, the electric grids and digital lines that feed our commerce and bind us together. We will restore science to its rightful place, and wield technology's wonders to raise healthcare's quality and lower its cost. We will harness the sun and the winds and the soil to fuel our cars and run our factories. And we will transform our schools and colleges and universities to meet the demands of a new age. All this we can do. And all this we will do.

Now, there are some who question the scale of our ambitions — who suggest that our system cannot tolerate too many big plans. Their memories are short. For they have forgotten what this country has already done; what free men and women can achieve when imagination is joined to common purpose, and necessity to courage.

What the cynics fail to understand is that the ground has shifted beneath them – that the stale political arguments that have consumed us for so long no longer apply. The question we ask today is not whether our government is too big or too small, but whether it works – whether it helps families find jobs at a decent wage, care they can afford, a retirement that is dignified. Where the answer is yes, we intend to move forward. Where the answer is no, programs will end. And those of us who manage the public's dollars will be held to account – to spend wisely, reform bad habits, and do our business in the light of day – because only then can we restore the vital trust between a people and their government.

Nor is the question before us whether the market is a force for good or ill. Its power to generate wealth and expand freedom is unmatched, but this crisis has reminded us that without a watchful eye, the market can spin out of control and that a nation cannot prosper long when it favors only the prosperous. The success of our economy has always depended not just on the size of our Gross Domestic Product, but on the reach of our prosperity; on our ability to extend opportunity to every willing heart – not out of charity, but because it is the surest route to our common good.

As for our common defense, we reject as false the choice between our safety and our ideals. Our Founding Fathers, faced with perils we can scarcely imagine, drafted a charter to assure the rule of law and the rights of man, a charter expanded by the blood of generations. Those ideals still light the world, and we will not give them up for expedience's sake. And so to all other peoples and governments who are watching today, from the grandest capitals to the small village where my father was born: know that America is a friend of each nation and every man, woman, and child who seeks a future of peace and dignity, and that we are ready to lead once more.

Recall that earlier generations faced down fascism and communism not just with missiles and tanks, but with sturdy alliances and enduring convictions. They understood that our power alone cannot protect us, nor does it entitle us to do as we please. Instead, they knew that our power grows through its prudent use; our security emanates from the justness of our cause, the force of our example, the tempering qualities of humility and restraint.

We are the keepers of this legacy. Guided by these principles once more, we can meet those new threats that demand even greater effort, even greater cooperation and understanding between nations. We will begin to responsibly leave Iraq to its people, and forge a hard-earned peace in Afghanistan. With old friends and former foes, we will work tirelessly to lessen the nuclear threat, and roll back the specter of a warming planet. We will not apologize for our way of life, nor will we waver in its defense, and for those who seek to advance their aims by inducing terror and slaughtering innocents, we say to you now that our spirit is stronger and cannot be broken; you cannot outlast us, and we will defeat you.

For we know that our patchwork heritage is a strength, not a weakness. We are a nation of Christians and Muslims, Jews and Hindus, and non-believers. We are shaped by every language and culture, drawn from every end of this Earth; and because we have tasted the bitter swill of civil war and segregation, and emerged from that dark chapter stronger and more united, we cannot help but believe that the old hatreds shall someday pass; that the lines of tribe shall soon dissolve; that as the world grows smaller, our common humanity shall reveal itself; and that America must play its role in ushering in a new era of peace.

To the Muslim world, we seek a new way forward, based on mutual interest and mutual respect. To those leaders around the globe who seek to sow conflict, or blame their society's ills on the West, know that your people will judge you on what you can build, not what you destroy. To those who cling to power through corruption and deceit and the silencing of dissent, know that you are on the wrong side of history; but that we will extend a hand if you are willing to unclench your fist.

To the people of poor nations, we pledge to work alongside you to make your farms flourish and let clean waters flow; to nourish starved bodies and feed hungry minds. And to those nations like ours that enjoy relative plenty, we say we can no longer afford indifference to suffering outside our borders; nor can we consume the world's resources without regard to effect. For the world has changed, and we must change with it.

As we consider the road that unfolds before us, we remember with humble gratitude those brave Americans who, at this very hour, patrol far-off deserts and distant mountains. They have something to tell us today, just as the fallen heroes who lie in Arlington whisper through the ages. We honor them not only because they are guardians of our liberty, but because they embody the spirit of service: a willingness to find meaning in something greater than themselves. And yet, at this moment, a moment that will define a generation, it is precisely this spirit that must inhabit us all.

For as much as government can do and must do, it is ultimately the faith and determination of the American people upon which this nation relies. It is the kindness to take in a stranger when the levees break, the selflessness of workers who would rather cut their hours than see a friend lose their job, which sees us through our darkest hours. It is the firefighter's courage to storm a stairway filled with smoke, but also a parent's willingness to nurture a child, that finally decides our fate.

Our challenges may be new. The instruments with which we meet them may be new. But those values upon which our success depends – hard work and honesty, courage and fair play, tolerance and curiosity, loyalty and patriotism – these things are old. These things are true. They have been the quiet force of progress throughout our history. What is demanded then is a return to these truths. What is required of us now is a new era of responsibility – a recognition, on the part of every American, that we have duties to ourselves, our nation, and the world, duties that we do not grudgingly accept but rather seize gladly, firm in the knowledge that there is nothing so satisfying to the spirit, so defining of our character, than giving our all to a difficult task.

This is the price and the promise of citizenship.

This is the source of our confidence: the knowledge that God calls on us to shape an uncertain destiny.

This is the meaning of our liberty and our creed, why men and women and children of every race and every faith can join in celebration across this magnificent mall, and why a man whose father less than 60 years ago might not have been served at a local restaurant can now stand before you to take a most sacred oath.

So let us mark this day with remembrance, of who we are and how far we have traveled. In the year of America's birth, in the coldest of months, a small band of patriots huddled by dying campfires on the shores of an icy river. The capital was abandoned. The enemy was advancing. The snow was stained with blood. At a moment when the outcome of our revolution was most in doubt, the father of our nation ordered these words be read to the people:

"Let it be told to the future world that in the depth of winter, when nothing but hope and virtue could survive that the city and the country, alarmed at one common danger, came forth to meet it."

America. In the face of our common dangers, in this winter of our hardship, let us remember these timeless words. With hope and virtue, let us brave once more the icy currents, and endure what storms may come. Let it be said by our children's children that when we were tested we refused to let this journey end, that we did not turn back, nor did we falter; and with eyes fixed on the horizon and God's grace upon us, we carried forth that great gift of freedom and delivered it safely to future generations.[1]

Thank you. God bless you.

And God bless the United States of America.

Barack Hussein Obama

---

1. Obama, Barack. *Inaugural Address*, January 20, 2009. Retrieved online on from *The Avalon Project at Yale Law School*, https://avalon.law.yale.edu/21st_century/obama.asp on July 31, 2025.

Lift Every Voice and Sing

JAMES WELDON JOHNSON

Lift every voice and sing
Till earth and heaven ring,
Ring with the harmonies of Liberty;
Let our rejoicing rise
High as the listening skies,
Let it resound loud as the rolling sea.
Sing a song full of the faith that the dark past has taught us,
Sing a song full of the hope that the present has brought us.
Facing the rising sun of our new day begun,
Let us march on till victory is won.

Stony the road we trod,
Bitter the chastening rod,
Felt in the days when hope unborn had died;
Yet with a steady beat,
Have not our weary feet
Come to the place for which our fathers sighed?
We have come over a way that with tears has been watered,
We have come, treading our path through the blood of the slaughtered,
Out from the gloomy past,
Till now we stand at last
Where the white gleam of our bright star is cast.

Lift Every Voice and Sing

God of our weary years,
God of our silent tears,
Thou who hast brought us thus far on the way;
Thou who hast by Thy might
Led us into the light,
Keep us forever in the path, we pray.
Lest our feet stray from the places, our God, where we met Thee,
Lest, our hearts drunk with the wine of the world, we forget Thee;
Shadowed beneath Thy hand,
May we forever stand.
True to our God,
True to our native land.[1]

---

1. Johnson, James Weldon. "Lift Every Voice and Sing, from *James Weldon Johnson: Complete Poems*. Penguin Books, 2000.

Into the Light

Hayes Anderson and Ovie Elaine Boleyjack Bell

Index

A

Acklin, George and Dorothy Sawyers, 197
Adams farm, 98
Adams, Herschel farm, 46
Adkinson, Carol Cunningham, 203
Adkinson, Marguerite, 209
All Williamson County Chorus, 159
Allen, Josie, 226
Allison, W.T., 222
Alsup, Sandy Thomas, 64
Amos, Walter, 247
Anderson, Annie Bellenfant Claybrooks, 226, 227
Anderson, Annie Hardemon, 239–240
Anderson, Annie Kate, 223, 225
Anderson, Annie Mary, 227
Anderson, Bertha Floyd, 228
Anderson, Betty, 227
Anderson, Betty Lou Johnson, 223
Anderson, Betty Sue, 118, 223, 225
Anderson, Brenda Gail, 223–225
Anderson, Calvin, 226
Anderson, Crockett, 222–223
Anderson, Cynthia "Sinthy," 223, 228
Anderson, Daisy, 277, 279, 280
Anderson, Devon, 224
Anderson, Dorothy Braden, 228
Anderson, Dorothy Floyd, 227
Anderson, Edward, 124, 126, 228, 271
Anderson, Elizabeth Lavender, 226, 228
Anderson, Ella, 128, 129, 137
Anderson, Ella Catherine, 223, 225
Anderson, Ethel Evans, 228
Anderson, Eula Pearl Sheffield, 223
Anderson, Florine Rucker, 223
Anderson, Frances K., 228
Anderson, Frank, 227
Anderson, Fredia Diana Fulton, 202
Anderson, Gertrude, 277
Anderson, Hayes, 128, 137, 304
Anderson, Haze, 226
Anderson, Hazel, 129, 137
Anderson, Howard, 137, 227, 271
Anderson, James Wilson, 196, 223
Anderson, Jane, 226
Anderson, Jeffrey, 69
Anderson, Jesse, 125, 202, 227, 278, 279, 280
Anderson, Jesse, Jr., 131, 202, 229
Anderson, Jesse, Sr., 229
Anderson, Jessie, 40, 278, 280
Anderson, Jessie James, 190
Anderson, Jimmy, 12, 13, 39, 226, 287, 288
Anderson, Joe, 39, 137, 223, 226, 287, 288
Anderson, Joe and Hazel, 191
Anderson, John, 202, 228–229
Anderson, John Abe, 202
Anderson, John and Elizabeth, 227
Anderson, John Frank / John F., 123, 228
Anderson, John Frank, John F. family, 226–229
Anderson, Josie, 137, 194
Anderson, Juanita, 131, 280
Anderson, Ladunia, 280
Anderson, Leah, 202
Anderson, Lonnie, 137, 223, 225, 226, 287, 288
Anderson, Lonnie and Juanita Johnson, 192
Anderson, Lonnie B., 127
Anderson, Lonnie S., 128
Anderson, Loretha, 229
Anderson, Loretha Lynn, 202
Anderson, Lucille Bradley, 228
Anderson, Lytle, 227
Anderson, Lytle R., 170
Anderson, Lytle Webster, 226
Anderson, Martha, 87, 89
Anderson, Martha Louise Ridley, 69, 269
Anderson, Mary, 229, 276–278, 279
Anderson, Mary Cunningham, 227

Anderson, Mary Elizabeth, 75
Anderson, Mary Elizabeth Cunningham, 113–114, 204–205, 227–230
Anderson, Mary Gertrude Starnes, 226, 227
Anderson, Mary Jane, 222–223, 229
Anderson, Mattie Ruth, 128, 137, 223
Anderson, May Clara, 223, 225
Anderson, Nick, 223–224, 228
Anderson, Odie, 277–279
Anderson, Odie Lee, 124, 185, 280
Anderson, Powell, 123,
– family, 226
Anderson, Powell E., Jr., 69
Anderson, Powell Edward, 227
Anderson, Powell, Jr., 138, 226, 287–288
Anderson, Powell, Sr., 226
Anderson, Rachel, 223
Anderson, Regina, 131
Anderson, Rev., 282
Anderson, Richard B., 228
Anderson, Rosie, 227
Anderson, Ruby, 228
Anderson, Serenity, 83
Anderson, Shanna, 83
Anderson, Shawn, 69
Anderson, Sheila Wright, 228
Anderson, Sue, 138
Anderson, Vickie, 278, 280
Anderson, Virginia
– see McClain, Virginia Anderson, 227
Anderson, Webb, 227
Anderson, Wesley, 39, 190, 192, 228
Anderson, Wilson, 118–119, 222–225
Anderson, Wilson and Betty, 225
Anderson, Woodrow Wilson, 223
Anderson, Zachary, 278
Anderson, Zachery, 202
Arrington, 5

B

Ballard, Hank, 255
Barnes, Jessie, 278
Barnett, Ernestine Covington, 127, 128, 234, 235, 236
Barnhill, Juanita, 159
Bates, Mattie, 103
Batey, Anastasia, 78 Batey, James, Sr., 77–78
Batey, Juanita Vaughn, 217–221

Battery Plant, 213
Battle, Elizabeth Ogilvie, 222
Battle, Thelma, 6, 102, 103, 109, 130, 245
Batts, Ella Louise Wray, 231
Batts, Robert, 282
Baugh, Frances Lee, 60
Baugh, Izella Covington, 234 Beach, Damon, 202
Beach, Johnetha, 202
Beach, Loretha, 202
Beach, Pierre Murphy, 202
Beal, John, 283
Beal, Louise, 103
Beasley, Walter, 32
Bedford, A.M., 166, 274
Bedford, Betty, 166
Bedford, Hobert, 123, 287
Beechcraft Flying Service, 249
Bell, Elaine, 16
Bell, Ovie, 22
Bell, Ovie Elaine Boleyjack, 1, 2, 3, 7, 11, 15, 20, 23, 33, 38, 42, 45, 50, 55, 66, 70, 90, 160–161, 264, 265, 266, 292, 293, 294–295, 304
Bellenfant, Joe Billy (William), 216, 217–219
Bellenfant, Joe W., 218
Bellenfant, Joe William, 219
Bellenfant, Mandy, 226
Bellenfant, Mrs. Joe W., 218
Betts, Ann, 17, 19
Biden, Joe daughter, 266
Biggers, Barbara, 129, 138, 200
Biggers, Barbara Faye, 154
Biggers, Bishop Waymon, 186
Biggers, Earleen Hatcher, 244, 246
Biggers, Faye, 121
Biracial Families, 215–221
Black businesses of Kirkland, 183
Blackman, Annie Hardemon, 239
Blackman, Ida M., 168
Blackman, Robert, 167–168
Blue, Martha, 283
Bolerjack, John, 42
Boleyjack boys, 255
Boleyjack grandchildren, 260–263
Boleyjack, Albert, 126, 262
Boleyjack, Albert Lee, 49
Boleyjack, Alma, 138, 153
Boleyjack, Annie, 40, 98–99
Boleyjack, Annie L. Thompson, 45–48
Boleyjack, Arch, 42–44, 98–99

Boleyjack, Arch, Historic marker, 42
Boleyjack, Betty, 98–99
Boleyjack, Brown Lee, 59
Boleyjack, Ella, 157, 262
Boleyjack, George, 98–99, 126
Boleyjack, George "Scoonie," 31–32, 38, 45–48, 53–54
Boleyjack, George William, Jr., 49
Boleyjack, George, Jr., 15, 16, 98
Boleyjack, George, Sr., 39, 42
Boleyjack, Hattie, 262, 271
Boleyjack, Howard, 138
Boleyjack, Howard Landis, 49
Boleyjack, James Andrew, 49
Boleyjack, Joe, 39, 262–263, 271
Boleyjack, Joe Clifton, 49
Boleyjack, John, 40, 48, 66, 71, 262–263
Boleyjack, John H., 26, 28, 31, 38, 53, 70, 80
Boleyjack, John Haley, 50
Boleyjack, Larry, 48, 138
Boleyjack, Larry Neal, 50
Boleyjack, Lena Hardison, 59
Boleyjack, Linda, 159, 262
Boleyjack, Margaret, 42, 98
Boleyjack, Ovie, 200
Boleyjack, Ovie Elaine, 128, 262
Boleyjack, Sally, 42
Boleyjack, Thomas, 127, 128, 138, 262
Boleyjack, Thomas Jefferson, 50
Boleyjacks, 165
Bonds, Jessie, 278, 280
Bonner, Elizabeth, 60
Bostic, D.K., 272–273
Bostic, Elder Robert, 103, 277
Bostic, Gus, 273
Bostic, Minnie Mai, 239
Bostic, Robert, 277
Bostick, Addie, 70
Bostick, Addie Wilson, 20, 70–71
Bostick, Brent, 6
Bostick, Ed, 102
Bostick, Edgar Benson, 70
Bostick, Edward, 70
Bostick, James Robert "Guy," 70
Bostick, John Willie, 40, 187
Bostick, Mattie, 71
Bostick, Nancy, 91
Bostick, Zephiniah and Short, 102
Bowen, Sadie Frances, 126
Bowens, Alene, 277

Bowens, Annie Pearl, 168
Boyd, Bertha, 188, 194, 195
Boyd, J.W., 13, 101
Boyd, William, 102
Boykin, Sophia, 75
Braden, Dorothy Anderson, 228
Bradford, Malik, 280
Bradley, Lucille Anderson, 228
Bright, Carolyn, 159
Britton, Britton, 75
Britton, Carol Ann, 138
Britton, Jesse, 138
Britton, Patsy, 138
Brooks, Garth, 88
Brooks, William, 13
Brown, Charley, 55
Brown, Dontae, 280
Brown, Ed, 55–56
Brown, Ed, Family, 55
Brown Ed, Stores, 55
Brown, Katie, 55
Brown, Larry, 55
Brown, Linda, 55
Brown, Mary, 55
Brown, Mr. and Mrs. Ed, 54
Brown, Philip, 159
Brown, Rev. Frank, 168
Brown, Ronnie, 285
Brown, Roy Lee, 282
Brown, Shirley, 55–56
Brown, Tom A., 282
Brown, Zachary, 280
Buchanan, Rosemary, 154
Burgess Cafe, 261–262
Burgess, Alma, 262
Burnes, Margaret Jean, 154
Burnes, Sadie Frances, 186
Burns family, 165
Burns, Angeline, 64
Burns, George W., 167
Burns, George, Jr., 168
Burns, Lawrence, 124
Burns, Margaret, 127, 128
Burns, Margaret J., 271
Burns, Nettie Mae, 167–168
Burns, Norma, 159
Burns, Raymond, 124
Burns, Rosa L., 167
Burns, Rosie L., 168
Burns, Sarah, 121, 129, 138

Burns, William, 13, 168
Burns, Wilma, 168

C

Caldwell, Bertha Mae, 208
Caldwell, Lee farm, 11
Campbell Patricia, 78
Campbell-Webb, Mary, 78
Campbell, Fulton, 78
Carney, Barbara Ann, 128
Carney, Betty Lou, 138
Carney, Jo Ester, 139
Carney, Joe and Rosie, 257
Carney, Joe Henry "Claude," 256–257
Carney, Maggie Lou, 256
Carney, Margaret Elaine (Oglesby), 254, 256
Carney, Rosie Marie Davis, 73
Carney, Theresa, 131, 139
Carraway, Leslie, 75
Carter, Frank, 193
Carter, Jack, 6
Carter, Mary Eunice Hatcher, 254
Cedars, The, 257
Cheairs, Henrietta, 60
Christmon, Ruth, 209
Churches
– Beech Grove United Methodist, 224, 247
– First Baptist Franklin, 59
– First Baptist Murfreesboro, 64
– Green Grove, 62, 68
– Green Grove Baptist, 17, 18
– Green Grove Primitive Baptist, 1, 63, 64, 67, 69, 74, 79, 272–275
– Little Harpeth, 277
– Locust Ridge Primitive Baptist, 168, 202, 208, 247, 284–286
– Mount Pleasant Missionary Baptist, 70, 114, 115, 174, 234, 240, 249, 261, 281–283
– Mt. Calvary Missionary Baptist, 61
– Mt. Zion Primitive Baptist, 277
– Pleasant Valley, 277
– Scales Chapel, 115, 282
– Shady Grove Primitive Baptist, 166, 170, 228, 230, 276–280
– Shiloh Missionary Baptist, 61
– St. Peter's, 277
– Watson Tabernacle, 247
– Westwood Baptist, 227, 228, 230
– White Chapel Primitive Baptist, 277

Cisner, Julius, 12, 13
Claiborne, Charlie F., 91
Clary, Jo, 159
Claybrooks, 165
Claybrooks Juanita, 188
Claybrooks, Ada Mae York, 92–93
Claybrooks, Annie, 170
Claybrooks, Annie Louise, 94
Claybrooks, baby, 94
Claybrooks, Bessie, 209
Claybrooks, Charles, 62, 95, 139, 274–275
Claybrooks, Deborah, 93, 121, 129
Claybrooks, Delicia Lashann, 93
Claybrooks, Delores, 92–93, 95, 127, 139, 193, 272–275
Claybrooks, Derrell, 93
Claybrooks, Donald, 94
Claybrooks, Emmett, 209
Claybrooks, Emmett Charles, Jr., 92–93
Claybrooks, Emmett Charles, Sr., 92–93
Claybrooks, Emmett family, 67
Claybrooks, Eulyn, 139, 271
Claybrooks, Ewellyn, 127, 128
Claybrooks, Faye, 94
Claybrooks, Georgia Mae, 209
Claybrooks, Grundy, Sr., 226
Claybrooks, Irene, 95, 187
Claybrooks, James, 92
Claybrooks, James Arthur, 94
Claybrooks, James Ben, 187
Claybrooks, Joyce, 94
Claybrooks, Kenneth Wayne, 93–94
Claybrooks, Kevin, 93
Claybrooks, Lamont, 139
Claybrooks, Linda, 139
Claybrooks, Linda Faye Baugh, 93
Claybrooks, Malinda Gwendolyn (Gwen), 92–93
Claybrooks, Mandy Bellenfant, 226
Claybrooks, Mary Ann, 39, 154
Claybrooks, Mary Elizabeth Patton, 193
Claybrooks, Millard, 193, 209
Claybrooks, Pearly Mae, 230
Claybrooks, Rev. Fred W., 93
Claybrooks, Shirley, 139
Claybrooks, Susie Bell, 94
Claybrooks, Terrence, 93
Claybrooks, Vivian, 94, 196
Claybrooks, Wanda Lane Ellis, 93
Claybrooks, Wayne, 95

Index

Cliffe, Mamie, 209
Clover Bottom Developmental Center, 69
Cobbs, Charleen, 64
Coe, Deloris, 159
Coffee, Adlai S., 282–283
Coffee, Brenda, 282
Cole, Natalie, 88
Coleman-Lackey, Cynthia, 172
Coleman, Cora, 179
Coleman, Cynthia, 280
Coleman, Darian, 280
Coleman, Donna, 278–280
Coleman, Elsie Mai, 168
Coleman, F.A., 179
Coleman, George, 172
Coleman, Jenny, 280
Coleman, Margaret, 277–279
Coleman, Margaret Jean McClain, 171
Coleman, Melanie, 172
Coleman, Quintin, 64
Coleman, Robert, 171, 172, 279
Coleman, Stephanie, 172, 280
Coleman, Virginia, 172
Coley, Anita Thompson, 212
College Grove Bank, 257
College Grove High School, 2
College Grove map, 1878, 198
Collier, Michelle, 282
Confederate Army surgeon, 174
Cook, Tish Webb, 135
Coolidge, Eula D. Scales, 207
Corder, Lady, 64
cotton pickers, cotton picking, 7, 9
Cotton, Ameerah, 65
Cotton, Miss, 101
Cotton, Pamela, 63–65
Covington Bernice, 139, 234
Covington-Barnett, 282
Covington, Aggie J., 124
Covington, Aggie Jane, 126
Covington, Aretha, 139
Covington, Betty, 123
Covington, Beulah, 233
Covington, Bruce and Jane, 252
Covington, Charles, 139
Covington, Charlie B., 124, 230
Covington, Clarence, 139
Covington, Darrell, 189
Covington, David DeWayne, 131, 189
Covington, Ernestine
 – see Barnett, Ernestine Covington, 127, 128, 234, 235–236
Covington, Greg, 140
Covington, Gregory, 189
Covington, Hazel, 283
Covington, Hazel Scales, 132, 233–234
Covington, Henrietta, 140
Covington, Izella, 124, 126, 234
Covington, Jane, 252
Covington, Jerome, 40, 126, 127, 234, 283
Covington, Jerome and Jessie, 189
Covington, Jerome David, 124
Covington, Jesse, 124, 140
Covington, Jessie, 116, 131
Covington, Joe, farm, 46
Covington, John Weakley, 80
Covington, Larry, 128
Covington, Lillian Floyd, 230
Covington, Mamie, 126
Covington, Mattie Mai, 140
Covington, Michael, 189, 287, 288
Covington, Mike, 140
Covington, Mildred, 126
Covington, Mrs., 114
Covington, Pearlie May, 124
Covington, Polly Mai, 123
Covington, Professor, 160, 234
Covington, Risdon Woods, 233
Covington, Theresa, 140
Covington, Tom, 276
Covington, Tommie, 123
Covington, Veronica, 140
Covington, W.B., 12, 116, 124, 132
Covington, W.B., Sr., 283
Covington, William, 189
Covington, William B., 2, 41, 114, 126–127, 133, 165, 213, 233–234, 235–236, 242, 252, 254–255, 258
Covington, William B., Jr., 124, 155–156, 234
Covingtons, 165
Crafton, Bettie, 227
Creations by G. Ridley, 88
Credle, Lorenzia, 75
Crinell, Leroy, 282
Crowder, Mary, 140
Cumberland Association, 166
Cunningham, Carol, 140, 202, 203
Cunningham, Eugene, 129, 140
Cunningham, Gene, 202, 203
Cunningham, James, 40
Cunningham, James A., 287

Cunningham, James Andrew, 201, 202
Cunningham, John and Pauline Rucker, 201–203
Cunningham, Marcus, 202
Cunningham, Mary, 227
Cunningham, Mary Elizabeth, 192, 201, 202
Cunningham, Mildred, 140, 202, 203
Cunningham, Pauline, 114, 117, 204–205
Cunningham, Rose, 191
Cunningham, Rosie, 201

D

Dalton, Baby, 110
Dalton, Bobby, 152
Dalton, Charley, 152
Dalton, Doyle, 152
Dalton, Elizabeth, 272–274
Dalton, Etter, 110
Dalton, Michael, 152
Dalton, Walter, 110
Dalton, William, 13
Dalton, Willie, 230
Dalton, Willie "Junior," 194
dance hall, 162–163
Davis, Earline, 140
Davis, Jerry, 141
Davis, Leon, 141
Davis, Mary, 17, 131, 278
Davis, Ronald L. F., 37
Davis, Sally, 129
Davis, Tommie C., 141
Davis, Viola, 141, 189
Decarlos, Antoine, 77
Democratic Convention, 266
Demonbreun and Hatcher families, 108
Demonbreun, Brenda, 154, 194, 217
Demonbreun, Carmack, 217, 287, 288
Demonbreun, Edward Allen, 287, 291
Demonbreun, Homer, 216, 218, 219
Demonbreun, Homer Maurice, 217, 287, 288
Demonbreun, Homer W., 218–219
– Last Will and Testament, 219–221
Demonbreun, Homer Waldorf, 218
Demonbreun, Homer, Sr. "Rooster," 217–219
Demonbreun, Sadie B., 117, 217, 283
Demonbreun, Tim, 127, 141
Demonbreun, Timothy, 217–221
Demumbrane, see Demunbreun
Dennis, Patricia, 79

Derryberry, Mr., 32
desegregation, see segregation/desegregation
Dobson, Aneva, 123
Dobson, Lau Carol, 159
Dobson, Rena, 123
Dobson, W.B. "Bill," 201
Dodson, John, 285
Dodson, Mary, 141
Dodson, Mary Louise, 128
Dodson, Willie, 141
Dotson, Mary Ann, 127
Dotson, Maudell, 2, 12, 108, 114, 116, 133, 134, 254
Dotson, Maudell Parrish, 131, 206
Dotson, Mrs., 242
Dozier, Henry, 74, 79, 274
Dozier, James, 79
Dozier, Mary, 79
Dozier, Samuel, 79
Drew, Charlotte, 283
Drone, Ms., 213
Dudley, Emma, 60
Duncan, Clifton E., 230
Duncan, Eugene, 141
Durango Boot, 209

E

Easley, John, 159
Easley, Larry, 283
Easley, Larry D., Sr., 283
Easley, Lauren, 282–283
Easley, Lesley, 283
Easley, Lindsey, 282–283
Easley, Robert, 110
Elam Mental Health Clinic, 64
Ellis's Cafe, 183
Ellison, Evelena, 123
Ellison, Sina Mai, 123
enslaved persons, 174
Esmon, Don, 159
Esmon, George, 13
Esmond, Betty, 200
Esmond, Betty Ann, 128, 141, 241–242
Esmond, Bo, 141
Esmond, Brenda, 141
Esmond, Charles, 241–242
Esmond, Clarence, 127, 128, 141, 241–242, 277
Esmond, Donna, 172
Esmond, Dorothy Jean, 186, 241
Esmond, Jerry, 129, 142, 241–242

Esmond, Jimmy, 241
Esmond, Jimmy D., 241–242
Esmond, Jimmy D. and Willie Mai, 241–242
Esmond, Louise, 241
Esmond, Mary, 241
Esmond, Robert, 142
Esmond, Rosie, 241
Esmond, Thomas, 241–242
Esmond, Willie, 241
Esmond, Willie Mai, 241–242
Esmonds, 165
Evans, Ethel, 228
– see Anderson, Ethel Evans, 228
Ewing-Beal, Lena, 283
Ewing-Covington, Johnny, 283
Ewing, Bernis, 131
Ewing, Diane, 142, 287, 288
Ewing, DiAnne, 282
Ewing, Essie, 283
Ewing, Joe B., 287
Ewing, Taylor Grant, 40
Ewing, Thomas, Jr., 142
Ewing, Tom, 122
Ewing, Tom Allen, Jr., 287, 289
Ewing, Tom, Sr., 283
Ewing, Will D., 282–283
Ewing, Willie B., 124
Ewing, Willie Frank, 287

F

Ferguson, Alton, 32
Ferguson, John, 32
Ferguson, John and Martha, 28
Fisher, Willie B., 277, 280
Fitzgerald, Charles, 13
Fitzgerald, Jane, 159
Fitzgerald, Louise Shaw, 73
Fleming, Edward, 13
Floyd, Annette, 169
Floyd, Arthur, Jr., 124
Floyd, Bertha Anderson, 228
Floyd, Bessie Lee
– see Jones, Bessie Lee, 167–168
Floyd, Bessie Lee Jones, 169
Floyd, Charles, 287
Floyd, Daisy, 185, 188
Floyd, Dorothy, 227
Floyd, Dwight, 169
Floyd, Isaac, 230

Floyd, James, 40
Floyd, Mary Ann, 154, 187
Floyd, Savannah, 77, 230
Floyd, Thomas, 287
Floyd, Yvonne, 169
Fort Campbell, 60
Frank, Ann Ferguson, 28
Freedmen's Bureau, 115
Frierson, Rev., 282
Fuller, Dan, 32, 33
Fuller, Sam, 6

G

Gaffney, Shaun and Annette, 64
Garrett, James Oscar, 142, 186
Gary, Rev., 282
Gates Tire Company, 77
Genesco, 74, 202
Gentry, Bubba, 32
Gentry, Mrs. Jimmy, 242
Georgia Boot, 209
German, Archy, 6
German, Nicholas Samuel, 190
Givens, Elaine, 159
Glenn, Andreaco Ramaun, 77
Glenn, Antoine Decarlos, 77–78
Glenn, Brandy, 78
Glenn, Bud, 13
Glenn, Carleesa Marshall, 77–78
Glenn, Charles M., Sr., 77
Glenn, Charles Milton III, 77–78
Glenn, Charles Milton, Jr., 77–78
Glenn, Charles, Jr., 142
Glenn, Dasmine, 77–78
Glenn, James and Linda, 78
Glenn, Nikitra Shantel, 77–78
Glenn, Steffon Milano, 77
Glenn, Willie B., 126
Global Walk in Forgiveness, Inc., 63
Goodwin, Bernice Covington, 139, 234
Gordon, Treva, 64
Gosey, Claudia, 159
Gosey, Evelyn, 159
Gray, Carolyn, 169
Greathouse, Bob, 264
Greathouse, Frances, 276–278
Greathouse, Mr., 213
Green Book, 178, 183
Green, Christine Scales, 207

Green, Elizabeth, 103
Greenlee, Bryan, 278–280
Greenlee, Della, 280
Greenlee, Tommy, 277–279
Griffey, Delores Thompson, 212
Grimes, David, 13
Grisham, Mrs., 269

H

Haley, Ben, 283
Haley, J.B., 283
Haley, Sadie, 127, 142
Haley, Willie B., 217–221
Hamilton, Charles, 159
Hamm, Joyce, 159
Hardeman, Charles, 13
Hardeman, Doris, 32
Hardeman, Herbert, 126
Hardemon, Annie/Ann, 239–240
Hardemon, Baxter Herbert [Jr.], 239–240
Hardemon, Baxter Herbert [Sr.], 239–240
Hardemon, Edward L., 239–240
Hardemon, Mattie Hughes, 239
Hardemon, Minnie Mai Bostic, 239
Hardemon, Oscar, Sr., 239
Hardin, Addie Bostick, 70
Hardin, Berry, 128
Hardin, Millie, 192
Harlan, Deonna, 75
Harper, Della, 159
Harris, Barton, 230
Harris, James, 129
Harris, Katherine, 127
Harrises, 165
Hartan, Sam, 110
Hartley, Serrila, 159
Harvey, Brandon, 246
Harvey, Marquinta Hatcher, Dr. – see Hatcher, Marquinta, 246
Hatcher Dairy, 255
Hatcher, Alan Tyrone, 142
Hatcher, Almeda, 244
Hatcher, Andrew, 243–244
Hatcher, Buford, 127
Hatcher, Charlie, 243–244
Hatcher, Clarence, 243–244
Hatcher, Earleen (Biggers), 246
Hatcher, Eli Hugh, 246
Hatcher, Elliot, 244
Hatcher, Era Emma "Sadie" Odell Kinnard, 244
Hatcher, Ester Lee, 244, 246
Hatcher, Gail, 142, 193
Hatcher, George Abram, 252
Hatcher, Gwen, 142, 193
Hatcher, Isham, 244
Hatcher, Jackie, 142, 255
Hatcher, James, 244, 246
Hatcher, James Ewing, 243–244
Hatcher, James Marvin, Sr., 244
Hatcher, Jasper, 168, 271
Hatcher, Jasper "Jay," III, 248
Hatcher, Jasper G., Sr.
Hatcher, Jasper G., Sr., Highway, 248
Hatcher, Jasper G., Sr., 244, 246–248, 284–285
Hatcher, Jasper, IV, 248
Hatcher, Jasper, Jr., 248
Hatcher, Jessie, 246
Hatcher, Jessie Mary, 244
Hatcher, Jimmy, 243–244, 254
Hatcher, John R., 244, 254
Hatcher, Johnny, 243
Hatcher, Kadafi N., 248
Hatcher, Kenneth Xavier, 248
Hatcher, Laeunia, 244–246
Hatcher, Laeunia (Thompson), 245
Hatcher, Lawrence B. / Buford, 244, 246, 257
Hatcher, Lorenzo, 244, 246, 287, 289
Hatcher, Marquinta, 246
Hatcher, Martha Jane, 244
Hatcher, Marvin, 142, 271
Hatcher, Marvin and Sadie, 246
Hatcher, Marvin P., Jr., 244, 246
Marvin P. Hatcher, family, 245
Hatcher, Marvin, Jr., 287, 289
Hatcher, Marvin, Sr., 287, 289
Hatcher, Mary Eunice, 254
Hatcher, Maudene, 245
Hatcher, Maudine, 244–245
Hatcher, Meredith, 244
Hatcher, Meredith and Mariah, family, 243-245
Hatcher, Nathaniel, 127, 143
Hatcher, Ned and Mariah, 254
Hatcher, Ned/Ed, 243–244
Hatcher, Regina, 193
Hatcher, Rosa Moss, 243–244
Hatcher, Sam, 243–244
Hatcher, Simon, 244
Hatcher, Susan, 244

Index

Hatcher, Thelma Thressa Thomas, 246–248
Hatcher, Verleen, 121, 129, 193
Hatcher, Vincent, 131, 143
Hatcher, Vinnie Starnes Reams, 244
Hatcher, William and Lucy Rucker, 244, 254
Hatcher, Willie, 246
Hatcher, Willie E., 245
Hatcher, Willie Ewing, 244
Hatcher, Winnie (Vaughn), 244, 246
Hawkins, Farolyn, 78
Hawkins, Joerina, 78
Hayes, Coach, 13
Haynes, Eva, 159
Henry Horton Highway, 17
Herbert, George T., 184
Hettley's Tavern and Grocery, 177
Hettley's Gas Station, 176
Hettley's Store, 176
Hettley's Tavern and Grocery, 176
Hill, Bernita J., 61
Hill, Deacon Eddie L., 61
Hill, Dr. Cornelius, 64
Hill, Zema W., 230, 276
Hill, Zula M. Garnett, 61
Hillsboro High School, 61
Hodge, Leon, 13
Hodge, Zack, 13
Hogans, Evelyn, 75
Hogue, Charles, 61
Homer Demonbreun farm, 107
Hopkins, Cora Page, 17, 57
Hopkins, Millard, 17, 58
Hopkins, Mr. and Mrs., 57
Hosford, Karen, 270
House, Bob, 276
House, Bybee, 110
House, Martha Ann, 17–19, 57
House, Robert, 129
Houston, Whitney, 88
Howse, Bertha, 127, 143
Howse, Bertha Lou, 208
Howse, Daniel, 287–289
Howse, Daniel O'Neal, 208
Howse, Loretta, 143, 208
Howse, Minnie Kathryn, 226
Howse, Robert, 143, 273–274, 287, 289
Howse, Robert E., 208
Howse, Robert William, 208
Howse, Tom, 230
Hughes, James, 143

Hughes, Langston, 10, 25, 265
Hughes, Louise, 191
Hunt, Sandra, 285
Hyde, Charles, 195
Hyde, Peter/Pete, 6, 273

I

Integration, 199–20, 267, 269–270
Intermarriage, 174
Ito, Joichi, 43
Ivery, Connie, 159

J

Jack Shaw, 6
Jackson, Kenneth, 77–78
Jackson, Mr. and Mrs. Dudley, 93
Jamison, Uncle Edward, 30
Jarrett, Thomas, 285
Jenkins, Bessie, 168
Jim Crow laws, 33–37, 160
Jim Crow South, 23
Jim Johnson Picnic, 224
John L. Jordan Store, 162–163
John Little farm, 98
Johnson, Annie M., 127
Johnson, Annie Mai, 164–165
Johnson, Beatrice, 192
Johnson, Bessie, 164, 271
Johnson, Betty Lou, 223
Johnson, Charles Lawrence, 208
Johnson, Clifton, 278–280
Johnson, Edward, 133, 134
Johnson, Elsie M., 168
Johnson, Eugene and Maggie, 164
Johnson, Eula, 277–279
Johnson, Eula Jones, 114
Johnson, Frank, 143
Johnson, Fred, 56
Johnson, James, 15
Service Station, 15
Johnson, James Weldon, 302–303
Johnson, Jesse, 192Johnson, Jessie, 152
Johnson, Jimmie, 164
Johnson, Jimmy, 128
Johnson, Martha, 164, 283
Johnson, Mary Ruth, 68
Johnson, Mildred, 68
Johnson, Pattie, 154
Johnson, Paulene, 164

Johnson, Peggy, 143
Johnson, Reginald, 127, 143
Johnson, Richard, 152, 192
Johnson, Wanda, 121, 129, 143
Johnson, William B., 68
Johnson, Willie Eve, 283
Jones-Ewing, Lizzie, 283
Jones, Alice, 277
Jones, Anderson, 277
Jones, Andrew, 285
Jones, Anita L. Carter, 193, 254–255
Jones, Anthony, 82–83
Jones, Ashley, 278–280
Jones, Bessie Lee, 167–168
Jones, Bettie Jean, 167–168
Jones, Beulah, 124
Jones, Brenda, 159
Jones, Carolyn, 278
Jones, Chance, 82
Jones, Charles Lee, 167–168
Jones, Charlie Frank, 167–168
Jones, Chasity, 278–280
Jones, Chera, 83
Jones, Cohen, 82
Jones, Colie, 112
Jones, Corbin, 83
Jones, Darnell, 280
Jones, Elizabeth, 123
Jones, Eula, 124
Jones, Eula Lee, 126
Jones, Fannie Lou, 123
Jones, Frances Biggers, 112
Jones, Frances Kay, 199, 213
Jones, Hill, 276
Jones, Houston, 143
Jones, Jalen, 82
Jones, Jerry, 143
Jones, JoAnn, 199, 213
Jones, John L., 168
Jones, Juanita Ridley, 81
Jones, Keland, 83
Jones, Kristle, 278
Jones, Lamont, 82
Jones, Lewis, 122, 276, 277
Jones, Lolie, 112
Jones, Louie and Texarue, 188
Jones, Marcus, 167–168
Jones, Martha L., 144
Jones, Marvin Henry, 167–168
Jones, Mary, 195

Jones, Mary "Mai," 167–168
Jones, Mary and Joanne, 191
Jones, Melvin Eugene, 167–168
Jones, Michael, 82
Jones, Nancy, 192
Jones, Nettie Mae, 167–168
Jones, Peggy, 199, 213
Jones, Ramona, 199, 213
Jones, Robbie D., 1, 173, 183
Jones, Sadie, 123
Jones, Sadie Pearl, 123
Jones, T.B. farm, 7
Jones, Tanaa, 83
Jones, Thomas, 82, 83, 167–168
Jones, Thomas Edward, Sr., 169
Jones, Tina, 278
Jones, William, 168
Jones, William C., 168
Jones, William D., 144
Jones, William James, 12, 40
Jones, Willie, 279–280
Jordan farm, 242
Jordan Beauty Shop, 162–163
Jordan Teen Center, 162–163
Jordan, Addie Frances, 230
Jordan, Albert, 114
Jordan, Annie May, 123
Jordan, Bernard, 127, 128, 144
Jordan, Clatie Lytle, 162–163
Jordan, Clatie Mai, 165
Jordan, Edgar, 122
Jordan, Fannie Mai, 144
Jordan, Fred, 121
Jordan, Henry Ester, 11
Jordan, Irma, 122
Jordan, Jasmine, 202
Jordan, Jason, 202
Jordan, Jerry, 236
Jordan, Jerry Wayne, Sr., 144
Jordan, Joe Siah, 202
Jordan, John L., 5, 29, 30, 117, 136, 162–163
Jordan, John Willie, 110
Jordan, Michael, 129
Jordan, Mildred Cunningham, 202
Jordan, Mildred Marie, 209
Jordan, Nora, 159
Jordan, R.L., 110
Jordan, Randall, 144
Jordan, Rosie Bell, 123
Jordan, Thelma, 196

Jordan, William B., Jr., 287
Jordan, Willie, 278
Jordans, 165

K

Kappa Alpha Psi Fraternity, 234
Kelton, Howard, 159
Key, Ezekiel, 83
King, Martin Luther King, Jr., 293
King, Mr., 213
King, Tandy, 213–214
Kirkland Baseball Team, 38
Kirkland farmhouses, 174
Kirkland map, 104
Kirkland Masonic Lodge, 184
Kirkland Roadside Businesses, 173–183
Kirkland School, 1
Kirkland Service Center, 181
Kirkview, 174
Korean War, 59
Kroger, 77
Kroger Warehouse, 247

L

L&N Railroad, 92
LaBelle, Pattie, 88
Lampley, Vickie, 159
Lane, Douglas, 13
Lane, Hattie Boleyjack
– see Boleyjack, Hattie, 153
Lane, Hattie Ruth, 49
Lanier, Earlene, 116, 124, 133 135, 190
Lanier, Emma D., 283
Lanier, Hurley, Jr., 124, 126
Lanier, Mamie, 124
Lanier, Mrs., 12, 158, 242
Lanier, Ms., 213
Lanier, Nannie, 2, 116, 127, 128, 129, 133, 254
Lanier, Nannie Lee, 114, 116
Lanier, Theresa, 124
Lavender, Elizabeth, 226
Lavender, Richard and Mary, 226
Lawrence, Felix, 230
Leach, Clara, 154
Leach, John, 144
Leach, Robbie, 144
Lee Robert Howard, 59–60
Lee, Brown, 56
Lee, Dinah, 60
Lee, Dr., 64
Lee, Eula Pearl, 126
Lee, Eula Pearl Lee, 124
Lee, Hettie Fudge, 59–60
Lee, James Alexander, 60
Lee, John Thomas, 277
Lee, Labora "Rick," 101
Lee, Leonard, 159
Lee, Ms., 213
Lee, Patricia, 144, 154
Lee, Robert Anderson, 59–60
Lee, Tom, 124
Lee, Tommy, 126
Lee, Willie Jean, 231–232
Lewis, Betty, 277
Lewis, Ken, 166
Little, John W., 46
Little, John, farm, 46
Lloyd, Annette, 192
Lloyd, Bertha, 62, 64, 192
Lloyd, Elder Richard, 93, 192, 274, 277
Lloyd, Richard A., 62, 64
Lockridge, Dorothy, 79
Lockridge, Ellis, 13
Locust Ridge Cemetery, 168
Lucas, Vel, 13
Luster, Larry, 287
Lyons, Irene K. Scales, 207

M

Mangrum, Barbara, 159
Mangrum, Bill, 159
Mangrum, Jennie, 159
Manier, Balim, 281
Map of College Grove (1878), 198
Map of Scales and Webb plantations, 175
Martin, Jerry, 75
Martin, Zoelithia, 75
Mason, Brandon L., 247, 285–286
Mason, Carolyn Wray, 231–232
Matthews, Delores Vaughn, 38, 39, 51–52
Maxie, 258
Maxwell, Shirley, 159
May Day Festival, 120
May Lizzie, 72
Mayberry, Christine, 144, 194, 196
Mayberry, Thomas, 128

Mayes, Ruby
— see Anderson, Ruby Mayes, 228
Mayes, Willie Gene and Dorothy, 186
Mayfield, Mr., 213
Mays Hosiery Mill, 213
Mays, Willie Gene, 195
McCaroll, James, 64
McCathern, Claude, 282–283
McClain, Claude, 144
McClain, Ed, 102, 123
McClain, Edwin, 227
McClain, Edwin and Virginia, 229
McClain, Edwin E., 170
McClain, Eugene, 124, 129, 193, 257
McClain, James, 123
McClain, Mamie, 126
McClain, Margaret, 124
McClain, Margaret J.
— see Coleman, Margaret J. McClain, 170
McClain, Margaret Jean, 126
McClain, Mary E., 110
McClain, Valerie Scales, 193
McClain, Virginia, 124, 126, 277
McClain, Virginia Anderson, 170, 227
McClain, William, 144
McCord, Alvin, 287
McCord, Charles, 145
McCord, Chevalier, 223
McCord, Clarence, 129, 145
McCord, Genita, 223–224
McCord, Jackie, 287
McCord, Maudene Hatcher, 245
McCord, Samuel, Jr., 223, 224
McCord, Sereta, 129, 145, 214
McCord, Seretha, 145
McCord, Shakiya, 223–224
McCord, Shila, 223
McCord, Tonia, 223
McEntire, Reba, 88
McLemore, Bobby, 145
McLemore, Ennie Mae, 145
McLemore, Florence, 60
McLemore, Mariah, 145
McMurray, Dave and Mary Scales, farm, 47
McMurray, Mary Elizabeth Scales, 53–54
Mercer, Ann III, 78
Ministers and Evangelists, 271
Mitchell, Elder James, 61
Moody, Miss, 112
Moody, Mrs., 165, 242

Moody, Ms., 213
Moody, Vella, 2, 114, 116, 133, 134, 254–255
Moore, Harold, 13
Moore, Rev., 282
Moreland, George, 75
Moreland, Vivian, 75
Morris, Ann, 78
Morton, Ira, 98
Morton, Jacqueline, 75, 76
Morton, JarKaveus, 75
Morton, Jonas "Pop," 187
Morton, Joshua Matthew, 74
Morton, Mack, 75
Morton, Martha Shaw, 73
Mother Board, 68
Mother's Board, 170
MP Brothers, 247
Muhanda, Louise Batey, 77
Murdic, Billy, 13
Murdic, John, 13
Murphy, Pierre, 202, 278
Murray, A.F., 282
Murray, Betty Boleyjack, 23, 49
Murray, Josie Ewing, 283
Murray, Josie L. Ewing, 192
Murray, Milton, 283
Murray, Nichole, 145
Murray, Paula, 282
Murray, Thomas, 283

N

Nance, Mary, 159
Nash, Mr., 273
Nashville Rescue Mission, 62
Negro Elementary Schools, 113
Nevils, Robbie Morton, 101
Nipper, Dr. Stephanie, 64
Nolensville Utility District, 17
Norris, Addie, 145
Norris, Aggie, 278, 279
Norris, Aggie Jane, 166
Norris, Annie Mary Anderson, 227
Norris, Antonio, 166
Norris, Brenda, 121, 129, 145
Norris, Brenda Janice, 166
Norris, Charles, 123, 145
Norris, Cordell, 253
Norris, Dexter, 131, 253
Norris, Erma, 283

Index

Norris, Esther, 145
Norris, Evan, 287
Norris, Fred, 252–253
Norris, George, 145
Norris, Holly, 278–279
Norris, Houston, 227
Norris, Ike, 13
Norris, Janice, 146, 280
Norris, Jennie, 278, 280
Norris, John, 146, 166
Norris, John C., 166
Norris, Joyce, 253
Norris, Louise, 278, 280
Norris, Mamie Robertson, 253
Norris, Marie, 146, 166
Norris, Mary, 131
Norris, Ramona, 194, 196, 253
Norris, Robert, 146, 166, 200
Norris, Ross, 114, 177
Norris, Sarah, 131
Norris, Shanita, 253, 287, 289
Norris, Tony, 287
Norris, Tiffany, 278
Norris, Travis, 253
Norris, William "Bill" and Elizabeth Floyd, 252
Norris, William, Sr., 252
Norris, William, Sr. and Martha Demunbreun, 252
North, Dorothy, 133, 134

O

Oasis Court and Cafe, 179
Oasis Motel, 180, 282
Oasis Restaurant, 179–180
Obama, Barack, 294, 295, 296–301
Obama, Michelle, 294–295
Odom, Lelia May, 40
Ogilvie, Addie Marie Ridley, 1, 19, 57–58, 84, 86–87, 147, 268–270, 292
Ogilvie, Anna and Samuel, 223
Ogilvie, Barbara, 186
Ogilvie, Betty, 186, 194
Ogilvie, Candace, Dr., 84–85
Ogilvie, Clara Ann, 191
Ogilvie, Dr. Candace, 100
Ogilvie, Frank, 227
Ogilvie, Frank and Marie, 78
Ogilvie, Frank III, 84–85
Ogilvie, Frank J., 271
Ogilvie, Frank J., Jr., 287, 289
Ogilvie, Frank J., Sr., 100
Ogilvie, Frank James, Jr., 84
Ogilvie, Frank, Jr., 146
Ogilvie, Frank, Sr., 56, 84, 229
Ogilvie, Frankie, 85
Ogilvie, George, 40, 186, 271, 277, 278, 279, 280
Ogilvie, Gerald, 277, 278, 279, 280
Ogilvie, J.S., 222, 228
Ogilvie, Kennedie, 85
Ogilvie, Libbie, 85
Ogilvie, Marie,
– see Ogilvie, Marie Ridley, 57, 75, 89, 232
Ogilvie, Mary, 278
Ogilvie, Mary L. Jones, 112
Ogilvie, Minnie, 277
Ogilvie, Minnie Anderson, 84, 170, 227, 229
Ogilvie, Minnie Mary Anderson, 100
Ogilvie, Rachel, 223
Ogilvie, Rachel Webb, 223
Ogilvie, Sara, 84–85
Ogilvie, Valerie, 84–85
Ogilvie, Wanda, 278, 280
Oglesby, Anna, 146
Oglesby, Annie Mildred, 128
Oglesby, Bertha, 123, 278
Oglesby, Brianna, 75
Oglesby, Climmie, 123
Oglesby, Geneva "Sis," 212, 213
Oglesby, Gerald, 64
Oglesby, Larry, 146
Oglesby, Leon, 124
Oglesby, Margaret, 127, 128
Oglesby, Margaret Elaine Carney, 256
Oglesby, Margaret Louise "Pee Wee," 256–257, 258–259
Oglesby, Mary Lean, 124
Oglesby, Robbie, 146
Oglesby, Sarah, 124, 126, 277
Oglesby, Thomas, 128, 146
Oliver, Ernest, 146
Oliver, Nancy, 146
Outlaws, softball team, 13
Outlaws, the, 40
Overton, Janie, 60
Owen, Sarah, 60
Owens, Cynthia, 159
Owens, Daisy, 283

P

Page-Hopkins Place, 17
Page, Cora, 17
Parks, Irene, 272–275
Parnell, Rev., 282
Parrish, Noble, 209
Parrish, Robert, 6
Parton, Dolly, 88
Pate, Georgia, 51
Pate, Willie, 51
Patterson, 5
Patton, Anna Margaret, 110
Patton, Annie, 2, 88, 133, 134
Patton, Annie Elizabeth, 114, 116, 254
Patton, Annie Hunter, 130
Patton, Annie Mai Johnson, 164
Patton, Barnell, 129
Patton, Carl, 282
Patton, Carrie, 75
Patton, Charles, 127
Patton, Delores, 127
Patton, Edward Lee, 127
Patton, Elizabeth, 75, 280
Patton, Ella Mae, 75
Patton, Ella Mai Hardemon, 239–240
Patton, Fannie Bell Lee, 101
Patton, George, 11
Patton, Henrie Ester, 74
Patton, Herbert, 135
Patton, J.C., 13, 14, 40
Patton, J.C., Jr., 11, 12, 75
Patton, J.C., Sr., 11, 56, 74
Patton, Jack and Lily Jordan, 249
Patton, Jimmie, 110
Patton, Larry, 146
Patton, Larry Herbert, 155–156
Patton, Linda, 283
Patton, Mamie, 110
Patton, Martha Ann, 11
Patton, Mary, 110
Patton, Mildred Lee,
– see Webb, Mildred Lee Patton 249
Patton, Mrs. Thomas, 103
Patton, Ms., 213, 242
Peacock, Buela S. Scales, 207
Peacock, Curry and Gail, 64
Pearl Harbor, 59
Pendergrass, Thelma, 168
Perkins, 6
Perkins, Alexander, 75, 76
Perkins, Andy, 280
Perkins, Belinda, 278
Perkins, Claude, 13
Perkins, Henry, 278, 279
Perkins, Jackie, 278
Perkins, James and Henry, 195
Perkins, James K., 14, 40
Perkins, Jerry, 287
Perkins, John and Henry, 40
Perkins, Ke'aria, 75
Perkins, Lea, 147
Perkins, Mamie, 278
Perkins, Ruth Ann, 147
Perkins, Thomas H., 215
Perkins, Tina, 147
Perkins, Tom, 56
Perkins, Tyrika, 278
Perkins, W.O.N., 215
Perkins, Wash, 56
Perkins, Whitney, 278
Peters, Mary, 159
Petersburg, 5
Peterson, Ann, 66–67
Peterson, Judge Jim, 66–67
Phillips, Betty, 147
Phillips, Ernest, 147
Phillips, George Russell, 147
Phillips, Judith, 78, 147
Phillips, Kent, 78
Phillips, Michael, 147
Pickens, Marquia, 278, 280
Pointer, Montrell, Jr., 256
Polk, Beulah Lee Jones, 126
Polk, Frank, Sr., 75
Polk, Mamie, 75
Polk, Mamie F. Patton, 11
Pollard, Malachi, 204–205
Pope, Beverly Ann, 74, 76
Pope, William, 13
Possum Trot, 5, 39
Powell, Annette, 79
Powers, Faye, 159
Price, Mackenzie Dai'Shawn, 88
Price, Sisoukrath Xander, 88
Public Schools of Williamson County, survey, 105–106
Puckett Brothers Store, 56
Puckett, James, 56

Index

Pullman, George, 35

R

R.H. Boyd Publishing, 213
raccoon hunting, 31–32
Randolph, Margaret Ann, 49
Randolph, Margaret Boleyjack, 98–99
Ransom, Mattie, 278–279
Rawls, Emoni and Emaji, 82
Ray, Mary Jane, 159
Reams, Hattie Louise, 114, 116, 135
Reams, Jessie, 244
Reams, Manervie, 244
Reams, Mrs., 12
Redmond farm, 215
Redmond, Lillian, 103
Redmond, Lucy, 215
Redmond, Mamie Lou, 123
Redmond, Peggy Jane, 215
Redmond, T.E., 215
Redmond, T.J., 215
Redmond, Will, 215
Redmond, Young, 215
Reynolds, Bill, 13
Richardson, William, 64
Ridley, Addie Marie, 147
– see Ogilvie, Addie Marie Ridley
Ridley, Anna, 193
Ridley, Annie, 280
Ridley, Annie M., 127, 128
Ridley, Annie Mary, 57, 87, 89, 271
Ridley, Araminta, 69
Ridley, Araminta Shaw, 86, 89
Ridley, Babe, 17
Ridley, Dorothy, 147
Ridley, Dorothy J., 87
Ridley, Etta M., 128
Ridley, Frank J., 87, 89
Ridley, George, 88, 89, 147, 159, 271
Ridley, George E., 87–89
Ridley, George Edward, 88
Ridley, James, 57, 69, 129, 147, 152, 271, 287, 290
Ridley, James W., 87, 89
Ridley, James, Jr., 86
Ridley, Juanita, 87, 184, 194
Ridley, Marie (Ogilvie), 127, 192
Ridley, Martha (Anderson), 57, 127, 269
Ridley, Morton, 148
Ridley, Shawna Lee, 88–89

Ridley, Tina, 148, 280
Ridley, Will, 102
Ridley, Will "Babe," 15
Ridley, William, 87, 89
Ridleys, 165
Riley, William, 148
Roberts, Darius, 278–279
Roberts, Fred, 278
Roberts, Mai E., 168
Roberts, Mary "Mai" Emma Jones
– see Jones, Mary "Mai," 167
Roberts, Miesha, 278–279
Roberts, Renae, 278, 280
Robertson, Mamie, 253
Robinson, Edward, 13
Robinson, Jackie, 39
Rodgers, Marshall, 148, 287
Rodgers, Mildred, 168
Rogers, Marshall, 117
Rollins, Gail, 159
Rucker, Annie Bell, 123
Rucker, David and Nettie, 223
Rucker, Ella, 40
Rucker, Eula Pearl, 123
Rucker, Florine, 223
Rucker, Frank, 278–279
Rucker, Hattie, 192
Rucker, Howard, 148, 271, 278, 279, 280
Rucker, Jessica, 280
Rucker, Lillia P., 128
Rucker, Lillie Mai, 123
Rucker, Loletha, 280
Rucker, Louise, 148
Rucker, Lucinda, 114, 134
Rucker, Mildred, 278
Rucker, Mildred Hardin, 277
Rucker, Mrs., 125
Rucker, Mrs. Lucinda, 124
Rucker, Sammie, 148
Rucker, Sharon, 278
Rucker, Thomas, 278
Ruckers, 165
Rudy Farms, 13, 40
Russell, Bernice, 148
Russell, Betty Anderson, 227
Russell, Christine Lawrence, 230
Russell, Gus, 276
Russell, Henry, 227
Russell, Herbert, 129, 131–148
Russell, Hubert, 148

Russell, Jerry, 278, 280
Russell, Jimmy, 131
Russell, Joe Billy, 148, 192, 195
Russell, John, 127, 196
Russell, Lillie, 277
Russell, Patsy, Rosa Lee Jones, 230
Russell, Robert, 149
Russell, Sharon, 149
Russell, Susie Mae, 186
Russell, Will, 230
Rutherford County, 5
Rutledge, Dave, 31–32
Ryan, Jane, 159
Ryan, Tommy, 159

S

Sawyers, Annie, 277
Sawyers, Annie Lou Howse Johnson, 208
Sawyers, Arthur Lee, 208
Sawyers, Caroline, 208
Sawyers, Clara Belle, 208–209
Sawyers, Clifton, 209–210, 287, 290
Sawyers, Cora, 133, 135, 194
Sawyers, Cora Sue, 188–119
Sawyers, Dorothy, 149, 159, 194
Sawyers, Emma, 209
Sawyers, Hewitt, 188, 189, 271
Sawyers, James O'Neal, 208
Sawyers, John Henry, 209
Sawyers, Lena, 210
Sawyers, Mamie, 209
Sawyers, Paul, 127, 128, 149, 271, 287, 290
Sawyers, Paul David, 290
Sawyers, Ruth Ann, 209
Sawyers, Sara, 188, 209, 210
Sawyers, Sue, 116
Sawyers, Walter, 39
Sawyers, Will Amos, Jr., 208
Sawyers, Will Amos, Sr., 208–209
Sawyers, William, 208
Scales plantation, 174
Scales Cafe, 178
Scales Cemetery, 176
Scales family farm, 115
Scales Family, 174
Scales Roadside Inn, 179
Scales, A.G., 176
Scales, Abb, 116, 282
– see Joe Abb Scales, 116

Scales, Absalom, 281
Scales, Absalom Gollehugh, 174; house, 181
Scales, Absalum and Eliza D., 115
Scales, Addie B., 207
Scales, Alberta, 126
Scales, Alma Muse, 50
Scales, Annie Well, 114, 117, 135, 164, 188, 197, 242, 283
Scales, Bessie, 122, 123
Scales, Bobby, 124
Scales, Buela S., 207
Scales, Charlie Lavender, 182
Scales, children, 197
Scales, Christine, 207
Scales, Cora, 174
Scales, Della Wilson, 20, 207
Scales, Delora, 174
Scales, Dr. Sam, 174
Scales, Dr. Samuel Webb, 174
Scales, Earl, 123, 176
Scales, Edd, 114
Scales, Ella, 283
Scales, Ellis, 178, 252
Scales, Emma D., 123
Scales, Eula D., 207
Scales, Felix, 124, 271
Scales, Frank, 123
Scales, Georgie E., 207
Scales, Gladys, 283
Scales, Hazel, 123
Scales, Hetley, 115
Scales, Hettley Carter, 176
Scales, Huck, 123
Scales, Irene K., 207
Scales, James, 6
Scales, Jennie "Jane" Cardwell King, 175–176
Scales, Jerry, 174
Scales, Joe Abb, 116, 207
Scales, Joe Ellis, 123
Scales, Joe Frank, 207
Scales, John, 123
Scales, John Kirkland, 149, 155–156
Scales, John L., 207
Scales, Joseph G., House, 174
Scales, Josie Ann, 115–117, 154, 197, 281–283
Scales, Lilly Mae, 187
Scales, Louisa, 174
Scales, Mai, 123
Scales, Mrs., 157
Scales, Nellie Jane, 123

Scales, Perse "Percy," 176
Scales, Preston, 114, 136, 164, 259
Scales, Preston, Jr., 117
Scales, Robbie, 127, 149, 154, 183, 197, 283
Scales, Robbie Lee McClain, 178
Scales, Robert, 149
Scales, Robert Preston, 127
Scales, Sadie Pearl, 278
Scales, T.E. Jr., Esso Service Station, 183
Scales, T.E. Jr., Service Station and Cafe, 178
Scales, T.E., Jr., 178
Scales, Thomas Ellis, 174–176
Scales, Thomas Ellis, Jr., 183
Scales, Thomas Ellis, Jr. "Little Ellis," 178
Scales, Thomas Houston, 207
Scales, Urban Samuel, 181–182
Scales, Urban, Dairy Bar, 182
Scales, Urban, Service Station, 182
Scales, W.P., 53–54
Scales, Willa, 283
Scales, Willeva, 123
Scales, William Flem Herbert, 178
Scales, William James, 207
Schools
- Allison Chapel School, 107–108, 116, 208, 224, 246
- College Grove High, 69, 117, 213–214, 200, 223, 242, 252, 258, 264, 265, 266–267, 269–270
- Franklin High, 255
- Franklin Training, 99, 166, 202, 208, 227
- Green Grove, 77, 98, 101–103, 107, 109, 114, 116, 268
- Huntsville, 107, 111, 116
- J.C. Napier, 98
- Kirkland, 69, 77, 86, 88, 99, 107, 112–152, 158, 160, 164–166, 174, 202, 213, 224, 227, 242, 249, 252, 253, 254–255, 258, 268-270
- Kirkland School, fire, 114
- Kirkland, formulation, 115–117
- Kirkland, new building, 114
- Lipscomb Elementary, 158
- Life Christian University, 61
- Locust Ridge, 107, 108, 116, 252
- Nashville Tech, 61
- Natchez High, 69, 99, 161, 242, 258, 269
- Natchez High Shrine Bowl Champions, 13
- Nolensville Elementary, 107
- Page High, 117, 203
- Patton Chapel, 107, 110, 114, 116
- Pearl High, 249
- Queen's Chapel, 208
- Tennessee A&I College, 12, 51, 233–234, 249
- Tennessee State University, 12, 233
- Trinity Elementary, 258
- University of Memphis, 61
- Westwood Community School, 242
Scott, Yvonne, 285
Scruggs, Annette, 159
Scruggs, Lillian, 159
Scruggs, William, 13
Scruggs, Willie Mae, 77
segregation/desegregation, 26, 55, 114, 115, 160, 235, 242, 266, 299
Selmer, Walter, 13
Sewell, Paul, 159
Shady Grove Trail, 277
Shannon, Annie, 277
Shaw, Araminta
- see Ridley, Araminta Shaw, 72–73
Shaw, George, 72–73
Shaw, Hattie, 75, 76
Shaw, James, 50, 228
Shaw, Jennie Mae, 72
Shaw, Lemon, 75
Shaw, Louise, 72
Shaw, Mack, 72
Shaw, Martha, 72
Shaw, Mattie Lee Wilson, 20, 72–73
Shaw, Ovaline, 72–73
Shaw, Robert, 72, 73
Shaw, Thomas, 72–73, 102, 103
Shaw, Walter, 72
Shaw, Will D. and Sallie Wilson, 103
Shaw, Willie Dee, 72
Shaw, Woodrow, 72
Shaw. Sallie, 72
Sheffield, Eula Pearl, 223
Shelton, C., 123
Shelton, Cora, 283
Shelton, Julius, 123
Shelton, Mrs., 101
Shelton, Wayne, 127
Shiloh Missionary Baptist Church, 61
Shirling, Ginger, 1
Shrine Bowl, 12
Simmons, Melbra, 64
Slavery, 7
Slaves, 6
Smith Brothers Funeral Directors, 168
Smith, Bill, 278

Smith, Hattie, 278, 280
Smith, Hattie Floyd, 149
Smith, Henry L., 168
Smith, Melvin J., 168
Smith, R.G., 20
Smith, Royden G., Sr., 21
Smithson, Clarence, 209, 285
Smithson, Clarence and Sara, 209, 210
Smithson, Derrick, 149, 209, 211
Smithson, Jennifer, 209, 211
Smithson, Terrence A., 149
Smithson, Timothy Scott, 149, 209, 211
Smotherman, Carol, 1
Solomon, Ernestine, 283
Southall, Richard, 13
Sowell, Ellowese, 49
Spann, Janice, 159
Spann, Louise, 93
Spanntown Road, 17
Sparkman, Donna, 280
Spencer, C.B., 13
Spencer, Patricia, 159
Spencer, Willie, 159
Starnes, Epp, 53–54, 99, 102–103, 117, 136
Starnes, Jesse, 149
Starnes, Mal, Jr., 110
Starnes, Mamie Bostick King, 109
Starnes, Willie, 110
State Route 11, 173
State Route 16, 173
Stellar Gospel Music Awards, 88
Stinson, Jerre, 159
Strawther, Addie B., 124
Strawther, Jackie, 131, 150
Strawther, Joe Ernest, 124
Strawther, Michael, 131
Strawther, Mike, 150
Strawther, William, 124
Sturbridge Point, 215
Sulphur Dell Park, 14, 41
Sunset Park, 14
Survey of Public Schools of Williamson County, 105–106, 113
Sylvan Retreat, 174

T

Taylor, Harry, Store, 237–238
Taylor, Harry and Mildred, 237–238
Taylor, J.F., 274
Taylor, Norma, 78
Taylor, Pattie, 114, 116
Taylor, Pattie Davis, 101–103, 134, 254
Tennessee Poultry, 166
Tennessee Prison for Women, 62
Terry, Pastor and Sirvela, 64
Thomas, Eddie B., 283
Thomas, Edwin E., 282
Thomas, Hamp, 32
Thomas, Thelma Thressa
– see Hatcher, Thressa, 246–247
Thompson-Easley, Deborah, 283
Thompson, Aletha, 154
Thompson, Alma, 283
Thompson, Alma Wray, 122
Thompson, Anita, 212
Thompson, Chris, 280
Thompson, Cindy, 150
Thompson, Clarence Alexander, 212
Thompson, Clarence and Ovie, 99
Thompson, Delores, 127, 212–214
Thompson, Ella, 283
Thompson, Ella D., 218–219
Thompson, Geneva, 132, 230
Thompson, Geneva "Sis" Oglesby, 212, 213
Thompson, Hubert, 150, 236
Thompson, James "Pete," 150, 255, 287, 291
Thompson, Jessie, 133, 135
Thompson, Jimmy, 114, 117
Thompson, Jimmy G., Sr., 287–290
Thompson, Jimmy Green, 135
Thompson, Jimmy, Jr., 282
Thompson, Jimmy, Sr., 122, 282
Thompson, Joe, 123
Thompson, Joey, 280
Thompson, Laeunia Thompson
– see Hatcher, Laeunia, 246
Thompson, Lizzie Murphy, 260
Thompson, Nicholas Austin, 96–97
Thompson, Oscar, Oscar Lee, 123, 287, 290
Thompson, Ovie, 207, 237
Thompson, Ovie Jane Wilson, 20, 21, 260–263
Thompson, Pete, 150, 255
Thompson, Regina, 280
Thompson, Robin, 121, 129, 150, 212–214
Thompson, Sadie B., 123
Thompson, Sherrdon, 150
Thompson, Theodore, 127, 199, 213, 287, 291
Thompson, Thomas Theodore, 212
Thompson, William, 150

Index

Thompson, William and Alma Wray, 219
Thompson, William Clarence, 260, 263
Thompson, William Hubert, 40
Thompson, William Wilson, 207, 212–213, 263
Thompson, William Wilson, Jr., 212, 287, 291
Thompson, William, Sr., 122
Thompson, Willie B., 114, 117, 283
Tomlin, Sandra, 159
Triune, 5, 6
Tucker, Billy, 110
Tucker, Charles, H., 271, 287, 290
Tucker, Hazel, 226
Tucker, Hazel and Charles, 186
Tucker, Louis, 110
Tucker, Mackene, 110
Tucker, Olvie, 110
Tucker, Sallie Ann, 110
Tullos, Emma, 186
Tullos, Pete, 186
Turner, Bettie Jean Jones, 167–168
Turner, George, 78
Turner, Jason, 78
Turner, William, 78
Turpin, Mamie, 103

U

U.S. 31A, 173
U.S. 41A, 173
U.S. Army, 37, 59, 162, 202
Unknown, Cora Ann, 126
Unknown, student 1, 151
Unknown, student 2, 151

V

Varsity Cheerleaders, 200
Vaughn, "Tunnie," 96–97
Vaughn, Ada Mae, 51–52, 189
Vaughn, Annie, 75
Vaughn, Annie Margaret, 11
Vaughn, Annie Margaret Patton, 96–97
Vaughn, Charles, 124, 150, 252
Vaughn, Delores, 190
– see Matthews, Delores Vaughn, 38, 39, 51, 52, 190
Vaughn, Geraldine, 51–52
Vaughn, Gloria, 51, 152
Vaughn, Hutton, 39, 51–52
Vaughn, James T., 150
Vaughn, Jessie Hatcher
– see Hatcher, Jessie, 246
Vaughn, John Leslie, 39, 51–52, 189
Vaughn, Juanita, 150, 195
Vaughn, Lillian, 51
Vaughn, Mary Frances, 51
Vaughn, O.W., Jr., 127
Vaughn, O'Neal, 124, 189, 252
Vaughn, Richard, 51–52
Vaughn, Richard, Jr., 150
Vaughn, Robert, 189
Vaughn, Robert "Monk," 51–52
Vaughn, Sherry, 151
Vaughn, Thomas "Jack," 51–52
Vaughn, Tony, 282
Vaughn, Vera, 151
Vaughn, Virgil O'Neal, 51–52
Vaughn, Wesley, 152
Vaughn, Winnie, 51–52, 114, 117
Vaughn, Winnie M.
– see Hatcher, Winnie, 245, 246
Vaughns, 165
Videll, Mrs., 102
Vietnam, 202
Village of Flowers, A, 88
voting, 29, 30

W

Walden, Caroline Sawyers, 208
Walden, John Henry, 278, 290
Walden, Thelma Jordan, 162–163
Walker, Mrs., 123
Waller, Elton Lee, 61 Walter, Cathy, 265
Wanetta, 195
Warren, Peggy, 159
Warwick, Rick, 1, 2, 215–216, 217
Washington, William J., 75
Waterway, Sandra, 64
Watkins, Rev., 282
Webb family, 174
Webb plantation, 174
Webb Family Cemetery, 174
Webb, Donzetta, 151, 159, 249–251
Webb, Dr. William Smith, 174
Webb, Elliott, 151, 249–251, 271
Webb, Elliott G., Sr., 287–290
Webb, Geraldine, 128, 151, 249–251
Webb, Gertrude, 283
Webb, Gertrude Woods, 249
Webb, James, 174

Webb, Judge, 117, 136, 282
Webb, Judge, Jr., 114, 123, 249, 271, 287, 290
Webb, Judge, Sr., 249, 287
Webb, Judy, 151, 249–251
Webb, Mildred Lee Patton, 249
Webb, Rachel, 223
Webb, Tish, 114, 117, 123, 132, 135, 251
Webb, Tisha, 283
Webb, Tishie, 251
Webb, Tony, 249 251
Webb, Will Harris, 122
Webb, William Felix, House, 174
Webb, Zennia, 151, 249–251
Welch, Joseph May, family, 166
Werthan Bag Company, 239
Wetzel, Jaylan, 202
Wetzel, Lauryn, 202
Wheeler, Patricia Lee
– see Lee, Patricia, 153
Whidby, Sue, 159
Whitehead, Mary, 230
Wilkerson, Gianna Reign, 88
Wilkerson, Mon'Torre Dewane, 88
Wilkerson, Torey Wayne, Jr., 88
Williams farm, 11
Williams, ?, 151
Williams, Anthony, 75
Williams, Betty Lou, 98
Williams, Beverly, 131, 151
Williams, Brady, 75
Williams, Carl, 75, 76
Williams, Carlton, Jr., 75
Williams, Charles, 75, 76
Williams, Cheryl, 75
Williams, Colleen, 134
Williams, Dr. Novella, 64
Williams, Essex, 75
Williams, James Alfred, 189
Williams, Kenneth Eugene, 74, 76
Williams, Larry, 75, 76, 151
Williams, LeRoy, 75
Williams, Lillie, 190
Williams, Linda Boleyjack, 157–159
Williams, Linda Darnell, 50
Williams, Louie, 98
Williams, Louis farm, 46
Williams, Martez, 75
Williams, Mary Patton, 11
Williams, Mary Virginia Patton, 74–76
Williams, Naveysha, 75
Williams, Ponell Cecil, 74, 76
Williams, Sam, 40, 190
Williams, Sam, Jr., 190
Williams, Shatonya, 75
Williams, Shirley, 75
Williams, Thomas, 40
Williamson County, 6
Williamson County Board of Education, 116–117
Williamson County Public Schools, 105–106
Wilson, Della
– see Scales, Della Wilson, 207
Wilson, Mary Lee, 60
Wilson, Mr., 213
Wilson, Ovie Jane
– see Thompson, Ovie Jane Wilson, 260–263
Wilson, Sallie Ezell, 20, 21, 70, 72, 207, 261
Wilson, Thomas and Sallie, 70
Wilson, Thomas Jefferson, 20, 72, 207, 261
Wilson, William M. "Buddy," 207
Wilson, William McKinley (Buddy), 20
Wilson, Willie, 118–119, 133, 134
Wilson, Willie, Jr., 2
Windrow, Fannie Covington, 80
Windrow, Fannie Lou Covington, 47
Windrow, Horace, 47, 80
Windrow, Horace and Fannie Covington, 46
Windrow, R.L., 270
Windrow, Robert (Blue), 261
Womack, Cheryl, 64
Woods, Gertrude (Webb), 249
Woods, John, 13
Woods, Palmar, 123
Woods, Pauline, 123
Woods, Sweet, 123
Woods, Tevin, 88
Woullard, Martitia, 64
Wray sisters, 231–232
Wray-Batts, Ella Louise, 283
Wray, Carolyn, 132, 154, 159, 231–232, 282
Wray, Ella Louise
– see Wray-Batts, Ella Louise, 231, 283
Wray, Louise, 122
Wray, Lucille, 117, 283
Wray, Lucille McClain, 213–232
Wray, Myra Ann, 196, 231
Wray, Will Allen, 122, 231–232
Wray, Willie Jean, 231–232
Wray, Willie, Jr., 228
Wright, baby in arms, 280

Wright, R.A., 274
Wright, Sheila, 228
Wright, Trent, 279
Wright, Wesley, 280
Wright's Funeral Home, 168
WWII, 59, 249

Y

Yeargins, Annie Ruth, 196
Yeargins, Ivory, 277
Yeargins, Pearl, 230
York, Vicki, 159

www.ingramcontent.com/pod-product-compliance
Lightning Source LLC
Chambersburg PA
CBHW080451100526
44581CB00003B/104